22.95

FAITH IN A WINTRY SEASON

Karl Rahner

FAITH IN A WINTRY SEASON

CONVERSATIONS AND INTERVIEWS
WITH KARL RAHNER
IN THE LAST YEARS OF HIS LIFE

Edited by Paul Imhof
and Hubert Biallowons

Translation edited by Harvey D. Egan

CROSSROAD · NEW YORK

1991

The Crossroad Publishing Company
370 Lexington Avenue, New York, N.Y. 10017

Originally published as
Glaube in winterlicher Zeit:
Gespräche mit Karl Rahner aus den letzten Lebensjahren
© 1986 Patmos Verlag Düsseldorf

English translation © 1990 by The Crossroad Publishing Company

Printed in the United States of America

Library of Congress Cataloging-in-Publication Data

Rahner, Karl, 1904–1984
  [Glaube in winterlicher Zeit.   English]
  Faith in a wintry season : conversations and interviews with Karl
Rahner in the last years of his life / edited by Paul Imhof and
Hubert Biallowons ; translation edited by Harvey D. Egan.
    p. cm.
  Translation of : Glaube in winterlicher Zeit.
  Includes bibliographical references and index.
  ISBN 0-8245-0909-9
  1. Rahner, Karl, 1904–1984—Interviews.   2. Catholic Church-
-Doctrines.   3. Theology, Doctrinal.   I. Imhof, Paul.
II. Biallowons, Hubert.   III. Egan, Harvey D.   IV. Title.
BX4705.R287A5   1989
230′.2′092—dc20   89-7742
                                                                CIP

CONTENTS

Translation Editor's Preface

Shortly after a visit to the Rahner Archives in Innsbruck in 1984 and daily prayer at his crypt, I undertook the translation of Karl Rahner's *I Remember: An Autobiographical Interview with Meinold Krauss* (New York: Crossroad, 1985). That interview contains material found nowhere else; it is highly autobiographical and is Rahner at his most personal and intimate—a rare treat, for Rahner refused to write his autobiography or memoirs.

The interview captures vividly the Rahner I came to know and love for almost a quarter century. I translated it because it communicates the spirit of Rahner the man, the priest, the Jesuit, the theologian, and the Christian known and admired by so many people. It is the easiest, most readable way into his mind and heart. I recommended the book so highly because it can serve as an introduction to this remarkable theologian who has been called the Father of Roman Catholic theology in the twentieth century.

Shortly before Father Rahner died on March 30, 1984, I had finished reading *Karl Rahner in Gespräch*, two volumes of his television, radio, and newspaper interviews from 1964–1982. Although I had seen and heard some of these interviews during my years of doctoral studies under Rahner in Germany, the reading of them all in a short interval of time had a tremendous effect upon me.

Because of their lively, direct, and highly readable style, I was eager to make these interviews accessible to Rahner's already wide English-language audience. The Rahner who lectured, who wrote difficult theological essays, recedes into the background. Here the pastoral, "sapiential" theologian and popularizer takes center stage. In relatively easy language, he explains what Christians believe, why this is intellectually justified today, and how this can be experienced. We find him striving not only to help people understand Christianity but also to unite their hearts and spirits with its truth and good. The Rahner who listened to the catechism of the heart and who spoke directly and effectively to it dominates these interviews.

As someone who has been reading Karl Rahner for almost thirty years and teaching his thought for fifteen, these interviews appeared to me to be the easiest and the best introduction to this exceptional theologian. In a remarkably nontechnical and straightforward fashion, these interviews present an excellent cross-section of his speculative, pastoral, spiritual, and ecumenical ideas. A few also provide easy access to the philosophical underpinnings of his theology.

The reader can also grasp through these interviews both Rahner's architectonic, holistic grasp of the faith and the way he applies this unified vision to a vast range of issues as they arose in the important twenty-year period following the Second Vatican Council. Rahner's awesome mastery of the Church's tradition and his unusual sensitivity to the "signs of the times" permeate these interviews. They reflect both Rahner's and the Church's identity-in-transformation over the years. Thus, I assembled a team of Rahner scholars to translate the two German volumes which were published in one volume as *Karl Rahner in Dialogue: Conversation and Interviews, 1965–1982* (New York: Crossroad, 1986)

For the same reasons and with equal enthusiasm, I have done the same for the English translation of this third and final volume of Rahner's later conversations and interviews, *Glaube im winterlicher Zeit: Gespräche mit Karl Rahner aus den letzten Lebensjahren.* Twenty-three of these interviews were given during the last two years of his life; more than a third within a few months of his death! And since only six interviews in the German volume were given prior to 1982, the German subtitle, *Interviews and Conversations with Karl Rahner in the Last Years of His Life,* has been retained.

Some interviews contain heretofore unpublished autobiographical information. For example, the interview "The Importance of Thomas Aquinas" gives detailed information about Rahner's intellectual formation. Several interviews originated from Rahner's trip to Hungary just a month before he died, where in dialogue with Marxists he focused upon a shared "realistic humanism" capable of preventing a world catastrophe. Other interviews contain his mature reflections on liberation theology, demonic possession, Mariology, ecumenism, the new Code of Canon Law, the contemporary priesthood, married priests, the ordination of women, the immorality of even defensive nuclear weapons, and the like.

One theme stands out in these interviews: Rahner's rejection of the contemporary tendency to reduce God to a God of human needs, to one who exists only for our sake. He brands this as "anthroegoism" and "the most dangerous heresy of all." For Rahner, God must be loved for *his own* sake, even though this will not ensure the "good life."

Because the German volume contains interviews that repeat matter already found in *I Remember* and *Karl Rahner in Dialogue,* four of the interviews were not translated. On the other hand, I have added to this volume the 1974 interview, "Grace as the Heart of Human Existence," given on the occasion of Rahner's seventieth birthday, from the book *Herausforderung des Christen* (Freiburg i. Br.: Herder, 1975), because it is an exceptionally concise statement of how Rahner conceived theology and his life's work as a theologian. I sincerely thank Mr. Franz Johna of Verlag Herder in Freiburg for permission to translate and publish it.

I am also most grateful to Professor Heribert Breidenbach of Santa Clara University, to Professor Heinz Bluhm of Boston College, and to Dr. Hugh M. Riley of Munich for their help with some of Rahner's difficult German. The four of us (and the other translators of this volume) now have first-hand experience of what Rahner meant when he said that his brother Hugo could not have translated him into German because Hugo was inadequate as a speculative theologian! Finally, I wish to express my gratitude to Santa Clara University for the appointment to the Bannan Chair in the Department of Religious Studies for the academic year 1987–1988. This provided me the time and the resources to complete this work.

Although *Faith in a Wintry Season* stands on its own, I would recommend that the reader who is new to Rahner begin with Karl Rahner's *I Remember*, proceed to *Karl Rahner in Dialogue*, and then read this final volume of interviews. I have already successfully used this method in courses on Karl Rahner.

Harvey D. Egan, S.J.

Editors' Preface

At a time when the spectre of an ecclesial restoration seems to be appearing everywhere, these conversations with Karl Rahner offer a few points of reference suggesting how, in a "wintry season," one might avoid being misled by excessively conservative tendencies. Some things obviously would have to be rethought and reformulated today. Yet the interviews remain relevant because many of Rahner's excellent suggestions have not been taken up. Perhaps some of them still will be. The discussion, at any rate, remains open.

Already in 1973 Rahner spoke of a "wintry season." One might wonder whether such a thing is not a regularly recurring phenomenon in the life of the Church. It cannot always be spring, summer, or fall; there are also barren periods.

> That should not be disregarded, nor, still less, gloried in. Piety's wintry climate cannot be overcome by simply proclaiming high ideals and acting as if they could be realized with a little goodwill. Perhaps this period, at least for not inconsiderable groups of Christians, is already on the wane. It is possible that groups of young people, too, will come to experience religion in a more enthusiastic or pentecostal way. . . . Perhaps in the future there will coexist two different styles of piety. One will be difficult because, although carried by the grace of God, it will have to live and thrive in a world of technical rationalism and in close proximity to a concerned atheism; the other will experience spontaneously and with great intensity God, his Spirit, and the life-giving power of the gospel.[1]

Rahner's life with its ongoing involvement in church and society offers a context for the following conversations and interviews.[2] He was always ready to respond to the questions that were put to him. Sometimes different people asked the same thing. In such cases Rahner's answers varied little. In order

---

1. *Orientierung* 37 (1973): 202.
2. See Herbert Vorgrimler, *Understanding Karl Rahner: An Introduction to His Life and Thought*, trans. John Bowden (New York: Crossroad, 1986), and Paul Imhof and Hubert Biallowons, eds., *Karl Rahner: Bilder eines Lebens* (Zurich and Freiburg i. Br.: Benziger and Herder, 1985).

5

not to shorten the exchanges arbitrarily, repetitions, with a few exceptions, were left in the text.

The present book contains some conversations that for technical reasons were not able to be published earlier.[3] In *Faith in a Wintry Season* we put together from the surviving notes a colloquium on Mariology. It turned out that the amount of material on Mariology and ethics justified a more extensive publication on its own.

Without the people with whom Rahner spoke this book would never have existed. Our sincere thanks, therefore, are expressed first of all to them. We also thank Rosemarie Imhof and Elisabeth Meuser for their help in preparing the manuscripts and in seeing them through the printing. A special word of thanks must also be directed to the Karl Rahner Archives in Innsbruck. Through it some of the material became available to us for the first time. We would like especially to mention Professor Walter Kern and his academic collaborator, Roman Siebenrock.

Paul Imhof, S.J., and Hubert Biallowons

Translated by Daniel Donovan
University of Saint Michael's College, Toronto

3. Hubert Biallowons, Paul Imhof, and Harvey D. Egan, eds., *Karl Rahner in Dialogue: Conversations and Interviews, 1965–1982* (New York: Crossroad, 1986). This volume contains sixty-three interviews and conversations.

Part I

A THEOLOGIAN'S THEOLOGIAN

1 • Preacher of the Gospel

Interview with Dieter Müller, S.J., Munich (1984)

Father Rahner, in 1936 you received a doctorate in theology and a year later you completed the postdoctoral degree, the Habilitation, *in the area of dogmatic theology at the University of Innsbruck. You taught this area of theology there and after 1967 in Münster (Westphalia). Just what is "dogmatic theology," the area in which you worked?*

Dogmatic theology is scholarly reflection upon the contents of faith in God and Jesus Christ as proclaimed by the Church.

What is the role of this area in the education of a theology student who, for instance, intends to be a teacher, perhaps in a secondary school? What does dogmatic theology help one do?

Without giving the impression that I consider other theological disciplines such as exegesis—the scholarly unfolding and interpretation of the Old and New Testament—as second-class citizens, I think that radical and clear reflection upon the real content of the Christian message is one of the essentials for anyone who later, commissioned by the Church, intends to proclaim the message of Christianity, to arouse faith, to lay the foundations for a Christian life.

With regard to your work, you once said that scholarly theology in the strictest sense is at the same time the most kerygmatic, the most valuable for preaching. You wanted your scholarly work to serve, first and foremost, the preaching of the gospel.

There was a time, in the 1930s, when a theory was developed in Innsbruck which advocated a dual education for future priests: there would be a "kerygmatic theology" which would directly serve the task of preparing priests to preach. There would also be another scholarly theology based more upon philosophical and theological reflection. I never accepted this theory, although I grant that in practice there can be variations in theology and pedagogy.

I always emphasized the need for every future priest and preacher of the Word of God to reflect as intensively as possible upon the content of the faith being preached. This is what dogmatic theology does from a scholarly approach. Naturally it also depends upon the age and upon the gifts of the future priest.

9

"Gospel" means literally "good news." Why is this news "good?"

That is hard to answer in a few sentences. I think that in all human experiences of individual realities, their finitude is ultimately experienced along with them: health, the joy of life, success, scientific and historical research. . . . All human things—everything a human being actually can do with reason--ultimately display a finitude and consequently an inability to fulfill the total "capacity" of the human being. All these empirical experiences are subject to the transitoriness of time. Thus they are linked to disappointments and also to experiences of meaninglessness.

If Christianity ultimately (I say "ultimately," not "alone") announces that the absolute, infinite, holy, and living God is the total fulfillment of human existence, then with that comes a joy and a fulfillment of a fundamental kind that essentially exceeds everything else, and is in itself unsurpassable. Whether, and how far, an individual man or woman in the concrete situations of life, limited by one's lifespan, by one's work, depending also upon one's individual, intellectual and other abilities, is able to really appreciate such an awesome message is quite another question. Nevertheless, Christianity preaches an absolute joy—one can also say, an absolute future, an unlimited reality. This, then, is in an absolute sense "good news." How much a person understands it, how clearly it appears in toilsome daily life, as I said, that is a totally different question.

I'm thinking of factory workers whom I have gotten to know in a course offering practical experience in factory work and life, and I ask myself how this message, as the Church teaches and preaches it, can be understood as the good news at all.

I have to phrase my answer in a general and abstract way. According to the normal Catholic understanding of faith there are people who find eternal and absolute salvation in God, who, simply put, "get to heaven," although they know little or nothing explicitly or in clearly formulated sentences about Christianity. A Tibetan monk, for example, who has never seen the New Testament and never heard of Jesus Christ might perhaps have an idea of the "Word of God" which we would find questionable. According to the teaching of Vatican II, he nevertheless attains eternal life if he has not sinned in a fundamental way against his own conscience.

Now back to the factory workers. It's really not so surprising that in our world today many people have only a slight hunch, or not even a clue, about Christianity's good news, as we priests conceive it. But there is also something else we should consider. Even in the lives of ordinary people who seem oppressed and torn by life's troubles, there are moments in which something explicitly appears that destroys this pessimistic impression. For example, if some poor devil loves his wife and children with selflessness, instead of trying to keep his burdensome life together with cynicism and bitterness, if this person lives with patience and a rather anonymous hope in an ultimate meaningfulness, then even he has a very clear access to what we preach. Our task consists in this: to work these experiences into our preaching so that people can also explicitly accept Christ.

We were speaking of the necessity of a contemporary theological education. Can you tell us something about your years in formation? What differences are there with the contemporary situation?

When an elderly person today looks into the past and then back into our time, he or she sees, of course, a big difference between the past and the present in styles of life and education. Doubtless there is a considerable difference between the "preconciliar" Society of Jesus and the "postconciliar" one—to formulate it that way.

Obviously the contemporary Society of Jesus can and must, in many ways, have a different lifestyle than earlier. Answering why would demand a lengthy cultural-historical investigation. But I think that the generation of Jesuits of today and tomorrow must also ultimately retain the true mentality and the particular spirit of the Society of Jesus, as Ignatius intended, and actualize it in new ways. That's a difficult job. Our last general, Father Pedro Arrupe, worked hard to effect such a transition. He worked carefully but also introduced the necessary experimentation! Still, there's a lot to do.

On March 7, 1984, the Protestant pastor Martin Niemöller died. A man of his Church, he was also a passionate critic of it. Concerning his relationship to the Church, he once said that he had suffered as much under the Church since 1945 as he did in the years he spent in a Nazi concentration camp. You've also had difficulties with the Church. In your experience, are Niemöller's views understandable?

Comparisons are always quite difficult. And the relationship of a Protestant pastor to his Church is, in terms of the ecclesiology of Protestant Christians and theologians, different from that of a Catholic, a priest, and a Jesuit to the Roman Catholic Church. Consequently, the style, scope, and radicalness of criticism within the two forms of Christianity are different.

A Protestant exegete like Ernst Käsemann can certainly threaten to leave the regional Protestant Church in Germany without thereby ultimately contradicting Protestant theology. For a Catholic Christian, priest, and theologian something corresponding to this is a priori unthinkable! The latter has an "absolute" relationship to this Church. But obviously one can also express one's criticisms in the Church. Pope Pius XII once said openly that there must be something like public opinion in the Catholic Church too—without it the Church would suffer! That means therefore that criticism is legitimate and necessary, and, as criticism, looks for public exposure. We can disagree over "how" to do that. I think, however, that even if one disagrees about this or that concrete aspect, still a Catholic has the obligation to retain certain forms of respect toward the pope and the bishops.

In 1985 the diocese of Rottenburg/Stuttgart is holding a diocesan synod with the theme "Handing on the Faith to the Next Generation." What do you think is most important for this theme?

You're asking me too much! There must be good preaching. To have good preaching, one must first have studied good theology. And those who preach must be vital, devout, and radical Christian men and women living a deep spiritual life. Obviously there must also be a certain freedom within apostolic and pastoral activity.

One last question: As you look at your life to this point, for what are you most thankful?

I am thankful that God kept me in his grace and now leads me toward a blessed, meaningful end. Or, at any rate, I am hopeful of this—more I can't say.

Translation by Thomas O'Meara, O.P.
University of Notre Dame

2•Grace as the Heart of Human Existence

Interview with *Herder Korrespondenz* on the occasion of Father
Rahner's seventieth birthday, Munich (February 1974)

Professor Rahner, for more than forty years you've done research, teaching, publishing, counseling, and preaching in theology and in the Church. If you had to draw up a kind of interim "balance sheet," what would the bottom line look like? What, if you will, would be the debits and credits?

Whether it's an *"interim* balance sheet," as you put it, is doubtful. Celebrating one's seventieth birthday is already, more or less, the "bottom line." As for debits and credits. . . .

Still, though, we'd like your thoughts. You are a seventy-year-old German professor who no longer teaches. But then teaching was only part—though an important part—of your activity. You're still active in theology. New publications are about to appear; other larger works will follow. And surely there are a lot of manuscripts and private writings shoved away in a drawer somewhere that should be published. . . .

Oh, no! After seventy years I can't imagine being fresh as a daisy or doing something in theology entirely different from what I've already done. Indeed, there are my lectures, tentatively titled "Introduction to the Concept of Christianity,"[1] which I originally gave in Munich and later in Münster. If I finish that project, which isn't certain, that will be the end of it. As for a compendium of theology which others, not I, call "mine"—well, it wouldn't contain much more than what someone immersed in "my" theology wouldn't already know, even without the *Introduction*. That's more or less the bottom line.

. . . All things considered—the origins, experiences, and results of your theology—what you have accomplished is surely more than "only" theology. From the very beginning your way of doing theology has been viewed as involvement in faith and church reform. In your later years that involvement has grown.

Yes, I often hear such comments. But you see, if from the start I had worked out a theology which was directed toward a specific goal, then of course people could ask: Did he reach the goal? To what extent did he reach it? How far short did he fall? But if there was no such "plan," if one simply gave oneself to life and its daily demands, then it's difficult to speak of a

---

1. E.T.: *Foundations of Christian Faith: An Introduction to the Idea of Christianity,* trans. William V. Dych, (New York: Seabury, 1978).

balance sheet, debits and credits. Aside from the lexicographical works, I have published primarily small, individual works. I haven't even published many larger, more comprehensive works. The extent to which my theology is correct, how helpful it was to Christianity, the Church, peoples' religious lives is, in the final analysis, for others to judge.

Let me repeat something here I recently said to the members of the Order of Merit.[2] I had to speak about "my" theology. In essence it was *one* thought: I wanted to do theology in a serious and ecclesially responsible way, but I absolutely did not, nor could I, really anticipate what would come of it. One is a theologian and raises questions. For example, What is the relationship between the papacy and the episcopacy? What is a sacrament? What is grace? Then on the basis of one's very simple professorial work one comes across a certain theological question, writes an article about it, thinks it's more or less reasonable, and publishes it. But it is entirely impossible to say to what extent that article penetrates public consciousness, changes things or moves people.

Earlier that may have been true. Now, however, we live in postconciliar times, some distance from Vatican II. Your theology has had broad influence. What effects and reactions have there been to Rahnerian theology in Germany and in the entire Church?

Here again I believe that's for others to judge. Obviously one inaugurates certain things, but their long-term effects can't be foreseen. You, not I, say that my theology has a certain significance for the Church's theological and religious life. You also rate that significance rather high. Still, your opinion can be disputed. Some say that I've started something really big and judge it positively. Others say things have gone haywire, that I've pushed things too far, led only to confusion or pluralism in the Church.

What is correct is another question. The fact that I was at the Council is more or less accidental; there was no way I could have known there would be one. God knows I didn't become a theologian in order to be a theological innovator or prophet, and I surely didn't want to be the pioneer of a new theological era. I am a Jesuit, a priest, a member of a religious order. I had work to do, lectures to give. I was, heart and spirit for the most part, interested in everything I had to do. Like others, I have said, advocated, and propagated things that I considered correct, and I hope on the whole they were and are. But it is worth noting that I neither could, nor wanted, to foresee the long-term effects of anything I've said.

---

2. The West German Order of Merit for Arts and Sciences, of which Rahner became a member in June 1970.

Although the Church and its proclamation weren't the specific impetus, certainly they were the context for your theological thought and activity. You weren't spared conflict with the Church's magisterium. Your study on Mary's bodily assumption into heaven, written during the time of Pius XII, was never published. On the eve of the Council a Roman censure hung over your head. How do you view this experience?

Here, too, I can't say anything sensational one way or the other, either positively or negatively. In hindsight, after all is said and done, while things were happening it was not possible to anticipate what would come of the difficulties I had with Rome, other theologians, the censure, and so on. A theologian who doesn't merely parrot the obvious, but who thinks this or that on his or her own accord and at his or her own risk, can't expect smooth sailing; can't expect that there will be no difficulties with coworkers, with the Church. I hope this doesn't sound like an old man's euphoric, serene retrospection, but I can't find anything negative to say here. Quite frankly it wasn't that dramatic. If a high official at the end of his life takes a backward look, it becomes obvious that at one time he had a great opportunity. But he also had doubts. He had patrons, but also opponents.

Crudely put, your original discipline was more philosophy than theology. After further study of philosophy with Martin Heidegger in Freiburg and the rejection of your dissertation Spirit in the World, *which, I might add, still endures as one of your classical scholarly works, you moved into theology. Was this a real break with philosophy, or is philosophy still a basic, if not the primary, impetus of your theology, a kind of* conditio sine qua non?

Here I believe I must distinguish between what I thought and wanted from the start and what my religious superiors had in mind as my life's work, my actual profession. It's true that until 1936, through the fourteen years of my Jesuit studies, I was destined to lecture in the history of philosophy at Berchmans College in Pullach. I was completely happy and willing to do this and during my years of study I looked and worked toward that end or "destination," if you will. After finishing my theological studies with J. B. Lotz, I was sent to Freiburg where we had the good fortune to have Martin Heidegger as a teacher. Already during my philosophical studies in the Jesuits I became engrossed with what at that time was the totally new philosophy of Joseph Maréchal. As a consequence of this study and "destination," then, I acquired a certain basis for theological thinking which was imprinted, not insignificantly, by Maréchal and Heidegger. Without ever becoming a philosophy professor I was then reassigned by my superiors. But it wasn't as though I had been a philosopher and then changed professions. The fact that I became a lecturer in dogmatics at Innsbruck in 1937 was the result of pure practicality, dictated by necessity and personal decisions.

A spectacular transition from philosophy to theology didn't take place. During my studies in Valkenburg I was already interested in theological questions, above all in spiritual theology, in the history of piety, in patristic mysticism, and also in Bonaventure. I had also written a small, lousy, but at least according to the standards of the time, adequate theological dissertation.[3] But there was no break, as you put it. Aside from the above mentioned Freiburg dissertation, right from the start, already in *Hearers of the Word*,[4] my philosophy stood entirely in the service of my theology. For this reason, I couldn't tell you now what developed over the years from my philosophical studies, except for a few basic ideas. Even while studying with Heidegger, I was uncertain. I'm also uncertain that you can find any Heideggerian influence on me now, aside from some rather abstract philosophical structures that one might problematically call transcendental method.

You just said that philosophical thinking has always stood at the service of your theology. Isn't the opposite also true? Doesn't your philosophical thinking—imprinted by Kant, Joseph Maréchal, and Heidegger's transcendental philosophy—also influence your theology? In contrast to the general lack of philosophical-speculative thinking on the theological landscape over the last fifteen years, your theology is powerfully metaphysical. Conversely, this same theology is reproached for being narrowly speculative, for neglecting actual history, the historical-critical side of theology. . . .

Yes, good. You're entirely correct. In this respect my theology is unique, and broadly speaking its individuality can be designated rather negatively. Strictly speaking, it is true that I have never been an exegete and only in a very limited sense have I done work in dogma and historical theology. In this respect I readily admit that my theology has limits. It is speculative reflection on data available in the general faith-consciousness and scholastic theology.

I might say, too, that I have not used the new historical-critical method and discovered new data, insights, and tendencies either from Augustine, Pascal, or Thomas that I had first to describe and then reflect upon further. To that extent my theology is reflection on the data that was always readily available in sound scholastic theology. As you know, I have written a five-hundred-page volume on the patristic history of penance which has been published recently.[5] But such work, which I do gladly, isn't very typical. For that reason, Hans Küng has upbraided me on numerous occasions saying that in distinction from the Tübingen school, which he purports to represent, I am not a historical but a speculative theologian.

3. "E Latere Christi. Eine Untersuchung über den typologischen Sinn von Jo 19, 34," Th.D. diss. Innsbruck, 1936. Unpublished and untranslated.
4. Trans. Michael Richards (New York: Herder and Herder, 1969).
5. *Theological Investigations 15: Penance in the Early Church*, trans. Lionel Swain (New York: Crossroad, 1982).

Since the beginning of the infallibility debate there has been a kind of delayed "confrontation" between the Innsbruck neoscholastic tradition and the Tübingen school. But Rahner is long gone from Innsbruck and Küng's intellectual origins (at least a thread of his education) were earlier more closely bound to and stamped by Roman scholasticism. Still, the first and perhaps the theological contribution you have made has been to unfold the scholastic-Thomistic theological tradition and, by using the structures of modern thought, to transpose large portions of it into categories of modern philosophical thought. And behind this "transposition" stands the philosophy of existence of the early Heidegger.

Yes. But if I'm going to sing my praises here I should say that this didn't happen by presenting a thought-system different from scholastic theology. It wasn't the result of an explicit decision or of a systematically formed philosophy. It happened because I tried to ferret out the inner power and dynamism which is hidden within scholastic theology. Scholastic theology offers so many problems and is so dynamic that it can develop within itself and then by means of a certain qualitative leap can surpass itself. As a result, one can make considerable progress beyond the supposedly much simpler scholastic theology.

Earlier you mentioned the Tübinger school. You've maintained a real, if not intentional, distance from critical exegesis and the historical-critical method. Doesn't the future of Catholic theology, especially in view of its ability to be ecumenically verified, at least in the German-speaking world, lie precisely in a dynamic mediation, if not reconciliation, between scholastic theology developed further in its inner dynamism by contemporary hermeneutical methods and historical-critical research? We're also thinking here of a demythologizing exegesis, which is not, however, merely an end in itself.

But of course! Obviously that's not to say anything against a real exegesis that moves beyond pure philology, the difficulties of the scriptural text, toward a living theology. It's immaterial whether this happens as it does with Schlier, or Schnackenburg, or Vögtle. Obviously, there is this kind of exegesis. I want to distance myself as far as possible from the accusation that I consider exegesis secondary or superfluous.

The same holds true for all historical theology. Again and again one should look to Origen, Irenaeus, Augustine, Thomas, Bonaventure, and perhaps also Suarez. One should look with new eyes and perhaps discover theological elements which are in the history of theology and the Church's consciousness but have not been expressed clearly enough. To discover something through such historical research, to make it live and introduce it into today's ecclesial, ecumenical, and human consciousness, is obviously a task which deserves the utmost respect. For myself, however, I claim the right not to do such research, or to reflect less on it. For my part I don't want to do much more than to release the inner dynamism that still exists in the ordinary, apparently sterile, homogeneous (in the pejorative sense) scholastic theology.

How, in your opinion, can we achieve a fruitful interchange between both "theologies?"

Well, now, one of the basic convictions of my anthropology is that an absolute system is impossible. Consequently, I'd be the last one to write a prescription here. However, if historical theology, given the relativity and questionableness of what has come down to us from earlier eras, would strive to respect the theological substance of those who lived earlier, then already much would be achieved. Some historical works today are one-sidedly critical. They contain too little of the enthusiasm a student should have in the presence of the great masters. The willingness to grow and to learn must also accompany the ability to be critical.

You see a large part of your task as disclosing the inner dynamism of scholastic theology. But isn't there more here than meets the eye? Isn't there a driving force and goal in your work which goes beyond this? Alongside the philosophical-speculative dynamic of your theology isn't there also a spiritual concern that is clearly at work? Simply stated: Alongside interpreting existence in the categories of contemporary and Thomistic philosophy, isn't also the "nontheological" master, Ignatius, with his spirituality of finding God in all things and his theological ethos of decision, essential to your theology, including how you address basic moral questions (e.g., the justification and limits of situation ethics)?

By all means! I would want to distinguish though between what I have done—and that is approximately what I tried to describe to you before—and the specific dynamic which gave impetus to this work. Very generally and simply I would say, without knowing whether it should be praised or censured, whether it limits or enhances my theology, that behind everything I have done there stands an immediate pastoral and spiritual interest. And may I add here that I hope that I have remained faithful to the Ignatian spirituality of my order, at least to a certain extent.

What I wrote to my order on August 31, 1973, is a theme that lies very close to my heart, even if I can't say much more about it here.[6] Just let me add, though, that when Ignatius heard about the election of Paul IV he said every bone in his body shook. It should also be said, however, that one can be a Jesuit who numbers the Petrine office among the Church's indispensable realities and still be critical of Rome.

6. See "Ignatius of Loyola Speaks to a Modern Jesuit," in *Ignatius of Loyola*, introduction by Paul Imhof, color photographs by Helmuth Nils Loose, trans. Rosaleen Öckenden (Cleveland: Collins, 1978), pp. 11–38.

. . . Can one also say that one of your primary and all-pervasive interests and efforts involves a pastoral mediation of theology, spirituality, and piety?

I would say that though I didn't have an explicit plan in mind, I was theologically concerned from the very beginning with questions dealing with pastoral, ecclesial, and personal religious life. In my early years, at least, I preached a lot; in Innsbruck almost every Sunday for ten years. I have given Ignatius's Spiritual Exercises rather frequently, which I can't do today as often for a variety of reasons. Might I say that I regard my devotional works, *The Eternal Year,*[7] *Encounters with Silence,*[8] *On Prayer,*[9] *Spiritual Exercises,*[10] and many similar works not as secondary by-products of a theology that is sort of an art for art's sake, but at least as important as my specifically theological works. I believe that in some chapters of *On Prayer* there is at least as much theology tucked in—painstaking, thoughtful theology—as in my so-called scholarly or scientific works.

I would also say, mischievously but earnestly, that in a certain sense I always wanted to be a dilettante in theology. I claim the right to this dilettantism, fully aware that there are vast numbers of technical problems which cannot be mastered today, either methodologically or practically. I recently said to some colleagues in Munich who aren't theologians that if one added up what a scholarly theologian must ideally know today, after forty years of my theological work I have become ten times dumber. Forty years ago the ratio between what I knew, and the problems, available information, and methods, was maybe 1:4; today it's more like 1:400. That gives me the right to be a dilettante, and to say I am.

And to a certain extent I would reproach my colleagues for not being dilettantes. They work in narrow, very specialized theological disciplines and surely that is very praiseworthy. Then again, might I say, there are fine Christians and pastors who attempt to deal with all the remaining theological problems which face any number of Christian people. This is perhaps an unfair reproach, I admit, but maybe I can explain what I mean: To a certain extent I want to be a deeply thinking dilettante—and one who at the same time thinks deeply about his dilettantism and factors it into his thinking—but all with reference to theology's ultimately foundational questions.

Generally, a theologian of your stature, aside from this or that specific question, has little chance of remaining a dilettante. To put it differently, isn't it a question of the relationship of the universalist to the theological specialist? Uniquely, yet necessarily

---

7. Trans. John Shea, S.J. (Baltimore: Helicon, 1964).
8. Trans. James Demske, S.J. (Westminster, Md: Newman, 1966).
9. New York: Paulist, 1968.
10. Trans. Kenneth Baker, S.J. (New York: Herder and Herder, 1965).

inconclusively, your theology seems to be a breakthrough in a universalist tradition and its inner dynamism.

Certainly one can formulate the problem as politely as you just did. But I don't believe we're saying exactly the same thing. Earlier, circumstances prevailed where the universalist could convey his universalism, at least approximately, through the scholarly methods of the time, methods for which he was rightly responsible. Today, of course, there is also a universalist task, but one has to be aware of the fluidity of the boundaries. This universalism can no longer be conveyed through the methods of theological specialties. I see a distinctive feature of my work as speaking theologically through my method and with responsibility to the Church in *this new* situation.

We can't discuss the problem in detail, though it certainly might be necessary and exciting. However, we can raise the issue of whether in the future the mediation of the universal over and between individual theological disciplines can succeed and, furthermore, to what extent it is a universalism of your making. If a theological universalism ceases, or is no longer present in sufficient measure, the question then arises whether the unity of theology is lost and your contribution to the Church's proclamation gives way again to a more abstract, overly specialized process.

If I can be a bit naughty here, let me say the following. Some of my colleagues, also some bishops, grumpily scold me saying I have spoken on just about everything there is to speak about in theology and the Church. And, they claim, that can't be good. To that I say, of course one should be conversant in all questions which pertain to the technical aspects of theological scholarship, and the conversation should be carried on with the utmost competence and enthusiasm. But that's not all. I find it rather humorous as I look back that, although I'm not a pastoral theologian, I published the multivolumed *Handbuch der Pastoraltheologie*, edited *Sacramentum Mundi*, was the principal editor of *Lexikon für Theologie und Kirche*, and so on.

And now I would say, because there is *one* faith and because the human being is and remains *one*, though he or she is by and large incomplete and has not adequately integrated the plurality of his or her perceptions, impulses, and situations, there must and can, to use your formulation, always be a universalistic theology. But I also think that without therefore denying the significance of the individual technical theological disciplines there must be a method (I haven't reflexively hammered it out) which at least *indirectly* achieves such a unity of theology. This method would not force the individual theologian first to go through the sum total of the individual theological disciplines, which would be a dizzying task even for the more competent specialist.

Your reference to the one *faith, the* one *human being, and the resulting necessity for a theological method which at least indirectly achieves this unity leads us into the methodological-systematic structure of Rahnerian theology. Briefly stated, your basic hermeneutical principle is a transcendental theological anthropology. If we are correct, the fundamental concern of your anthropology is to show that being thrust toward or "referred" to the absolute mystery of the self-communicating God ("referred" in the sense of a basic existential) is the condition of possibility of human desires, actions, and existence. Is this in a nutshell the shape of your theology?*

Transcendental anthropology does correctly characterize my theology, but under the following two presuppositions: (1) that a religion which is essentially historical, which has become historical, also carries within itself elements which are not necessarily deducible a priori, but are accepted as concrete historical facts and (2) that I hope I see this and to some extent incorporate it into my theology. By no means do I claim transcendental anthropology as the only possibility. I see it only as a way to clarify something that is, properly speaking, embedded in every theology if that theology is Catholic and correct. I make no claims here for originality. But if this transcendental anthropology is correctly seen and appreciated, then it appears to me that it contains something that perhaps hasn't been adequately seen or worked out in scholastic theology.

What I mean is this. At least at one time, grace, assisting grace, and the outward circumstances shaped by God's grace in human life were conceived extrinsically, as discrete realities that occurred now and then, and which could be lacking completely in the sinner or the unbeliever. My basic theological conviction, if you will, is in opposition to this. What we call grace is obviously a reality which is God-given, unmerited, free, dialogical—in other words—supernatural. But for me grace is at the same time a reality which is so very much a part of the innermost core of human existence in decision and freedom, *always* and above all given in the form of an offer that is either accepted or rejected, that the human being cannot step out of this transcendental peculiarity of his being at all. From this conviction, then, first arose what I call "anonymous Christianity" and the fact that I consider no religion—it's immaterial which one—ungraced, although this grace may be suppressed, or expressed in a depraved way. From here also developed what I have called the transcendental moment of historical revelation.

In the sixties there was considerable objection to your basic hermeneutical principle, that is, the transcendental approach of your theological anthropology, especially among Catholics but also among Protestants. One objection to Hearers of the Word *came from Wolfhart Pannenberg. He said that despite the emphasis on history in your transcendentality, it was at the expense of historicity.*

I would say that there are few philosophical, anthropological, and theological problems more difficult than the relationship between transcendentality and history. Consequently, I'm not surprised if someone wants to point out that my theology doesn't adequately handle this difficulty. I certainly don't suffer under the delusion that I have spoken the final, adequate, and totally incontestable word on this matter.

I am, however, convinced that history only becomes history in contrast to nature through what one calls transcendence. And I am further convinced that transcendence is not the business of human beings *alongside* history, but is lived and realized in concrete history and in freedom. Furthermore, if I admit, underscore, emphasize, and attempt to bring this basic, reciprocal relation between transcendence and history to fruition in theology (and as far as I'm concerned I've done that as well as I can), then it's obviously not hard for me to concede that in the concrete carrying out of this basic problematic shortcomings can creep in.

Another objection to your transcendental method, above all leveled against your metaphysical epistemology as set forth in Spirit in the World, *but in a way against Rahnerian theology as a whole, is voiced by those who say that you view the human being so much in relation to the world of objects that the principle of interpersonality comes up short. . . .*

Oh, yes. That I believe is the charge made by Eberhard Simons, Alexander Gerken, and others. Let me say two things here: first, I don't want simply to be stereotyped by *Spirit in the World* and *Hearers of the Word*. These were rather lopsided works of my youth. Second, we are dealing here with matters which, correctly understood, are so abstract and formal that they remain open to elucidation through what is called, for example, historicity, interpersonality.

Let me mention an entirely different example, the principle of contradiction, which I believe is always and everywhere applicable. But if I start to apply this principle to trinitarian theology or to the human personality, then the principle can and must also apply that these have to be brought into confrontation—entirely and correctly—with a fuller and more concrete anthropology or theology. In this sense the accusation matters to me. In the sense I stated it, I accept it. Beyond this, well, you do it better!

In your theology one encounters a variety of what you yourself call basic or primordial words. One of these words is grace. You recently described it as the heart and center of your transcendental theological anthropology. Other such primordial words include "mystery," "love," "freedom," perhaps also "guilt." And when I think about your spiritual-theological treatise on devotion to the heart of Jesus, I am reminded of the psycho-anthropological word heart. *These words are, to use a rather primitive comparison, the Morse code of Rahnerian theology. The predicative function of such words has already become clear in the example of grace. But what is their value in the entirety of your theological statements? Where are they rooted in life?*

Let me shed some light on the substance of your question by giving a concrete example. Thomas had one specific article in his *Summa* which dealt with God's incomprehensibility. And to. Thomas it was obvious that this incomprehensibility, therefore God as the absolute mystery, was not even abrogated by the beatific vision. Now, without entering into a more subtle interpretation of Thomas it is still true that this statement is onl̥ une of many that Thomas made. It appears in a specific place and, of course, is significant and exciting.

In my efforts to do more radical reflection, the concept of mystery, which of course is part of traditional theology, but also such concepts as freedom, hope, and humanity's insurpassable plurality, are assigned a different value. To a certain extent they are used in a primordial way. They become concepts in such a way that somehow, to the extent I accomplish it, they permeate the whole of my theology.

Speculative-systematic theologians are not a priori expected to have a closeness to life. I'm thinking here of the existential clarity of your theology. Isn't your concern for terms which relate to basic human ways of existing and experiences a bit far afield for a speculative-systematic theologian?

I believe that in great philosophy or theology, whether in Kant or Hegel, Augustine or Thomas, such basic human ways of existing and experiences are invoked and find shape in the length and breadth of their thought. I'm not saying my theology is great, but I simply can't imagine that my way is unique. When Thomas prays: *Adoro te devote latens Deitas* ("Reverently I adore you, O hidden God"), or when Bonaventure provides a glimpse into his entire philosophy and theology in his *De Reductione artium ad theologiam* (*The Reduction of the Disciplines to Theology*), one sees that they are sustained by a simple, basic, but living passion and experience. If something akin to that is generally found in my work, well, it's nothing unique to me.

In his anthropological study of your theology, Klaus Fischer, quoting you, claims that your problem might be an "existentially efficacious fundamental theology."[11] Without discussing what Fischer says in detail, you are also interested in examining humanity's transcendental-religious structure. Thus we might ask whether alongside (or behind) the philosophical, spiritual, and pastoral interests there is not also a driving

---

11. Klaus Fischer, *Der Mensch als Geheimnis* (Freiburg: Herder, 1974), p. 277.

concern in your theology for a contemporary Christian apologetic in the best sense of the word.

You're always discovering new aspects in my theology! It's starting to make my head swim. But, yes, good. I don't think that fundamental theology can be practiced today as it was before. Earlier one described a once-and-for-all Christian revelation in a purely formal way without going into *what* is revealed. But one can no longer do that today. Consequently, every individual theme of systematic theology must also be seen together with its fundamental theological aspect; it must be described as credible and should not *only* be grounded on the formal authority of Scripture, the magisterium, and so on. If one attempts to do this, if one is convinced of the proclamatory task of all theology, and theology is not practiced for "scholarly" or "professorial" ends, then all theology is also an "existentially efficacious fundamental theology."

If one asks not only about the basic impulses of Rahnerian theology, but really wants to grasp what it's all about, albeit crudely, a whole series of "catchwords" come to the fore: human being, God, Christ, Church. God—at any rate as the mystery of humanity's existential being thrust toward, or "referred" to, the Absolute—is the all-pervasive theme of your theology and anthropology. Not so clear, however, is the relationship within your transcendental-anthropological constructs between natural theology and revelation theology, between the God of creation and the God of revelation or, as exemplified in the doctrine of grace, the relationship between nature and grace.

When we perceive Christian grace as the bearer and support of human existence and self-fulfillment through God's self-communication, as he is in himself—when we see it as the constitutive, transcendental, necessary, basic structure of humanity—then naturally the relationship of grace and creation, of natural knowledge of God and of revelation theology, of grace and nature, is no longer simply additive or measured in levels, like the stories of a house.

But that's how grace was understood in the scholastic theology of the last century of Baroque theology. (I claim this wasn't the case with the high scholastics, but scholars argue about it.) There is no human self-fulfillment in which God's self-communication, grace, is not already reflexively or unreflexively at work, or when moments of revelation are not already involved. For human beings who "have" grace as an unavoidable existential of their existence it is not possible within what they reflexively verbalize about themselves and their world to distinguish neatly what is owed to revelation and what is merely natural knowledge of God, what is natural and what is graced, liberating freedom. Distinctions between revelation and natural metaphysics, nature and grace, natural law and supernatural moral law are methodologically correct because grace is unmerited, but they are secondary and relatively supplementary distinctions.

But in the understanding of the relationships between nature and grace a rift has opened between you and other theologians who mistrust your transcendental starting point. This rift has led to wide-ranging antagonisms or, should we say, misunderstandings with the practical consequences. Your thesis of a supernatural existential is constitutive of your theology of grace and, for that matter, of your whole theology. Moreover, through the supernatural existential you seek to penetrate to the Christian core. You describe the supernatural existential as something continually co-constitutive of the human being. Somewhat overstated, others see your theory of the "anonymous Christian," which is entirely based on this thesis, as a reduction of the Christian to the human, or, more precisely formulated, as at least a gradual reversal from a theocentric into an anthropocentric theology.

Yes, good. Let's take your last point first. The synod in Würzburg recently dealt with something similar, though not directly as a result of my theology. I am thoroughly convinced that if one works out a correct anthropology, legitimately grounded "from within," from itself outward, and not imposed from the outside, then there's no way such an anthropology can be contrary to a theocentric theology. Why? Well, because right from the outset the human being is not only radically, unequivocally open to God as the absolute mystery, surrendering to it, but also because the dynamism of God's self-communication, what we call grace, Holy Spirit, is also at work from the outset. Thus, if and to the extent a person once experiences this inner offer of grace and historically objectifies it in a continuing process which, finally, is precisely identical with human history, then a person is already in the realm of revelation and theology—a theocentric theology.

I would also take exception to the notion that there can be an antinomy between theocentric and anthropocentric theology. A German bishop once said that God can always give human beings more answers than they have questions.

. . . In a certain sense what you just said might be the flip side of your conclusion in Hearers of the Word, *that is, that God gives human beings no more answers than they have questions.*

As a general rule of thumb what the bishop said is certainly correct, but not entirely so. You see, if God, from the very beginning dwells within the innermost core of my existence through what we call grace, God's self-communication, and Holy Spirit, and if he comes to me not only from the outside, but from the very heart of my existence, then that is a revelation theology which so radically flows from the wellspring of the self that no more answers can be given. Of course this doesn't mean that the individual alone, apart from the entirety of revelation history, can objectify and verbalize this revelation.

Your idea that the supernatural existential as the basis for the grace relationship of the anonymous Christian is the starting point for Hans Urs von Balthasar's critique of your theology. According to him, your transcendentally grounded salvation optimism subsumes the doctrine of redemption, the whole of soteriology in fact, under an incarnational theology. He also claims that your integration of love of God and love of human beings, according to which the "primary act of God's love" is the categorically explicit love of neighbor, is such that this primary act of God's love remains rather secondary over against what he calls the "thematic-religious act."

Of course those are two different issues. Concerning the first criticism I would say that for me transcendentality is always transcendentality that attains its goal *in* actual history that ultimately cannot be deduced a priori. As I understand it, transcendentality always occurs also as a guilt-laden history of freedom. Thus what one calls redemption, grace, forgiveness, cross, and so on are always totally involved. Now, the extent to which I have adequately included all this in my all too brief theological deliberations is another question.

However, I don't agree with the theological assessment that if one earnestly accepts this interaction of history and transcendentality and its mutual conditioning, one must necessarily give short shrift to true Christianity as the history of guilt and forgiveness, of the cross and the incomprehensible self-outpouring of God's love. Moreover, at the Benedictine college in Rome Anselm Grün, the Benedictine from Münsterschwarz, wrote a dissertation which shows that I plainly haven't neglected the theology of the cross.[12]

With respect to the other criticism, the one about the integration of God's love and love of neighbor, well, I think it's superfluous. As a primal occurrence, prior to reflection, radical love of neighbor always attains and must attain God. But obviously the reverse is also true. I must love God who loves me and my neighbor. With respect to the specific fulfillment of love of God and love of neighbor, we have, from the outset, a perichoresis, that is, a mutual conditioning of both elements. But then I must *also* say, at least theoretically, that God's love is more important than love of neighbor. I have never really disputed that.

The next criticism comes not so much from von Balthasar, but from those who reiterate what he says in a variety of ways. If I may put it somewhat untheologically, they raise the value of the "merely" human in your theology of grace at the expense of its religious and theological dimension. At the same time, moreover, they maintain your theology of grace is a prognosis of a considerable decline in "explicit religiosity" in a rational-technical world becoming more "worldly." A few enlightened contemporaries, who defend a primitive horizontalism that certainly has nothing to do with your

---

12. *Erlösung durch das Kreuz: Karl Rahners Beitrag zu einem heutigem Erlösungsverständnis* (Munsterschwarzach: Viet-Türne Verlag, 1975).

theology, have argued in recent years that their position has been vindicated—supposedly thanks to you. And then again there are those anxious minds, including the minds of some bishops, that have expressed a definite mistrust of the kind of Christianity that is primarily or merely shored up by neighborliness. Occasionally this mistrust falls back on erroneous appeals to your theological authority.

Sure, there are probably those who appeal to my work in pursuit of their own interpretations and opinions, and there are of course also those who discover horizontal tendencies in what I say. I don't need to repeat, however, that my ultimate intent is miles removed from such accusations. At every turn I have fought expressly against a primitive horizontalism. I have said it is the unique heresy of our time. Whether every statement I make successfully embraces the themes of hope or love of neighbor by including all the information which a Christian believes and must believe, well, that's another question. I'm not a theologian who thinks he can be *so* systematic that he can formulate a speculative basic principle from which anything and everything that is important for humanity can be deduced. Even if indeed there are such principles, I never grasp them clearly and adequately—at least not initially. I must always search for the new on the basis of what I have learned and in so doing attempt to improve my original statements.

Occasionally there are also objections from the opposite direction. In recent years the statement has frequently been made that Rahner has not only opened up the existential-theological aspect of scholastic theology, but through his transcendental process of deduction has shown that attempts to settle ecclesiological questions hierarchically are no longer tenable. Cases in point include your exposition of the authority of Humanae Vitae, *your involvement in the infallibility debate, and the dispute over the role of papal nuncios.*

In order to respond I think it's important to distinguish between specifically doctrinal questions and those which deal with politics, Canon Law, and pastoral issues. With respect to the latter, I have not by and large behaved as a reactionary. Like others, I have operated within the framework of a judicious orthodoxy; an orthodoxy, I might add, that leaves even the village churches intact. I have often wondered whether it was wise in this or that concrete situation to waste my powder or save it for more important targets. On these important questions I may have been more conservative, cautious, and patient, but I certainly wasn't cowardly.

With respect to doctrinal questions it's crucial to determine whether and to what extent one has a legitimate right to attempt to probe church doctrine speculatively—defined or not defined—so that it can really be made understandable. Such an attempt—using today's methods, standing in today's hermeneutical horizon—to assimiliate a binding teaching is still an absolutely legitimate task. Whether I have in fact advocated something that isn't true and have speculatively exceeded the bounds of traditional teaching is, of course, open to question and can be discussed only on the basis of concrete examples.

One might point, for example, to Hans Küng's treatment of the infallibility question. But Küng isn't the only one who occasionally gets the impression. . . .
The infallibility debate contains some very important and difficult open questions which need further discussion. But I believe it's possible to discuss them without calling Vatican I's definition into question. In this respect I stand with Lehmann, Kasper, Hünermann, as well as with Ratzinger and the rest of the systematicians. Küng, on the other hand, regardless of what the younger generation thinks about it, stands more or less alone, in opposition to his colleagues between the ages of forty and sixty.

Klaus Fischer, in the book we mentioned earlier, poses what he sees as the basic hermeneutical problem of your Christology:

> *How is the message of Jesus Christ, God become human, brought closer to people today so that they grasp this message as the possibility for a new self-understanding. . . , so that they understand Christ as that truth on which their entire experience of existence is already based, without knowing it reflexively beforehand? (p. 274)*

This basic question was no doubt the guiding principle of your earlier publications. It was already in Hearers of the Word. *Nevertheless, your specific Christology developed only in your post-Innsbruck years. Was this accidental, to a certain extent the outgrowth of your teaching, or was there some particular theological reason for it?*
First of all, let me emphasize once again that a christological foundation was already laid in *Hearers of the Word.* I said there that I understand the human person ultimately as a transcendental being who must turn to history and as a being that can comprehend itself as the addressee of a possible revelation from God. I also said that the human person is that creature who receives in history the final reality of God's answer to the human question. In so doing, I have at least sketched out the essentials of a Christology. Thus it can be easily seen that in my Christology, for whatever reasons, some things were arrived at relatively late. But then again, some things which always seemed important to me didn't appear so late, for example, "Dogmatic Reflections on the Knowledge and Self-Consciousness of Christ"[13] and "Christology Within an Evolutionary View of the World."[14]

13. *Theological Investigations 5: Later Writings,* trans. Karl-H. Kruger (Baltimore: Helicon, 1966), pp. 193–215.
14. Ibid., pp. 157–92.

Putting it somewhat crudely, recent developments in Christology have seen a shift from a Christology from above to a Christology from below.

Ah, yes, that's the second point I want to make. I think the question of whether there has been a shift in my Christology is a fair one. However, I can't address it because I don't really know whether or not I have moved in recent years from a descending Christology, as I call it, more and more toward an unpretentious, prudent, less speculative ascending Christology. I would say this, however: my earlier statement that God became human and world—which of course is also correct today—is, in a metaphysically dynamic framework, a more original and almost self-evident statement. Now, however, I would prefer to say that in Jesus, the Crucified and Risen One, I know whereof I should live and die. Of course a metaphysical Christology still retains its validity. It's not by turning to a simple human encounter with Jesus, with the concrete elements of his life, death, and resurrection, that I then come to believe that God *himself* is my future and the forgiveness of my guilt.

Still your Christology radicalizes in a transcendental-anthropological way the transcendental starting point through the concept of the "Christ idea."

I am thoroughly committed to the transcendental validity of the "Christ idea." But I am convinced that one only comes to this transcendental idea in the encounter with concrete history. I first know what music is when I have experienced Beethoven, Bach, and Mozart. Moving out from the concrete historical encounter I can then ask metaphysical questions. I must then show that this concrete historicity (i.e., history that is called Jesus) has an inner relationship to a primordial, if you will, transcendental constitutive element of humanity. It is in this sense that I understand the concept of the Christ idea and hold to it firmly.

What, for you, is the significance of the category of the future as the medium for eschatological understanding? I'm thinking especially here of the theology of hope and the political theology of Moltmann and Metz?

If the dimensions of future, past, and present exist, then it is obvious that rational human beings must, also in theology, grant currency to them in their mutual relationship and irreducibility. In my recent conversation with Roger Garaudy in the *Paulus-Gesellschaft* I made it abundantly clear that for my theology God is the absolute future. I also attempted to remove it from a Marxist inner-worldly dynamic of the future. I think I also had a few things to say about the essence of hope and eschatology which went somewhat beyond what is customary in scholastic theology.

However, strictly speaking, I am not a political theologian, nor am I a liberation theologian. And the reason I'm not isn't because I have anything against it, nor is it because I think nothing more can come of it than hasn't already sprouted in my little cabbage patch. The real reason is that every person has only a limited amount of time, a limited capacity to work, a finite potential. It is obvious that later theologians, theological methods, and points of view emerge that some theologian will then take further. For example, if I had a few doctoral students, such as Johann Baptist Metz and others for whom I no longer pave the way, that doesn't keep me from acknowledging their originality without envy and recognizing the need to say something new or to restate the old in new ways.

Ecclesiological concerns and problems bring us to the subject of the Church. Professor Rahner, the Church has been a constant ingredient in your theological endeavors. It is the spiritual-intellectual sphere in which your theology moves. You have always understood faith and church reform as the theologian's concrete task. But given the psychological and official character of today's Church, to what extent can theologians actually influence and broaden church reform?

Behind your question lurks the difficult and perplexing problem of the relationship between theory and praxis. This relationship hasn't been clearly articulated in theology. Western theology, not that I've made it any better, has given preference to theory. It hasn't adequately taken into account the autonomous freedom of praxis, concrete historicity, experiments, and the logic of existential decision-making. Thus the so-called modern theologian can incorrectly assume that his theories can deliver practical directives like so much freshly baked bread for the Church's practical life and use.

But the "modern" theologian who sees and emphasizes the autonomy of praxis, concrete decision-making, and societal structures not only can and must see one of theology's essential tasks as opening up more areas of freedom for possible, practical church action. But that same theologian should also be engaged in freely criticizing these practical directives, when they are too quickly perceived as being the practical directives for all action in every age and place. On a certain level, then, the theologian's task is negative. Whether I have moved in this direction I think is doubtful. But let me at least say that I have referred to experiment in the church,[15] commented on the logic of existential decision-making,[16] and so on. These are at least a couple of examples of what I've said on this matter.

15. See "Experiment in the Field of Christianity and Church," *Opportunities for Faith*, trans. Edward Quinn (New York: Seabury, 1974), pp. 214–22.

16. See "The Logic of Concrete Individual Knowledge in Ignatius Loyola," *The Dynamic Element in the Church*, trans. W. J. O'Hare (New York: Herder and Herder, 1964), pp. 84–170.

In the critical examination of the relationship between theory and praxis in the Church, you, like other leading theologians of your generation, had some influence on the Second Vatican Council concerning decisions on faith and church praxis. However, you also contributed some important basic elements to this effort. One is reminded of your attempt to provide "short formulas of the faith" and your recommendation, which was considered by the Council, to reform theological studies by providing so-called introductory or basic theological courses.

As far as effects on the Council are concerned, well now, it seems to me that the significance of individual theologians has become a bit mythologized. No one really knows who was responsible for this or that statement. One collaborated with colleagues, tussled over a clear statement on the collegiality of bishops, the question of the relationship between Scripture and tradition, the theological basis for liturgical reforms, concelebration, but I don't really know the extent to which an individual theologian should be held up as particularly important in any of these areas. We went so quickly from one thing to another. The Council's texts themselves were so rapidly put together and there was so much to do that there was no real way of knowing who deserved or didn't deserve credit for one part or the other.

If that's your view of it, we must accept it. However, we would still like you to make a few comments on translating theological reflection into church praxis.

Yes. First, then, a word about basic formulas of the faith. Joseph Ratzinger once said that they were only attempts, formulated examples, not short formulas of the faith, only short formulas of Rahnerian theology. . . .

Perhaps not short formulas of Rahnerian theology, but ideal suggestions and themes with which, as it were, to experiment with Rahnerian theology.

Good, doing both at once might not be a bad idea. What I really mean here is that there haven't been short formulas of the faith which haven't also been the short formulas of a specific theology. Theology and faith statements are not so unambiguous and chemically pure that they can be separated from one another in such a way that short formulas of the faith are not also short formulas of a theology. I would even go so far as to say—and I think I could prove it—that the Apostles' Creed itself was conditioned by a definite time or by the theology of a specific era. After all, such short formulas are nothing more than attempts to make clear that Christian beliefs can be stated from other perspectives and by entirely different formulas from the unabridged ones to which we are traditionally accustomed. In reality, they should demonstrate that the theologian and the preacher has a much larger and wider operative field of possibilities than is usually thought.

Concerning the basic formation of theologians, I am reminded of what we talked about at the beginning. Such formation must, in a certain reflective sense, provide for a dilettantic theological universalism which is part of all theological specialties and which must be communicated to the next generation of theologians. Thus it is almost obligatory that there be something like an experience of grace, a genuine mystagogy which is, to a certain degree, a reflective—though not that of a narrow research discipline—basic, reasonable justification of one's own faith.

And what do you see as the possibility for developing such a program in light of the situation of theological faculties, theology generally, and the hierarchy's willingness to promote it?

Of course there's a big difference between what one would like if one could have it, what one wants, and what one practically, given the current situation of university theology in Germany, can hope for and expect. I have the impression that the concern for basic courses or, as the Council put it, "A General Introduction into the Mystery of Christ," more or less remains on the far horizon. Oh, here and there, there are some introductory lectures, but these have always been around. Precisely the thing we're talking about, however, presuming the Council knew what it specifically wanted, unfortunately remains mere theory.

Nevertheless, I still consider the program important. If I were to describe it in broad strokes I would say this: Isn't it possible to imagine, given all the freedom and possibilities for forming young theologians, that the first year or two would be spent not in scholarly, narrowly academic study, but under the guidance of a "master"? This master could be a combination of theologian and spiritual guru who would communicate to the young theologian what exactly Christianity, spiritual life, prayer, receiving the Eucharist, and basic theological reflection (reflection on the possibility of Christianity which is intellectually honest and sober) are all about. I don't know how much time one needs to do this, and I'm also not willing to decide whether it should be at the beginning or stretched out over the entire course of theological study. At any rate, I do think something like this is possible. Perhaps there are such spiritually gifted people within the profession who are such "masters."

There are lots of theologians, but spiritual masters are certainly fewer, even among professors.

I would say that there are many theological professionals who are privately devout and honest Christians. However, in their relationships with young theologians this part of their life is much less evident. Here, I think, there is an essential void which can be traced back over the last 150 years to the academic notion that scholarship was basically neutral. Today, though, things are different. Previously, young theologians who wanted to become spiritual, devout, and good Christians came from and remained in an obviously Christian milieu. They went to seminaries and were admirably drilled in the Christian life. But they didn't need theology divided into various disciplines and inculcated by professionals.

Today, however, people are entering theology seeking to find out what Christianity is really all about; perhaps they seriously question whether, in fact, one can pray, ask what it means to have a personal relationship with Jesus. Maybe they have certain basic social-political or social-critical views and live them out, maybe not. How will Christianity, obviously a presupposition for theological study, be communicated to these young theologians? I certainly don't deny that through God's grace and a kind of befuddled instinct they might on the whole make it to ordination. But one shouldn't rely on God's grace and individual instinct alone.

Professor Rahner, perhaps at this point we can ask you a rather personal question. It concerns developments in the Church in recent years. During the Council, people were busily engaged theologically, but some observers, even during the Council, expressed doubts and reservations about whether the Church at the Council was really dealing with the kinds of questions that could enliven not only the Church but also contemporary faith. Has this feeling—I guess it's a kind of painful experience of the lack of concurrence or convergence between the Church and the religious needs of the time—a feeling you might share with others, become more acute in postconciliar developments?

Well, now. I need to acknowledge the Council's very positive significance in overcoming the lack of historical convergence between people and the Church today, but I must say that I at least share your concern. The Church contributed a great deal to removing this lack of convergence and it would be unjust to expect a Council completely to abolish all ills. But if I'm honest, I have to say that I get the impression that, because of its defensive posture, the Church is in danger of retreating into a new ghetto. The Church doesn't want this lack of convergence, but in point of fact it grows again anyway.

Do you see the problem more in terms of the Church's refusal to accommodate, or in its inability to allow productive disagreement?

Certainly the Church can't, as it were, capitulate or accommodate itself to the spirit of the times. On the contrary, I would say that radical opposition to the tendencies of the time can, "progressively," be *the* opportune moment and the specific way of overcoming the deplorable lack of convergence. However, if I'm conservative in a way that preserves the Church's life and teaching without becoming involved with other people, then I am not correctly conservative. Then in God's name I simply confuse Christianity with opposition to people's inadequacies and sins, with a false convergence which finally serves to justify merely holding on to the conventional.

In recent months you have retired from some important advisory positions in the Church. You have resigned from the International Theological Commission and given up your work on the Faith Commission of the German Bishops' Conference. Do you question the usefulness or flexibility of such organizations?

A big distinction has to be made between the two commissions. But the first and most basic reason for resigning was my age. . . .

The General Synod, in which you continue to be active, advises pastors to resign their position when they reach seventy. But the Church can't refuse the collaboration and wisdom of its top theologian.

Yes, sure, but I'm no sage. The young can also do what needs doing today. I make no bones about it, in its actual work, not its ideas, the International Theological Commission is more or less ineffective. Where the guilt exactly lies remains to be seen. No Roman commission has ever asked the Theological Commission for advice. It stews, if you will, in its own juices. It deals with problems and speaks about them in more or less praiseworthy ways, but that's about it. The Theological Commission also does what I can do in a variety of other theological groups or organizations.

The Faith Commission of the German Bishops' Conference, however, is different. This commission has (or at least must have) a necessary task. . . . It is also obvious that the German Bishops' Conference is not as uninterested in its Faith Commission as Roman commissions are in the work of the International Theological Commission. I might also add, though, that, perhaps because of the press of business and the necessity for swift decision-making, it has happened more than once that the German bishops have overlooked the work or advice of their Faith Commission. Anyway, the chief reason I resigned—though the head of the commission, Cardinal Volk, and I are good friends—was my age. I have the right to leave this work confidently to my younger colleagues.

In conclusion, Professor Rahner, we'd like your thoughts on the Church's future. In one of your last publications, The Shape of the Church to Come, *you pleaded for an open and fraternal Church. In addition to approving a lot of things in the Church, you also had some criticisms. These criticisms lead you to a kind of intellectual kinship with people on life's treadmill and in scientific laboratories, people in whose activities and in whose life horizon God, as it were, is not present. Your conviction is that people should seek to measure and test what supports their faith and spirituality in such situations. Is this the point at which the Church must find its new impetus for the future?*

When all is said and done, I don't know. But I think that in the future there will be basically two fundamental types of spirituality and piety. Of course they are related to one another and can never be separated into their chemically pure components. The one type, though decidedly Christian, and though those who practice it pray and receive the sacraments, is what I have called a wintry spirituality. It is closely allied with the torment of atheists, though obviously people who practice it are not atheists. The other type is found among the newer enthusiastic or charismatic movements, such as Catholic pentecostalism. In this type of spirituality there is an almost naive immediacy to God, bordering on a naive faith in the power of the Holy Spirit. Whether it is completely correct or not, well, it remains to be seen.

Which type should take precedence in the Church?

Most likely both types will endure. I might say, though, that pastoral theology and strategies of pastoral care should not be confined only to the second, enthusiastic-charismatic type. In its preaching and conduct the Church must earnestly deal with the demands of wintry spirituality as well. Those who belong to this type are above all those Christians who are going through the purgatory and hell of modern rationalism. The Church must consider these people, too. It shouldn't only concentrate its efforts on those who belong to the first type.

Presently it appears to me that there is a recognizable tendency for the Church to draw back into its own ghetto. This presents the danger that the Church will come down only on the side of the pneumatic-charismatic movements. I have no objections to these movements, and I certainly don't have the right to contradict Cardinal Suenens, the American bishops, or Paul VI if they see a hopeful breath of the Holy Spirit in charismatic groups. But the Church must, more than it has to this point, consider how well it addresses these people of a willing but troubled faith, who certainly are unable to have their faith strengthened by a charismatic kind of piety.

In recent years there has been a clearly discernible proliferation of contrasting spiritualities which in the long run might present the Church with a new challenge to its unity. However, for an even longer time there has also been a divergence of theological streams into ideological channels which are often, as one might expect, conditioned by the times. Consequently, some speak of the dangerous realities of a "bad theology." And by "bad theology" they don't mean theology as such, but poor applica-

tion or cheap popularization. How does the Church actualize and represent the entirety of the Christian message in this context? To what extent can it? Or, in other words, in light of its own inherent weaknesses, what is theology's challenge today?

Your question is put in such a way that it is difficult to answer in a few sentences. As I see it, there is a pluralism in theology which for now and for the foreseeable future is insurmountable. I can't go into the reasons for it here. On the other hand, there is certainly a pluralism of bad theologies, theologies which are more shortsighted, oversimplified, and arrogant (also vis-à-vis the magisterium), than they should be. The inevitable question, then, is what is justifiable and unjustifiable pluralism in theology?

We are less concerned about the question of pluralism—though it's certainly an important part of the problem—and more concerned about believers, preachers, and catechists who have to come to grips with operative theologies colored by ideological trends or formal scholarly study and who, as a result, have difficulty in their faith consciousness or their proclamation of the total Christian message. Of course we also think of bishops and theologians who are dismayed by such diversification in the proclamation.

Yes, all right. If your question is what believers, bishops, pastors in the pulpit, and religious educators in schools should do, then I would say first that even today there is an obvious, unquestionable core of central Christian truths that can be explained by a theology that is not only sound and thoroughly orthodox, but also contemporary and assimilable,

By way of example, there are Catholic exegetes—should I mention Schnackenburg?—who have a mastery of contemporary scholarly, theological methods, who out of their own perspective and dynamic take pains with the entirety of the Christian message, are acknowledged as competent, and whom one can't reproach for doing outmoded or unassimilable theology. I think there are people in all theological disciplines to whom the waverers and those beset by their uncertainties can look and thus maintain an adequate unity between the Christian faith and its reflective theological interpretation.

Obviously this simple statement has not eliminated the problems you see. In the Church, among educated laity, religion teachers, and educators there are always those, who, if they are honest, have a difficult time with traditional theology and an immediately tangible orthodoxy. I think one has to be much more patient with these people than those who hold high positions in the Church seem to be. One should have patience with anyone who seeks to serve the Christian message—with a priest, for example, who wants to be a servant of the Church but who confesses that he hasn't always or in fullest measure totally agreed with or adequately synthesized his life and feelings with the

Christian faith. Obviously, it is presumed that such a person wants to live in the Church and doesn't absolutize his personal opinions.

That's fine for individuals and their association with church officials. But for the Church as a whole the basic problem remains: How can the Church do justice to its proclamation if, in this age of acute confrontation, the Church and its theology must toil so arduously to reach the level of a believable, total expression of the Christian message in its preaching?

Perhaps I haven't completely understood your question. I would venture to say, however, that through examples from church history I could show you that there have always been times in the Church that have resulted in conflicts and confrontations between people and theology, between hierarchy and theology, between individual orders, and so on. Furthermore, I don't think I'm deluding myself when I say that the contemporary turn of events—I need not describe them more in detail—is so far-reaching that I fear the conflict situation necessarily accompanying this turn of events far less than I do the conflict situation itself being insufficiently clear or being insufficiently perceived.

Of course, between Christians in one and the same Church, and among Christians generally, there should be love and tolerance. Doubtless, not only the "outmoded" but also the so-called liberals and progressives are often intolerant and loveless toward those in opposite camps. But the impossibility of coming up with a prescription for avoiding such conflict situations should not mislead us into the useless and, as far as I'm concerned, stupid notion that we no longer know what the true, acceptable and life-giving substance of Christianity is. But then I don't want to start preaching a sermon.

One final question. What primary task must theology fulfill in today's world?

It is obvious that theology today, in addition to continuing its scholarly and ecclesial tasks, tasks it has always had, has the primary task to present the basic substance of Christianity positively and with vitality. This basic substance must be thought through anew and defended because it is not as if the world and many who might call themselves Christians do not dispute it. The question of whether we are completely united on the essence of the sacraments or of indulgences, on the relationship of primacy and episcopacy, or on the ways Rome in particular cases should exercise its teaching authority, can indeed still be important. However, these questions need not be answered in definitive unity and clarity.

Very simply, theology's primary task is to speak about the living God as our absolute future and the final guarantor of our existence, and to proclaim that this God is not merely the absolutely distant, asymptotic goal with whom, for all practical purposes, we can have nothing to do. Rather, God is the one who gives himself to us as our eternal life, as the one to whom we can entrust ourselves by looking at the crucified and risen Christ.

Now, that is a very pious formulation of a theme that is inexhaustible for so-called clever and scholarly theology. But if one responds by saying that love of neighbor is a matter about which Christianity and the Christian faith—in Jesus—know something insurpassable, new, and by no means obvious, then one has already specifically stated the basic substance of Christianity. On the one hand, this basic substance is very obviously taught in the Church and, on the other—and even more importantly—can be lived and, time and again, bring unity to so-called theological pluralism.

Translated by Bernhard A. Asen
St. Louis University
and Harvey D. Egan, S. J.
Boston College

3 • The High Point of an Eighty-Year-Old Theologian's Life

Interview with the editors of *Vida Nueva*, Madrid (March 1984)

From the high point of your eighty years, how do you see your life in reference to the future and to God?

The real high point of my life is still to come. I mean that abyss of the mystery of God, into which one lets oneself fall in complete confidence of being caught up by God's love and mercy forever.

What, in your opinion, were the most important moments of your life?

According to human reckoning there were many: birth, baptism, religious vows, ordination to the priesthood. . . . But God alone knows precisely the most personal and most important moments of my life. I can at most in complete privacy surmise what they are.

Let's talk about your work. Which persons or historical figures have, in your opinion, most influenced your work?

As regards philosophy I'd like to mention Joseph Maréchal, S.J., and Martin Heidegger. With regard to spirituality, without a doubt, Ignatius of Loyola.

Father Rahner, for many years you've been a professor of theology at different faculties and universities. In addition, you have many disciples. Can you sum up in a few words what you regard as your most important contribution to theology?

This is really not a question I can answer. It's something that others have to do—from a critical perspective. But in order not to dodge the question completely: what is most important is contained more or less in my *Foundations of Christian Faith*. One should read it carefully and go on from the starting points I present there.

You are eighty years old. Is there something that you yourself feel lacking in your theological work and your work as a priest?

I'd like to have had more love and more courage in my life, especially with respect to those who have authority in the Church. But I'd also like to have shown a deeper understanding of the contemporary person and his or her way of thinking.

How do you assess Vatican II and the time since then?

Actually that ecumenical Council has not really been put into practice in the Church, either according to its letter or according to its spirit. In general, we are living through a "wintry season," as I have often said. Still there are unquestionably communities in the Church where the charismatic element is very much alive and offers occasion for much hope.

Do you believe then that a new ecumenical council is advisable?

To the extent that I can assess the mind of Rome at this time, I feel that a new council would be premature. It would actually be no more than a synod of bishops with an advisory voice.

What do you think of the present situation of your order? What do you specifically think about the former general of your order, Pedro Arrupe?

The Society of Jesus still lives, just as the whole Church does, in a situation of transition. There's nothing remarkable about that at all. With strength and gentleness my order will certainly get through this stage successfully in the end. Pedro Arrupe was a magnificent general. We will be in a position to appreciate him better when we can evaluate him in retrospect. Spain can be proud of this Jesuit general.

Since we are already talking about the future, in your opinion, what possibilities lie ahead for the Church, especially the European Church, in the years to come?

The possibilities of the Church in Europe shouldn't be equated with those of the universal Church. Only if the Church has courageously transformed itself into a universal Church and ceased to be a European Church with "exports" throughout the world will it really be the explicit or anonymous "soul" of the world. In Rome, of course, there prevails a tendency to be excessively European.

In your estimation, where do the greatest dangers for the Church lie today?

The chief danger for the Church might well lie in its seeking itself and cultivating its "power" or "influence," regardless of whether this is along the lines of an overpowering conservativism or along the lines of a trendy progressivism. In both cases the Church would have failed to see that it is not a goal, but a means, a means of worshiping and loving God for God's own sake instead of being seen only as a way of promoting human success.

Father Rahner, what question do you ask yourself at this moment of your life, when you've just completed eighty years?

Ask myself a question, here and now? Well, I have a question, and I wish I knew the answer to it as well: What can I hope for? I can only say, for God's light, eternity, and mercy. And I hope to be able to pray along with Teresa of Avila: "Let nothing disturb you . . . God alone suffices," and with Ignatius of Loyola, "Take, Lord, and receive . . . , give me only your love and your grace; that is enough for me." Both these prayers are more than just words; they embody a whole way of life.

Translated by Roland J. Teske, S. J.
Marquette University

4•The Importance of Thomas Aquinas

Interview with Jan van den Eijnden, Innsbruck (May 1982)

For us in the Netherlands—and surely for you in Germany as well—Thomas Aquinas has moved completely off the theological stage, though he stood almost right at its center ever since Pope Leo XIII's encyclical Aeterni Patris. *The question is how something like this could happen.*

The study of the history of the influence of a theologian of the stature of a Thomas Aquinas is a difficult and lengthy undertaking. We thought that it would be highly rewarding to be able to show how the teaching of Saint Thomas influenced the personal history and the work of an important contemporary theologian.

In your bibliography, Father Rahner, there are few titles that explicitly refer to Thomas apart from Spirit in the World *and* Hearers of the Word. *Yet in your* Theological Investigations *Aquinas is very often quoted. Hence my question: What role did the "Angelic Doctor" play in the time of your studies? How did your relation to him develop at that time?*

I should say, first of all, that my intention of becoming a priest and a Jesuit had nothing to do with Thomas. I grew up in a good Catholic, but by no means a closed-minded family, side by side with a brother who became a Jesuit three years before I entered the order. Yet this did not have as much of an influence on me as one might suppose. I joined the Society of Jesus and then completed the standard training in the order. It was certainly not unimportant that I was already slated by my superiors to teach the history of philosophy at Pullach. I continued to have this assignment both during the two years I was a Latin teacher for the novices in Feldkirch and during the four years of theology in Valkenburg as well as during tertianship. With this assignment in mind I finally went for two years to Freiburg instead of to Rome where it was then generally the custom for future Jesuit professors to go. Hence, although I was supposed to teach philosophy, during all these years I still had been no more concerned with Thomas Aquinas than was normal for any student of my order with a somewhat scholarly interest in theology. Quite the contrary. I had during the two years between the study of philosophy and theology conceived the plan that, if I was to be a professor of the history of philosophy, I would deal with the difficult period of Baroque scholasticism. There are hardly any works on this period. One or two appeared in the nineteenth century, but there is practically nothing available on the history of scholasticism from the sixteenth and seventeenth centuries up to the decline of Baroque scholasticism at the time of the French Revolution. Hence I began to have a look at—"study" would be too strong a the Jesuit philosophers of the sixteenth and seventeenth centuries what had already appeared on them, prepared long excerpts from Sommer-vogel (*Bibliothèque de la Compagnie de Jésus*), and set up a card catalogue on the pertinent Jesuits. It has, of course, been lost.

During my philosophical and theological studies I enjoyed the neo-scholasticism that was taught to us Jesuits in the first half of the twentieth century. To be frank, this movement is hard to characterize. It rests upon a philosophical foundation that, of course, has something to do with Thomism. But at least with us in Germany it bore a Suarezian stamp. The Jesuits in Rome taught a "Thomism of the Twenty-four Theses" according to the Congregation of Studies of 1914, in which the real distinction between *esse* and *essentia* (existence and essence) played a fundamental role. But we were teaching a somewhat thin and pale neoscholasticism of a Suarezian sort. It was, nonetheless, quite clearly and unquestionably in conformity with all the Church's teachings. A good example of this is the *philosophia latisensis*. Such pluralism became possible after the death of Pius X. Our general, Wlodimir Ledochowski, obtained from Benedict XV the famous declaration that the twenty-four theses I mentioned were not obligatory for everyone in the Church. That sort of Thomism was, after all, heavily influenced by Cajetan.

Even the theology I studied in Valkenburg involved a line of thought carefully worked out in a neoscholastic manner. To be honest, I prefer it to much that is done in our faculties today. Admittedly it was a theology confined within quite limited bounds in terms of its questions and answers. We had little to do with the modern period. We had, of course, heard of Kant and Hegel, but by and large only to reject their views. The same holds for the modernism of the first twenty years of our century. But even our contact with Thomas must really be described as extraordinarily slight. If, for example, you looked at the *De gratia* of Hermann Lange, S.J., one of my teachers in Valkenburg, you'd see that it discussed Thomas in a very precise historical fashion. Basically it was a matter of a sort of reverence, a mere decoration. I certainly didn't have a living and inspirational contact with Thomas then.

Didn't you yourself at that time read any of Thomas's works?
I really can no longer answer that with much accuracy. And if you were to ask me if I took a course on Aquinas, at that time I'd have to admit that I do not know that anymore either. A sort of latter-day controversy broke out between Johann Stufler, S.J., in Innsbruck, and his Thomistic opponents in the Bañesian camp. Of course we heard a little of such things and perhaps got involved with it. But no one attached great importance to that controversy.

Let's continue my history with Thomas. After my theological studies and the tertianship that followed, I was supposed to prepare myself in the narrower sense for my assignment. As far as I can recall, there was then only one professor of the history of philosophy in Pullach. Such a situation would be impossible today. Up to then I was able to set, so to speak, the points of emphasis in my training as an expert in the history of philosophy. No demands were placed upon me from any side. Moreover, Father Johannes B. Lotz was supposed to become a professor of ontology in Pullach. But one thing I remember well. In the third year of my philosophical studies in Pullach I read with extraordinary eagerness and with great care the fifth volume by Joseph Maréchal, S.J., *Le point de départ de la métaphysique*. I made long excerpts from it which, of course, I no longer have. During this reading, I believe, I encountered Thomas for the first time in a more personal way that fascinated me; this was, of course, mediated by Maréchal's method. I certainly no longer recall very clearly, but it is entirely possible that my dissertation on Thomas originated with this reading. I believe that I was influenced by this Maréchalianism more clearly and earlier than Father Lotz, who was then at work in 'Freiburg as well. In my case this Maréchalianism was transformed into what others later called "transcendental philosophy and theology." To the extent that this Maréchalianism stems from Thomas and to the extent that Maréchal again and again tries to prove his thought through Thomas, I can certainly say that Thomism formed my philosophy and, at a step removed, my theology.

I now no longer clearly recall precisely why I worked on Thomas Aquinas's theory of knowledge. Certainly it meant a lot that Gustav Siewerth had earned his degree in Freiburg with a work that was Thomistically inspired in the genuine sense. And since we are speaking of Freiburg, Max Müller had recently completed his studies and become the assistant to my dissertation director, Martin Honecker! Lotz and I chose Honecker, although Heidegger, of course, interested us more. And accordingly, during both those years we did not study with Honecker, but went to Heidegger's lectures and seminars. There was, of course, good reason for the choice of Honecker as dissertation director. We chose him because it seemed safer to us in the first bloom of the Nazi era to place ourselves under the wing of a Catholic professor, such as Honecker. Heidegger was no longer rector of the university, but he had, nonetheless, been the first rector of the University of Freiburg under the aegis of the Nazis, namely, in the years 1933 to 1934. When we enrolled in the university, we simply could not yet size up Heidegger. Without question, he behaved toward us in a correct and friendly manner. Lotz and I were completely accepted as members of his graduate semina. But we did not know all this at the beginning of our studies. Moreover, there were still other reasons why we were doing doctoral work in philosophy, although we were enrolled in the theological faculty—something which was then a distinct possibility even juridically. One was safe from the Nazis and didn't, for example, have to carry a tin cup through the streets for the Nazi Winter Relief Fund.

And so I began to do my doctoral dissertation, and you know, of course, that my manner of interpreting Thomas, even of reorganizing him to some extent and pushing his thought further, in the end led to Honecker's rejection of my dissertation. In view of what happened, however, the frequently repeated claim that I was transferred to Innsbruck and into dogmatic theology because of that rejection is false. I had submitted my work toward the end of the summer term in 1936. I then had to go to Innsbruck, since my superiors had changed my assignment and I was to earn a further degree in dogmatic theology. Innsbruck needed a professor after the retirement of Johann Stufler and Joseph Müller, the predecessors of Franz Mitzka and myself. These reasons led to my reassignment. And only after I had begun to prepare my doctorate in theology, did I receive the letter from Honecker, telling me that he did not accept my dissertation. So even if he had accepted it, I'd have become a dogmatic theologian in Innsbruck, and quite gladly.

Yes, but didn't it strike you as a little strange to have first studied philosophy and then to be told to prepare yourself for the chair of dogmatic theology?

No, not really. Then such things were not regarded as terribly upsetting. Quite the contrary even; for, remember, my brother was already a church historian in Innsbruck. And, to be frank, I myself had no great inner attraction to the history of philosophy. Certainly, I would have been a quite respectable historian of philosophy, but my heart didn't bleed when I was reassigned by my superiors. Moreover, I finished my doctorate in theology very quickly, by December, 1936. I then published my dissertation on Thomas through the small Innsbruck press, Felician Rauch. The press printed *Spirit in the World* without any subsidy from me, but only because I had the little booklet *Encounters with Silence* printed by them at the same time.

I remember that a German professor of philosophy at the Gregorian by the name of Alois Naber was the order's censor, and he allowed *Spirit in the World* to be published without emendation. That was something in those days—by no means just a matter of course. In my years as a student of philosophy Maréchal was still a suspect author for our Jesuit scholastic philosophy. In particular, he was basically suspected of denying or obscuring the strict supernaturality of the beatific vision, since he had once again stirred up the question in Thomas Aquinas of the natural desire for the beatific vision of God. My former teacher of the history of philosophy in Pullach, Bernhard Jansen, for example, was one of those who expressed such reservations about Maréchal.

But let's continue with my biography. I was at Innsbruck, and in the first two semesters I lectured for four hours a week on the tract *De gratia*. This is where you might ask how far Thomism, as Maréchal and my own studies transformed it for me, made its influence felt in my treatises and, through them, in my entire theology. In this regard you should always keep in mind that before the Second Vatican Council, hence, in that epoch between Pius VII and Pius XII that I like to call "Pian," one was always held to a certain kind of reverence for Saint Thomas. It was thought that you had to prove the orthodoxy of your theology in this way. This reverence was by no means equivalent to insincerity or dishonesty. Rather, it belonged to a theological style of speaking that everyone expected. On top of that, through men such as Heinrich Denifle, Franz Ehrle, Johannes Hartmann, and my teacher, Heinrich Weisweiler, who was also a medievalist, we felt that we all had a basic dependence upon Thomas Aquinas. And so Aquinas was by no means someone whose name we had maybe come to know only as an idea out of the history of philosophy.

I believe my dissertation in philosophy can to an extent indicate how my generation viewed its relationship to Thomas. This relation differed from that of the classical Thomists, especially that of the Dominicans. For them Thomas's writings were something like a second Scripture upon which one was supposed to comment. Just think of Reginald Garrigou-Lagrange. I by no means want to deny that even this sort of contact with Thomas was something important. We Jesuits certainly were acquainted with and studied a work, such as Garrigou-Lagrange's *God*. But Thomas was read by my generation, unlike the Dominicans, as a great Father of the Church. This was certainly true of Max Müller, Johannes B. Lotz, Gustav Siewerth, and even of Erich Przywara, who exercised an important influence on the generation before me, an influence which found expression not so much in individual doctrines as in a particular style of thinking.

We read the works of Thomas; we allowed him to alert us to certain problems, but ultimately we approached him with our own questions and statement of the problems. And so we didn't really practice a Thomistic scholasticism, but tried to maintain toward him a stance comparable to that toward Augustine, Origen, and other great thinkers. We really appreciated Thomas; he was for us by no means a boring and dry scholastic, but someone with whom we wanted a real encounter just like that with Plato, Aristotle, Blaise Pascal, and so on. Accordingly, our relationship with Thomas involved a quite specific sort of "inspiration" or "normativeness," if you prefer that. And I think that a similar relation to Thomas would be advisable even for the present generation of theologians. In this connection I recall a description of life in a Dominican community where it was said that the young folk are more interested in Rahner than in Thomas. I regard this as regrettable. I am no

Father of the Church; I do not count myself among the great figures of the history of theology. But Thomas unquestionably belongs there, and you can learn a lot from him even today.

Do you regret that the present generation no longer has a relation to Saint Thomas such as you received through your studies?

Yes, but as regrettable as it is, one has to recognize the fact—perhaps inevitable given the times—that contemporary theologians simply do not know Latin. For that reason they, of course, fare much less well than we did with the texts of Saint Thomas. The scholastic philosophy and theology that I learned was still taught in Latin. I could still speak Latin right off on the Theological Commission at the Council, while Dominicans from France fared poorly at it. As far as that goes, we could read Thomas as well as or even more easily than a book in German. The situation is different today. I can't say whether, in view of the times, it was inevitable that Latin has become, despite all the exhortations on the part of the Church, as foreign to the young theologians as, for example, Hebrew or Coptic. I don't hold it against, say, an African theologian from Nigeria when he cannot handle Latin. But I still have to say that to do theology in a scholarly manner one simply has to have a really intensive knowledge of the Latin language. Only in that way can one read a medieval theological classic or a text in Denzinger with no hesitation. If, for example, someone wants to do exegesis today, he'll surely be told: If you can't read the Old and New Testament fluently in Hebrew or Greek, you cannot start with us. Moreover, a Protestant theologian once told me that twenty or thirty years ago it was customary for them to be able to read the texts of the Council of Trent in Latin. This is, of course, no longer taken for granted for them anymore than for us.

The decisive question, however, is: What could contemporary theologians learn from Thomas? Only the answer to this would justify an intensive study of Latin.

That is a very difficult question, and I probably cannot answer in on the first try. I can't, of course, claim that one can learn from Thomas what I myself don't know.

But you yourself have learned from Thomas. . . .

I'd like to put it this way: no scientific theology can be done if it does not incorporate philosophy. I think that an Eberhard Jüngel, perhaps to a lesser degree, Jürgen Moltmann, a Gerhard Ebeling, and so on, would agree completely. The purely exegetical theology practiced among us during the last twenty-five years is, I think, dying out. For it starts off from a positivism in faith, if I may put it that way, similar to what was practiced in the Protestant theology of the last fifty years--perhaps because of Karl Barth's influence. Such a theology starts off with a *sacrificium intellectus* (a "sacrifice of the intellect"); one takes up the Bible fully aware that one's own colleagues in exegesis are undoing Sacred Scripture with the help of historical criticism and, nonetheless, one immediately declares it the Word of God. In this way Scripture becomes the sole starting point in a positivistic sense for any theological discussion. I regard this as a real piece of nonsense. As regards the relation of fundamental and dogmatic theology, I, of course, differ from my former teacher, Karl Prümm. Theology necessarily implies a philosophy, and it makes no difference which philosophy one is dealing with. What is important is that philosophy give an account of its own reflection and be brought into theology after it has been subjected to such philosophical reflection. We have to learn at least this from Thomas.

Would you say that you learned this from Thomas?
Certainly I learned this from Thomas insofar as I have, through Maréchal, Kant, and German idealism, studied—let's be content to formulate it negatively—a "transcendentally tainted," philosophical Thomism. I readily make use of this Thomism in theology. I say, for example, in my theology that I cannot start off in a purely positivistic fashion from a so-called historical experience or only from a so-called narrative theology or even from a "political" theology that ultimately lacks self-understanding; I must also do philosophy. Heidegger may like to say that metaphysics is dead. It has not died, and it will continue to remain alive. On the contrary, metaphysics goes around causing trouble in unreflective form when it is not done explicitly. Whether philosophy should be studied first for three years before starting theology, as we did, is a topic we can discuss some other time. Even if there were no metaphysics today as Anglo-Saxon positivism, for example, and many a philosopher of science would have it, I'd do the philosophy that I need right within my theology.

The question of how the theologian learns to philosophize is, of course, first of all a methodological problem. One could, for example, attempt to interpret the whole of Christian existence in a "first-level" reflection process during a sort of basic course. Only afterwards would one do philosophy in a narrower sense or theology. The sequence in unimportant. There is also the possibility that one first study a theology that is oriented in a more positivistic, biblical fashion or in terms of the magisterium and that one then reflect on its premises and unarticulated presuppositions and go on to philosophy.

Let me give a few examples. Johann Baptist Metz wanted or wants to do a fundamental theology that comes after theology. Joseph Ratzinger, on the other hand, wants to do fundamental theology before theology proper. For this reason, Cardinal Ratzinger did not allow Metz to go to Munich. Let me put it this way: what classical philosophy, beginning with the pre-Socratics up to the present day, has done under the name "metaphysics" must be done somewhere in theology. And Thomas has done precisely this and done it in a splendid manner. So at least to that extent and for that reason one should try to learn from him. If young theologians can no longer begin with this Thomistic heritage, that's a bad sign—not for Thomas, but for present-day theologians.

Beyond this basic impact of Thomas as a philosopher upon your theology, were there also particular topics about which you learned from him?
Of course. There is a whole list of particular topics in philosophy and theology on which Thomas can be very stimulating. Here is something that I have always found important; I appeal to it even now. Unlike the Jesuit scholastic theology that I learned in Valkenburg, Thomas and later Thomistic theology regarded it as perfectly obvious that a formal object is given along with supernatural grace and that this formal object cannot be attained by any purely natural power of knowing or willing. Here you can see my clear dependence upon Thomas as well as how I go beyond him. For I am convinced that grace is a new formal object and one that natural knowledge cannot attain. Hence I also hold that right from the beginning the history of revelation runs parallel with grace and salvation history, whether Thomas explicitly admits this or not. Of course no modern theologian would deny this connection. In other words, grace has always been given, and this supernatural formal object is always at work somewhere in the totality of human consciousness. Thus there has never been a time or a place that was not a part of the history of revelation. The history of revelation did not first start with Abraham. Consequently, I view the relationship of Christianity to other religions quite differently from someone like Jean Daniélou.

And I'd like to say that I am at this point being radically Thomistic, and I stand quite apart from the typical Jesuit line of thought. This line may have begun with Francisco Suarez and Luis de Molina, and it continued on up to my teacher, Hermann Lange, and his treatise *De gratia*. Without pinning myself down in terms of history, let me say that Jesuit theology, perhaps beginning with Baroque scholasticism, denied the connection that I just sketched. I find this creates a gap, at least in practice, between nature and grace, a gap that is really terrible. The failure to understand the teaching of Saint Thomas led to a strict separation between the human and the graced supernatural by a modern, seemingly humanistic real distinction between them. I believe the original and mortal sin of Jesuit theology lies right here.

I must, of course, add that men like Garrigou-Lagrange unquestionably clung to the Thomistic teachings. But in the last analysis they failed to understand them. They accepted the insights that I sketched as particular statements, but not as something they applied to the basic tenor of their own theology in an original way! Thomas himself has to be interpreted. He has magnificent things that he mentions here and there in passing, but he doesn't incorporate these insights into the basic framework of his theology.

For example, a student of mine, Pius Siller, wrote a doctoral dissertation on the incomprehensibility of God. He makes it clear that somewhere in a commentary on Sacred Scripture Thomas expresses more profound and radical ideas than in his own *Summa* where—while doing a somewhat scholastic theology—he passes over a great deal. That means one really has to learn many things from Thomas despite Thomas!

Are there views of Thomas that you would completely reject?
There are some which, to be frank, I have found and continue to find unsatisfactory. For example, recently someone told me that Thomas denies that one can have hope for another. In other words, according to him the supernatural virtue of hope permits and allows one only to have hope for one's own self. I regard this as a horror. If I didn't have the confidence to have hope for you, I wouldn't dare to have hope for myself. I believe that Thomas has not thought this matter through. As another example, Thomas has a certain intellectualism which does not, in the last analysis, square with a correct understanding of the ultimate ground. For example, Thomas sees the nature of the beatific vision as consisting of intellectual knowledge alone. In doing so, he denies nothing of the reality. But I think that, if Thomas had on this question made radical use of the interchangeability of being as true and being as good (*ens verum et ens bonum*), he might have formulated otherwise or possibly even seen more clearly the nature of the beatific vision. I believe Thomas has or could have a metaphysics of freedom that is really magnificent, even if it is not completely worked out. Yet the Thomism of the schools has not seen this clearly enough.

Allow me a question about your personal relation to Thomas. Did you as a teacher also "study" Thomas for your lectures?
I spent my longest time as a teacher in Innsbruck. There the emphasis was upon lecture courses and not upon seminars and courses on particular topics. If I recall correctly, I didn't spend much time on Thomas in such courses.

Apart from *Spirit in the World* and *Hearers of the Word*, I took up particular topics mainly because I was forced to do so by external circumstances. I haven't studied Thomas, Duns Scotus, Origen, or Augustine for their own sakes, but to deal with the concrete questions of contemporary human beings.

As far as concerns the lectures, I was obliged for reasons of organization to lecture on the same four tracts, but never on Christology, never on the Trinity, and so on. These were always handled by a colleague. Dogmatic theology was taught by two professors, mornings and afternoons. It was the same with fundamental theology. Furthermore, consider that along with the review session we lectured in dogmatic theology ten hours a week for six semesters, and yet we really never felt we had enough time to go more deeply into things in terms of the history of dogma or the history of ideas or philosophy. Then you may be able to understand that, in my opinion, too little dogmatic theology is now offered in the study of theology. With us in Innsbruck and also in Valkenburg, where I studied theology, dogmatic theology was the area of concentration. We may have also studied a little exegesis and church history. But during the time of my studies in Valkenburg we were taught, for example, in liturgy no more than was necessary to administer baptism, and three weeks before ordination we were taught how to say Mass. It doesn't have to be this way today. But how is one supposed to give Thomas any emphasis in today's program of studies?

One of your students, Herbert Vorgrimler, has said of you in his biography that modern theology is characterized by a stronger turn toward earthly reality and that this has to do with a rediscovery of Saint Thomas, which is in turn essentially linked to Karl Rahner's dissertation Spirit in the World.

That is two questions. To the latter, I suppose you can say that transcendental Maréchalian Thomism received a certain correction from *Spirit in the World*—and precisely insofar as "spirit" is emphasized in this work as transcendence that can only become aware of itself by the "*conversio ad phantasmata.*" And that should not be translated as "conversion to the sense image," but as "conversion to history, to the actuality of freedom, to one's fellow human beings."

I'd like to say something more about this theological turn to the world, regardless of whether or not it has anything to do with Thomas. I have repeatedly stressed, and I believe that I must say it even more clearly today, that modern theology's turn to the world too often fails to see that it all too quickly takes God as a stopgap for human beings, their happiness and their so-called self-realization. That is the greatest profanity and shamelessness toward God! I once lectured in Salzburg on "the uselessness of transcendence." I stressed that God is not there for us, but that we are there for him and that we are real Christians only when we let ourselves fall, in surrender and without condition, into the incomprehensibility of God along with Jesus the Crucified. All this modern chatter about self-realization and even the enlisting of the good God in politics, the Third World, and the like are from the devil! Of course we must do much more for the Third World, and we must take a critical stance toward our Western European bourgeois society. I have nothing against liberation theology or political theology. But didn't Johann Baptist Metz let himself be a bit taken in by Ernesto Cardenal? I was present in Frankfurt when Cardenal explained that the kingdom of God had begun in Nicaragua, that there were no prisons there anymore, that everyone loved one another. . . . I won't have anything to do with such nonsense!

We must not overlook the danger that the modern period leans toward the heresy I mentioned of allowing God only to play the role of a stopgap for those cases in which human beings can no longer manage alone. I will have nothing to do with such a pseudohumanistic and horizontal theology. Of course many of the younger theologians, such as Johann Baptist Metz or Peter Eicher, object that my theology is much too a priori and transcendental. They say that the encounter with the concrete God of history comes off badly—and right in the social-political situation in which we live. My answer is that I at least held open this perspective in principle and in no sense denied it. Moreover, I don't regard my theology as universal and as having general and final validity. Theologians always take up in their thought particular points of view and don't notice that they overlook others in doing so. That was the case with Thomas, and that holds, of course, for contemporary theologians as well.

Even if this topic deserves further discussion, I am afraid that we are moving too far away from our initial question, namely, to what extent is Karl Rahner an important, modern disciple of Saint Thomas?

I was never a commentator on Saint Thomas and have really had no relation to him such as the Dominicans may have had earlier. To put it bluntly, if I wanted to defend something and could appeal to Thomas to do so, that was all right with me, and that was what I did. As a concrete example, among other things I was convinced by my study of patristics that the aspect of *pax cum ecclesia* ("peace with the Church") should not be left out of the sacrament of penance. By the way, note that the Second Vatican Council also stressed this, for example, in *Lumen Gentium*. In short, I have been happy to appeal to Thomas in cases like this. He had many theological insights that were forgotten in the course of the centuries. Think, for example, of Thomas's basic conviction that to be and to be present to oneself are the same or that freedom is merely the self-actualization of the person. I believe the metaphysics of matter in Thomas—where matter is understood in the philosophical sense—needs to be taken seriously. If it is, it seems to me Thomas certainly provides a foundation for the theory that I once worked out that in death the human person does not become a-cosmic, but rather all-cosmic. In this regard Thomas's teaching is not completely consistent. If, for example, he had really taken seriously his own theory of the *anima forma corporis* (the soul as the form of the body), then he would not have been able to speak in general of an *anima separata* (a soul separated from the body). Here is a case where one can be truer to Thomas than Thomas himself.

Besides all these theological details that you connect with Thomas, I have the impression, especially after reading Hearers of the Word, *that your motives in doing theology are very similar to those of Aquinas. Like Thomas, you want to come to an intellectual grasp of reality as we confess it in the faith of the Church.*

Yes, unlike Hans Küng and such people I never really wanted to do a theology that called into question the teaching authority of the Church where it bound me unconditionally. I have, for example, in the course of my theological activity defended out of genuine inner conviction many a teaching of the Church. Of some of these I would now say that I can no longer see it that way. Perhaps I should have been able to size it up differently then.

For example, I worked very hard to defend and to interpret the teaching on membership in the Church in Pius XII's encyclical *Mystici Corporis Christi* (1943). I did this in a way I probably could no longer bring myself to do. Similarly, in another case I tried to accept John XXIII's *Veterum Sapientia* (1962). So too I previously tried to defend and support, perhaps intelligently, but ultimately incorrectly, the monogenism of Pius XII's *Humani Generis*. And still earlier during the war I had lectured in Vienna to pious nuns on the Heart of Mary. Now I wonder whether I'd still do this. Probably I would say no and wonder whether I should not have left it alone then. Nonetheless, there are also topics on which I have held opinions that diverge from teachings of the Church, though not from defined ones. I am thinking of *Humanae Vitae* (1968), the question of the ordination of women, and so on.

You already mentioned the stance you tried to take with respect to the teaching authority of the Church. That reminds me of Thomas who supposedly held that the theologian was subject to the magisterium (the teaching authority).

You have to consider Saint Thomas in a highly nuanced way. On the one hand, he was suspect as an innovator by the official theology, at least in Paris, on account of many teachings. Of course there was then neither a Holy Office nor a man like Cardinal Ratzinger. On the other hand, Thomas got along quite well with the popes of his time. All in all, he was certainly *one* theologian among many others, even if he was a very important and respected one. This means that the apotheosis of Thomas Aquinas goes back only to Leo XIII; it came about slowly in the course of history since Cajetan through the Jesuits and the Dominicans and the post-Tridentine period up into the nineteenth century. When Leo XIII says that Thomas is the sea into which all the rivers of wisdom flow, so that from now on one need only consult him, I regard this as exaggeration and nonsense.

But I must also say that I find Thomas attractive. For with all the spiritual devotion that can be found in him, he is more sober and realistic than many another medieval theologian, including the Franciscan Bonaventure. And yet I would certainly count this contemporary of Saint Thomas's as one of the few independent theologians along with the "Angelic Doctor." I read Bonaventure's *Itinerarium mentis in Deum* (*The Soul's Journey into God*) with a certain enthusiasm. As far as that goes, I am by no means ready to grant Thomas an absolute rank beyond comparison with other theologians. On the other hand, as I said, Thomas's sobriety and realism appeal to me; in this respect his spirituality emerges as more restrained than that of many another medieval theologian, including Bonaventure.

I think we have spoken enough about your own relation to Thomas. Let's turn to the question of the history of the influence of Thomas and its investigation.

Perhaps by way of preface to the question I might tell a story to make a point about the principal methodology for such an investigation of the history of a thinker's influence. A Dutch theologian, whose name now escapes me, once told me that unfortunately not a word about Pierre Teilhard de Chardin, S.J., shows up in my theology, though he clearly inspired all my thought. I could only answer that at least up to that time I had read practically nothing of Teilhard de Chardin. But if you concluded from this that Rahner's theology is independent of Teilhard, I would answer that I don't make any such claim.

For the investigation of the history of the influence of a thinker this means that there is obviously a kind of "atmospheric communication" of a meta-literary kind. As another example, I have long stressed in my theology the incomprehensibility of God. This point is found in Thomas as well, but I don't think he brought it sufficiently to bear upon the basic framework of his theology. Therefore someone could claim that in this respect I was influenced, not by Thomas, but by Søren Kierkegaard, or by John of the Cross. To that I could only say that I have read only a little of the latter, but that doesn't mean I haven't been heavily influenced by him in a meta-literary fashion. Or, after *Spirit in the World* appeared, Hans Urs von Balthasar wrote in his review that I was inspired by Fichte, though I had never read a line of his. Thomas, too, is obviously a thinker who would have been influenced in a similar way by others. Despite his brilliance he did not fall from heaven. He too lived in a concrete situation that was not interchangeable with any other in history, with all the things that seemed plausible to him, though we may judge him quite differently from our point in history.

I am afraid that we can't take into account such meta-literary influences in the study of the history of Saint Thomas's influence. Otherwise, the task will become immense. Hence we have set about "studying" only those theologians who can be shown by the normal scientific methods to have read and studied some or all of the works of Thomas. It goes without saying, of course, that some people have read Thomas without being influenced by him in the least. Who then really deserves to be called a disciple of Aquinas?

In reply to your last question, Josef Pieper of Münster comes to mind as an example. On the one hand, he is a straightforward expositor of Thomas; on the other hand, he is brilliant in a way. He has written a small, valuable book as an introduction to Thomas's work, and he has written it in a very beautiful way that appeals to the minds and hearts of people today (Munich, 1958). Pieper's writing is perhaps not very profound and speculative, but his philosophy and theology are still derived from Thomas. Today he is almost forgotten, though his works went through huge editions.

I certainly understand your objection to considering meta-literary influences of Thomas upon particular theologians. We might get further if we concentrated upon particular philosophical and theological topics. On some of these Thomas took a position in a way that was never taken up in the general thinking of the Church. But some of these were handed down elsewhere and can, precisely for that reason, be shown to be typical of Thomas. In other words, can't one prove a historical influence of Thomas by finding certain topics that Thomas, so to speak, predefined to an extent? And then might one not show that these have not simply disappeared as sayings of the Common Doctor from the general consciousness of the Church, but have been continually handed down somewhere as fruitful, exciting, and inspiring? For example, Father Johann Stufler, my predecessor in Munich, taught a strange, old-fashioned, almost dry-as-dust scholasticism. But in the twenties he wrote a book on God's acting in the activity of every creature, especially in the activity of free choice (*Divi Thomae Aquinatis doctrina de Deo operante in omni operatione naturae creatae praesertim liberi arbitri* 1923). He may have spotted something in Thomas that had gone unnoticed up to then, but that could have a fundamental, even a radical impact on theology. Stufler's book was a polemic against the followers of Domingo Bañez with his teaching of *praemotio physica*, according to which one can act only under the immediate influence of God. In Stufler's presentation of Thomas, God only acts upon the world insofar as he produces the powers of creatures and not as a particular causal factor within the world. That may be dangerous or at least problematic, but for me it's fundamentally plausible, almost a presupposition. Thomas may have seen it, but it was overlooked by the scholastic Thomists. It may now have been rediscovered, just as one digs up a treasure without realizing what he has found.

But won't it be quite difficult to discover such topics, and so might it not be easier and better to begin with specifically Thomistic topics?

Of course, if one wants to investigate the history of Thomas's influence, it's obvious that at least the first step should be what you've suggested. Where Thomas has been explicitly influential is where you find the primary data for the history of his influence. Here, of course, the question arises as to how far we must take account of the fact that the character of traditional Thomism has changed. For example, the previously mentioned *praemotio physica* of Bañez was long taken to be the true and genuine doctrine of Thomas himself. However, in the last thirty or forty years many scholars have said that this doctrine is not Thomas's and is really Scotistic.

Yes, that is the problem. Where has Thomas been correctly understood?

We could, of course, say that the misunderstandings that have as a matter of fact resulted are also part of the history of his influence, for somehow or other Thomas is responsible for them as well.

With that you've brought up a problem that entered quite early into our reflections, namely: What does the concept, "history of the influence," mean? What does "influence" mean? I think one can say that all the erroneous interpretations and misunderstandings are part of the history of his influence. But let's only speak of the influence of Thomas upon someone when he is correctly understood, as far as one can judge this objectively.

This is, of course, especially difficult in the case of great thinkers and theologians. Their attitude toward many things is ultimately quite ambivalent, and rightly so. For example, what my own teachers in philosophy taught can be easily determined. But take a man like Nietzsche. Is he simply an atheist? Or does his philosophy contain other points on which he is clearsighted and doesn't attack the truth of the Christian faith, but rather defends it from misunderstandings? Isn't the case the same with Thomas? Isn't he like a huge forest out of which anyone can cut what he wants. This, of course, makes the question about the history of his influence difficult. Furthermore, great minds will say many things that give the impression that they have not reflected on the contradictoriness or compatibility of all that they have said. Consequently, later readers can take from the whole work widely differing views. And precisely with regard to Thomas I must clearly say: it is almost a priori evident that he has contradicted himself without noticing it.

Hence Thomas is the source of many different streams of thought. Just think of people like my fellow Jesuit, Francisco Suarez, who considered himself just as truly and radically a Thomist as his opponent, the Dominican Bañez, though the latter may have been three-quarters Scotist without knowing it. And what was Cajetan? Is he the "true" classical interpreter of Thomas? Or does he make the historical Thomas into a Cajetanism?

Such contradictions in the work of Saint Thomas can be most easily shown in individual cases.

Yes, the scholastic Thomists, even in my time, held in Christology on the doctrine of the hypostatic union that *esse* (existence) is really distinct from *essentia* (essence) and that the divine *esse* of the Word is that by which the humanity of Jesus exists. We Jesuits always regarded that as the greatest piece of nonsense and ultimately as not Catholic. Up to the present it remains undecided in the history of interpretation whether this classical Thomistic theory is really Thomas's. I have never put it to the test, but these differing interpretations may rest on the fact that Thomas actually contradicted himself in different writings.

In this connection perhaps one should also ask what was really behind the controversy on grace between the followers of Luis de Molina, S.J., and those of Domingo Bañez, O.P. On the surface, the Jesuits and Dominicans were fighting like the devil before the pope. Princes were stirred to action, and so on. But one has to see this controversy in relation to the intellectual history of its time. Both the Jesuits and the Dominicans thought they could prevail over Calvinism with their theory. I think Bañezianism contained, even if in somewhat disguised form, the Augustinism that can readily be found in Michael Baius and Martin Luther, and so the Jesuits correctly concluded that you are basically Calvinists. The whole dispute, moreover, had something to do with the humanism of the time. The Jesuits had a theology that, for all its loyalty to the Church and the pope, was conciliatory toward a free and modern humanism. But beyond all these explanations one has to ask whether something quite different wasn't behind the controversy on grace, namely, a fundamentally different reading of Thomas.

The impact of Thomas upon the Jesuits surely brings up one of the most important questions one could ask in a conversation on the history of the influence of Thomas Aquinas. The Thomistic renaissance of the recent past, neo-Thomism, started with the Jesuits of the nineteenth century, not with the Dominicans. In your opinion how did this sudden return to a thinker of the thirteenth century come about? Was it a matter of trying to bring back the past, of defensiveness, as many believe?

Even apart from the justified curiosity of the historian, your question is important for the sole reason that an answer to it can further help to assess the Catholicism of the era of restoration in the post-Napoleonic period up to Pius XII. That means the historical judgment on the Thomistic restoration will almost coincide with the judgment upon the Catholic Church in the Pian epoch from, as I see it, Pius VII to Pius XII. But how did we get the idea of making Thomas the Common Doctor and the philosophical and theological representative of Catholic Christianity?

If I'm not mistaken, there was on the one hand a strong movement that was trying to bring back the past. But on the other hand, the appeal to Thomas was, at least on the part of Leo XIII, an attempt to be able to react better to the questions of the present.

Right. As strange as it sounds, in comparison to Pius IX, Leo XIII was a liberal and a man open to the world. There is, of course, always that sort of thing in the history of the Church. I regard the present pope, for example, as progressive in terms of society and politics, but as trying to bring back the past in theology. Such contradictions or divisions often exist in a person's mind and at times in the Church as well.

Certainly the problem ought not to be oversimplified as, for example, was done a few years back by an ignorant journalist, Manfred Barthel, in his book *The Jesuits* (Düsseldorf, 1982). According to him, from 1814 up to the present the Society of Jesus followed a wholly negative, stupid, and reactionary course apart from exceptions, like me and a few others. But even in the nineteenth century the Thomists and followers of Thomas who were seeking to bring back the past were no dummies!Why then was there suddenly a push for such a return to earlier theologians and philosophers? Actually Leo XIII only made this trend an official obligation. The result was that the teaching of Thomas became the official doctrine of even the Jesuits. (In practice this may have seemed something different.) The allegiance to a theologian of the remote past with the aim of bringing back the past was undeniable. The theological climate was set by a number of facts. Leo XIII had condemned in the decree *Post Obitum* (1887) forty-nine statements of the ontologist Antonio de Rosmini-Serbati. The Tübingen theology really did not measure up either, and to mention a final example, though John Henry Newman became a cardinal, he never had a really vital significance for his own time.

Of course one can say that many Christians felt threatened in the nine-teenth century by the modern spirit of the Enlightenment. They thought they could only survive by a return to the past. It may also be that many really saw in Thomas the *penseur moderne*, as they said. But why did this happen in such a striking fashion? I think that in the case of many theologians in Rome, intelligent French Thomists, one could show from their lives that they became Thomists after they had turned away from the world in a sort of existential conversion and had become hostile to it. To what extent this applies to Jacques Maritain, I cannot say. Yet his intelligent and profound, but also furious and fanatic, Thomism is strange. Perhaps we are really faced with a problem that is ultimately insoluble in terms of intellectual history.

It may be that we can't tell whether the motives for neo-Thomism were in the last analysis reactionary or progressive. But I have a final question: Can one really aim at a restoration of the past through a return to Thomas Aquinas? Thomas himself surely had no such aim.

Leo XIII would have said no. For Thomas had advanced the theology that had come before him so that we now find in him a master that cannot in principle be surpassed. And right there lies the oddity. Up to Pius XII—just look at *Humani Generis* (1950)—there prevailed in the Church the strange idea that there had been a history of dogmas and their development, but now we were at last in possession of concepts that could not be improved. If such an idea is deeply impressed on the psyche through a shock, as, for example, in the nineteenth century through the Enlightenment, it is quite understand-able that the return to a progressive thinker like Thomas could lead to conservatism.

Translated by Roland J. Teske, S.J.
Marquette University

Part II

INDIVIDUAL THEOLOGICAL QUESTIONS

5 • Liberation Theology

Interview with Ton Oostveen, Amsterdam (September 1978)

Father Rahner, many see you as the champion of liberation theology, to whom tough class warriors and disciples of Karl Marx can appeal as their ideologue or at least as their inspiration. Is that right?

Leftist groups may appeal to what I have written, and rightly so. But that still doesn't make me their theoretician. Someone like that would have to agree with such a group on all the basic features of their theological and sociological ideas and would have to have been their developer. And there can be no question of that.

Of what then?

My theology is not so specific that it can be simply distinguished from that of others. My insights go along with the spirit of the conciliar constitution *Gaudium et Spes*, on the mission of the Church in society and politics. They emerge from a concept such as "love of neighbor as bearer of the love of God." But one cannot construct a full-fledged political theology from this idea. If I differ from others, perhaps it is because and insofar as I express more reserve with respect to the thinking of German Catholics and the German bishops.

Among other things this reserve has to do with the fact that the many millions that Adveniat, the German Church's aid program, distributes to the Third World, winds up, at least in South America, in the hands of powers suspicious of and opposed to liberation theology, doesn't it?

I don't want to state my opinion as to whether and to what extent a Christian can be a Marxist or a Leninist as long as I don't know what such Christians understand by Marxism or Leninism. But one who completely accepts what Marx says goes too far for me!

A major objection against the Church's "classroom theology" says that it does not arise from the actual experience of human persons, as, for example, in South America where only the class struggle can bring freedom. At least the leftist groups see it this way.

Actually my theology doesn't reflect every social experience. But are Christians forbidden—at the risk of not being true Christians—to belong to a particular social group in Europe? Must I under threat of the worst punishments of hell necessarily break with my social milieu? Can I really be a Christian only in the manner of Camilo Torres? To that I say no!

If a Christian must stand on the side of the proletariat, wouldn't he like to know which proletariat: that of the German union leaders, that of the terrorists, or that of the Eurocommunists, like Enrico Berlinguer?

I don't want to deny that there are Christians who decide to live and to work outside the mainstream as members of the proletariat without obliging me to do so. We can praise and thank God for them. By being outside the mainstream such Christians can develop new experiences in love of neighbor, pastoral strategy, and so on. In this way they can develop an authentic theology. For this reason I am favorable toward groups of leftist Christians, such as Calama, without being their theoretician.

When Bishop López Trujillo declares that Marxism is unacceptable, he must first explain to me what he means by this. In any case, I recognize the basic Christian inspiration of a number of groups, the unselfishness of such persons who want to serve. I really don't know and cannot know more than this. Hence I hold that the Church need not officially recognize such groups, but it must certainly tolerate them. When one does not know and cannot know whether one is dealing with truth or error, the Church has to be patient with experiments.

What do you think of rejecting particular social orders that are feared as Marxist on the grounds of their being contrary to the faith?

I won't hide the fact that I stand further to the left—to use this silly expression—than most German Catholics. But that doesn't mean that I give up all relativizing and distinguishing. I want to say that I regard it as dangerous to characterize liberation theology as a "diabolical" manifestation. But that by no means obliges me to find everything good on the side of the leftists or to set right out for Cuba.

Can one tie German Catholicism's support of reactionary efforts in the Third World to other disturbing signs in Germany, such as, for example, loyalty checks for jobs, antiterrorist laws . . .?

You are thinking of the Adveniat question, aren't you? Well, good, but I don't know whether one can tie the Adveniat problem so quickly to the rightist movements in Germany. Still I have no doubt that one should keep an eye on tendencies to revive the past in the Roman Catholic Church of Germany. Obviously there are movements aiming at restoration that deserve support. But I take my stand on the side of all who are against a restoration that is decreed from on high.

The pope and the European Catholics, specifically in Germany and the Netherlands, are becoming more and more suspected of aiming at a restoration. Were I someone actively involved in the class struggle, I'd be likely to leave such a Church.

I doubt that it is good to view these conservative currents only from the viewpoint of the class struggle. Social developments are much too complicated for that. Besides, I would ask right off: Why should I approve at all the really unchristian horizontalism in contemporary theology? Do I have to agree with it just because it claims to be modern? When the bishops stand for the preservation of certain limits against this theological current, I am thoroughly in agreement with them. Anyway, the episcopacy has by definition the task of conserving, of protecting. That is perhaps not so essential, but I do not find it so bad either.

But isn't it the case that too many bishops still seem to lean to the right rather than to the left?

That could possibly be due to a century-long habit. In any case, I ask myself how that can bother the left? Given their concept of the Church, they have no need to be upset if the bishops don't carry the banners of their movement.

Besides, in Europe we had absolute monarchies for centuries and so a social order that no one is trying to restore today, not even the conservatives. Hence I think that one shouldn't be so quick to excommunicate today's social critics, even if their concept of society is offensive. But I would be opposed to a Marxist government imposed against our will. Where can I find Marxist governments under which one can still call Christianity free? Unfortunately this combination has nowhere been proved possible, whatever the Eurocommunists promise. True, leftist Christian groups claim that they would cooperate with all social powers. But I wonder whether, when they have come to power, groups hostile to religion will not again have the upper hand.

Since the tough class struggle doesn't leave very much room for differentiation, I'd like to hear from you what you think of the leftist dogma that the Church must be the partisan of the poor.

I, of course, want the Church of South America to be the Church of the poor.

What would you do if the Church, the official Church, made a decision against the workers? That's what is feared from Puebla (1979).

That really makes the question a tough one. The Church changes too, even if slowly. According to the example of Jesus the Church may not and must not regard all classes as equal to one another. She must take the part of the poor. But that is not to say that a particular social class is the bearer of everything good and beautiful.

The Church can stand now on this, now on that side. And the Church can or ecclesial authorities can, of course, make mistakes. Human weaknesses cannot be excluded. When there is question of financial support for those attacking liberation theology, I don't think that you can say that it is the conscious strategy of our aid program, Adveniat, to support right-wing political forces against the left. But I fear, nonetheless, that it happens unconsciously. And we want to warn against that.

In that way you relativize almost everything, but meanwhile with your open letter (cf. "Attack and Reply," published by the study circle Church and Freedom, Aschaffenburg, 1978) you threw a rock into the beautiful showcase of German Catholicism.

Liberation theology has opened our eyes to structural injustice. Previously that wasn't in our moral books, and it is very important. Meanwhile we still struggle over the relation of structural and personal sinfulness. When does structural sinfulness become your or my personal sin so that we have to answer for it before God? You go home and your wife treats you to a special offer from the supermarket, a wonderful South American banana. When you enjoy the banana, haven't you taken more from the poor South American banana picker than if you stole a thousand guilders from a fat cat from the Netherlands? Maybe, yes; maybe, no.

And so I hope that our open letter has contributed to the continued possibility of the progressive liberation theology needed in South America. Of course I have my concerns about what can happen in Puebla. However, I don't expect a radical turnabout, not even in Puebla. In the Church you always have to count on a certain shrewdness. The Church isn't going to dish up anything radical. And precisely for this reason I do not look for any catastrophe from Puebla. Besides, Vatican II can't be undone even there.

Translated by Roland J. Teske, S.J.
Marquette University

6• The Devil, Possession, and Exorcism

Interview with Reinhold Iblacker, S.J., Munich (September 1974)

Father Rahner, today's media are whipping up a devil craze. For example, you've seen William Peter Blatty's The Exorcist. *Does this film really have anything at all to do with what you as a professor of theology think and teach?*

I must say that it really shows nothing at all that is of concern to the theologian and the Christian. People say that you can almost see the devil at work there. But they see nothing of him at all if they look carefully. They see nothing more than sick people. They see illnesses perhaps with some parapsychological trimmings and decked out with religious formulas, but not evil and certainly not God. When I look into my heart, I discover more evil with which I have to reckon in all earnestness than when I hear sick people utter obscenities. And in the mouth of a sick person they have nothing to do with morality at all. Even if you look at the world, you can see much more evil. But you can also in certain circumstances discover a living relation to God in faith, hope, and love. These are fine things about which this film shows us nothing at all.

In The Exorcist *the following takes place for everyone to see: the doctors, the psychiatrists, who are working on this case and practicing their art, first claim that they are agnostic and scientifically neutral. But in the end they give up and hand the patient over to the Church and the people the Church has empowered to perform the exorcism. As a theologian, what do you say to that?*

If a learned psychiatrist claims that one can as a matter of fact get no further in a case, one could say the same thing of a thousand other psychiatric cases in which no one dreams of possession. But if one asserts that this science, along with parapsychology, is simply unable to explain the given phenomena, then I have to ask myself as a theologian whether I may or even must come up with a theological interpretation of the phenomenon. But the mere fact that a psychiatrist throws in the towel is still no proof that psychiatry basically fails and has to fail in this case. If the psychiatrists worked longer and applied more subtle methods, if they worked more in depth with these phenomena on their level, they might make further progress.

You said after seeing the film that it is really the psychiatrists who should be upset, not the theologians.

Yes, because they seem to give up too quickly in this case. Because they can here and now do no more, they hand the matter right over to the theologians and exorcists. And yet the psychiatrists are still supposed to consider the exorcism only as a special method of psychological or psychiatric treatment. They don't believe in the underlying causes that the real exorcists presuppose.

Do you think there is an attempt to reconcile what might be thought of as possession and what the experience of psychic disturbances teaches?

If you cautiously presuppose influences of the evil one in the world—however that is to be interpreted theologically—these would still have their effect through illnesses that psychiatry can deal with. Even given this presupposition, psychiatrists must approach these illnesses precisely as illnesses and with their own means and presuppositions.

William Peter Blatty, the author of The Exorcist *stated that his work has a special theological meaning, if one looks to the end of the priest-psychiatrist. Before he dies, he takes the possession upon himself. It is thus not only a death of atonement, but a possession of atonement; by taking over the evil he works for the good: a negative path to God.*

First of all, that is an interpretation of what is shown and, moreover, a very doubtful one. Of course we see that the exorcism as such is not working. Suddenly there comes a moral act of heroism which drives out the devil. At that point people think that they have proof that the Church's exorcism expelled the devil. Second, the supposed atoning death has nothing to do with exorcism in the ordinary sense. Third, there remains the question about the causal connection between this "atonement" and the healing that follows it. Such a connection can be explained in a thousand different ways, and it remains a completely open question whether the suggested explanation is the right one.

If we look not only to the film, but to the sort of persons who work as exorcists, they seem to claim with absolute certainty that persons possessed by the devil, by the personal devil, are no longer free in managing their lives. Does that not contradict any understanding, even a theological understanding, of human freedom?

Not of itself. If I say, for example, that a particular person is under the influence of drugs or is incapable of being responsible for psychiatric reasons, I am also saying that this person here and now cannot make use of his or her freedom in a sense that we can empirically grasp. But at that point the phenomenon really ceases to be of any theological concern. If you suffered an attack of madness and killed me during it, I would be quite dead. But, in that case, basically nothing different would have happened than if I had died from cancer or from any other disease. These are things that properly belong to the profane sphere. And when someone acting as an exorcist says that a particular person is so possessed by the devil that there is no more freedom, then everything that follows upon this really has no theological interest.

Is that a theological trick by which you're going to get out of difficulties in the future, or is it a conclusion that says something serious, something essential for human beings?

A person has to answer before God only for what one freely does, and only such actions are significant for one's eternal salvation. Hence, if I presuppose that a person is so occupied in his or her psyche—by whomsoever—and is held captive so as to be unable to act freely, these are things that by their definition are of no concern for the person's salvation, at least immediately.

You say, "occupied . . . by whomsoever." May I pursue this? Do you mean by whomsoever, or by whatsoever?

You can say as you wish, "by whomsoever" or "by whatsoever."

What do you mean when you say, "by whomsoever"?

If I suppose a contemporary and theologically correct understanding of the devil's existence, I can and must reckon with some influences of a demonic sort upon human existence. I say this on such a supposition. Whether this supposition is valid or not is quite another question and one that we cannot now discuss. For we are discussing the phenomenon of possession and not the theological question of the devil's existence.

But what would you as a priest and pastor say if a Christian said that possession is a proof of the devil's activity?

First of all, it seems to me clear that a person, who—to put it in plain language—is crazy, decks out and objectifies his or her craziness with the means available from when one was healthy. A religious person is much more likely than one who is not religious to come upon the idea that the voices heard while suffering schizophrenia come from outside, from the devil. In other words, if you produce phenomena like that in the film, there is the danger that other sick persons will deck out their twisted imagery with religious motives, concepts, and interpretations. And then naive people will argue that such a phenomenon is proof that one has a case of genuine possession in the traditional theological sense. In other words, if you are constantly speaking of the devil, you shouldn't be surprised that he or she turns up.

The phenomenon of evil, of real evil, of evil in the world that must be answered for before God is something completely different from possession. Even the theologians of the Middle Ages knew that possession had little and only indirectly to do with freedom and, therefore, with responsibility before God and with eternal salvation. The phenomenon of possession is in any case a very complex one. No one denies that there are case histories that sometimes include parapsychological events and that all these different phenomena are found together in a very peculiar combination. As a result the question arises whether behind all this there is something else called the evil one at work in a special way. An almost unanswerable question!

If there are exorcists who in the face of particular phenomena are absolutely convinced that it is the evil one, in my opinion they conclude too readily to the devil. They think they know from Holy Scripture and the Church's tradition precisely how to think of the devil's activity. And I think that they are too quick with their answer in both respects.

What do you mean when you say that exorcists think they know precisely how to interpret the statements of Scripture and tradition about the working of the devil?
I mean to say that one has first of all to ask how the demonic that is undeniably attested to in Scripture is to be brought within the intellectual horizon of a modern, self-critical person.

How do you picture such demonic powers? How would you seek to bring your ideas within the intellectual horizon of a person of today?
First of all, I don't picture to myself demonic powers. But I would say to a contemporary person that they are "thinkable" within his or her intellectual horizon. For if we are once again inclined to accept extraterrestrial intelligences, why should it be automatically impossible to conceive extrahuman intelligences of a higher sort that stand in another relation to the world and to matter than we do? Can I not also think of there being such superhuman but finite, created intelligences as ordering principles of particular areas of the world? And can we not also think that such spiritual "great entelechies" of the world are without a personal history and thus have decided for or against God?

But you don't see a necessary connection between human action and some influence of these spirits?
There is certainly no necessary connection between human freedom and such extrahuman personal influences. Such a necessary connection would destroy freedom.

But the so-called exorcists say there is a necessary connection and it legitimates their intervention.

I can only answer that in no case of possession that I have come to know has the proof been compelling that there was a special case of demonic influence. Hence exorcists should not seek to drive out the devil, but to make use of "natural" means. For until the opposite is proved, such phenomena are to be explained *naturally.* This demand for a "natural" explanation for an empirically given phenomenon is also a theological postulate until the opposite is proved. But I think that no one either has proved or can prove that these appearances clearly have as their cause some individual, personal, created and extrahuman reality. I do not thereby deny that, in a theological perspective, it remains fundamentally possible to trace evil, diseases, and guilt back to an extrahuman cause that is also at work and conditions the situation.

Father Rahner, you regard it then as practically impossible ever to produce a clear proof that a case of alleged possession is clearly to be traced back to a demonic cause. Does this not mean as a consequence renouncing any activity of exorcism on the part of a priest?

That depends on what you understand by exorcism. If you think of exorcism as I think of my prayer at the bed of a cancer patient, then I can see a justification for the existence of exorcists even in cases of alleged possession. For a cancer patient I first of all call a physician, but I still do not give up on my prayer for the sick person.

Translated by Roland J. Teske, S.J.
Marquette University

7 • Do We Need a Third Vatican Council?

Interview with Helmut Gumnior, Hamburg (1976)

Professor Rahner, your colleague, Professor Hans Küng, has suggested convoking a Third Vatican Council. What do you think of this suggestion?
All things considered, I am not in favor of this proposal. To me, from a practical and concrete point of view, given today's situation in Rome, it seems unrealistic and inopportune, despite one's understanding or at least partial sympathy for Küng's proposal.

Why do you say unrealistic?
Of course the Church can convoke a council at any time, but only the pope can do so. Given that fact, I think it is unrealistic to hope that the present pope [Paul VI], given his present Curia and his present advisors, would consider convoking a Third Vatican Council. The pope is too old.

. . . and also perhaps too preoccupied with the after effects of Vatican II?
I think, if I can speak somewhat provocatively, that the pope is still somewhat frightened by his experiences after Vatican II.

You must be referring to inner-church debates brought on by Vatican II, for example, disagreements about liturgical reforms that are at the heart of Archbishop Lefebvre's protests. But, in fact, isn't Küng right when he argues that there is a whole series of very delicate ecclesiastical questions (for example, celibacy, how the pope is elected, birth control) which could best be resolved by a new council?
A new council is not only unrealistic, it is also inopportune. I think that Küng's proposal is too premature. To use his words, it would require broader "mutual exploration." Besides, do you really think that nowadays, only a few years after Pope Paul VI's opposition to artificial contraception, that a directive contradicting the papal statement is conceivable? Could you imagine a council that would outvote the pope? So, whoever is hoping for new regulations about papal elections or appointments of bishops cannot hope realistically for a council but only for a gradual, patient development.

Still, we suppport Küng's suggestion that the pope be elected by all the bishops throughout the Catholic world instead of by the college of cardinals, and his other suggestion that the bishops should be chosen by the clergy and laity of a given diocese.

Can you imagine that today you could find a majority of bishops who would agree to abrogate Paul VI's recent regulations about papal elections by the college of cardinals, and that the pope would agree to that?

That doesn't mean one shouldn't discuss the idea.
Küng's insistence on "mutual exploration" of specific questions is all very well and good. Today lots of people find that attractive and amusing. But what is all that supposed to achieve?

Well, perhaps it could bring about some improvements. Nowadays, practically all important decisions in the Catholic Church are made by the pope and the bishops. But the Church is made up not only of priests; most believers are laypersons. Where, through what forum, can this majority express its views?
The laity must gradually and from below influence those in official positions and slowly affect their awareness. Precisely because such a change of awareness among those holding positions of leadership in the Church needs more time than what would be available at a hastily convened council with all its time constraints, I regard such an ecclesiastical assembly, even along the lines of Küng's proposal, as undesirable. The bishops and pope are not likely to be influenced hastily by protests from below or by expressed needs however justifiable they might be.

There seem to be, as far as we can judge, many Catholic faithful who are unhappy with their Church precisely because it only governs but doesn't consult. Wouldn't it be possible to admit laypersons as council fathers?
I think one should start considering such a proposal. Thought should be given to see how, if you will, those at the base of the Church might articulate their views more clearly, how they might be heard. Of course that presupposes, as Catholics are convinced, that an opinion at the base does not automatically replace the unchangeable truth of the gospel.

So you believe therefore that a certain democratization of the Catholic Church is necessary.
"Democratization" is a vague idea. Nobody knows exactly what is meant by the term.

. . . Shared decision-making! Or more accurately: lay representation in councils.
Let me respond first with a question of my own. Why can't the bishop be

regarded as a representative of the people for whom he serves as bishop? A second question: How can you concretely conceive of democratization in a Church that has several billion members? There are a thousand questions! Who is to be elected from the base? Would you include those who haven't attended church for thirty years and who bear a grudge against the pope. Should such persons be elected? Why couldn't democratization or shared decision-making be initiated at lower levels?

How? Where?

One could imagine that the choice of bishops could include a meaningfully designed and juridically structured participation by priests and people. Then bishops would participate at a council as real representatives of their dioceses. I don't object to the idea of laypersons participating in a council. . . .

. . . Even laypersons who, for example, push for a new directive about birth control?

As far as the problem of birth control is concerned, the reason why it is such a critical issue is not because a majority favors a new ruling. The reason why it is critical lies in an objective situation.

Do you mean overpopulation on the earth or growing hunger would argue for a new decision about birth control?

Yes, on the basis of those kinds of reasons a new directive would be desirable.

When you say "a new directive would be desirable," do you mean specifically the elimination of the prohibition against using birth control pills?

To answer your question, I would repeat what I said: when you take a sober look at the situation, you see that the directive is in point of fact being adjusted in the Church. But it would still be desirable to have a theoretical directive. Still, I wouldn't expect any adjustment to take place in the next ten or twenty years.

Are you saying that the pope's statement stands in the way?

At present we have *Humanae Vitae* and we cannot expect that in the next twenty years the prohibition against the pill would be reversed by some kind of an official statement.

Doesn't this situation, namely, that in the next twenty years nothing can be changed, indicate that something is amiss in the Catholic Church's way of making decisions?

No. What it proves is that really profound changes in the Church's mentality can come about only slowly. Changes in the Church can't be simply decreed as political decisions. In fact, they should be an expression of the faith perceptions of the entire Church.

Would you like to see in the Church more mobility, more elasticity, in light of a very rapidly changing world?

Precisely. That is exactly my own wish.

Hasn't the decision of 1870 regarding papal infallibility turned out to be unfortunate for the Church?

No. Even today the dogmatic decision of that time still exercises a binding force on me. Of course the practical atmosphere, the practical style and procedures used by the Roman Curia are other issues.

Do you mean that the Curia has appropriated too many rights?

You have to understand that a society such as Catholic Christianity has the right to take its own tradition and history seriously, and thus can change only slowly.

Does the Church really have that much time?

That's another question altogether. Perhaps the Church will have to pay in the future for the fact that it reacted too slowly to many things. I have to admit that this possibility weighs heavily upon me.

So nothing can be changed?

That's not what I said. nothing can be changed here and now by a quickly convoked council, as Hans Küng thinks.

Translated by Michael A. Fahey, S.J.
University of Saint Michael's College, Toronto

8 • Witness to the Council

Interview with Thomas C. Fox, Innsbruck (1982)

Father Rahner, many younger Christians cannot fully appreciate the significance of Vatican II because they never experienced the time before the Council or at least not consciously. You are one of the men who participated in this Council of renewal. What kind of expectations did you have as you went to the Council?

It's hard to answer that in a few words. Before the Council and at its beginning there were a number of schemas that had been worked out by preconciliar commissions. Even before the Council I had been named a *peritus* of the Council, although the commission of which I was a member never invited me to attend a meeting in Rome before the Council. The Roman theologians apparently worked out their preconciliar schemas in isolation. Of course I lack the competence to judge most of those schemas. But to the extent I can judge, I thank God with all my heart that these schemas were rejected at the very beginning of the Council and that it formulated its own decrees and declarations by means of its own commissions.

As regards dogmatic theology, these preconciliar schemas were solid and neoscholastic, but in many cases quite reactionary. For example, what is called monogenism (the teaching that all humanity springs from *one* human being or at least from one human pair) was supposed to be defined. And so, in fact, I went to the Council as Cardinal Franz König's *peritus* with limited expectations. I was, of course, pleased that a council had even been convoked.

Did the Council live up at least to your limited expectations?

Right from the first session it very rapidly became clear that the Council had its own sense of responsibility and initiative which Pope John XXIII did not block. So at the beginning of the Council my expectations increased. The way it worked out did not disappoint me. I've never been a theologian opposed in any way whatsoever to what is properly Catholic faith. And so, obviously I wasn't disappointed when the Council in its properly dogmatic theology stated and affirmed the ancient and binding teaching, even if I was not particularly happy, as others on the Theological Commission to which I belonged, that Pope Paul VI again emphasized papal primacy in various sections of the Constitution on the Church where it really was no longer necessary.

I was also happy that in the Decree on Revelation the question about the exact relationship of Scripture and tradition (after lively disagreements in the Theological Commission) remained an open question. I was pleased that

74

Mariology remained part of the Dogmatic Constitution on the Church, and also that John Courtney Murray prevailed over Cardinal Ottaviani on the question of religious freedom. Finally, through my efforts it was spoken of in number 48 of the Constitution on the Church that the restoration of the world has already been irrevocably inaugurated, that the end of times stated in 1 Corinthians 10:11 has already begun for us, and that the sacrament of reconciliation also implies reconciliation with the Church (something that only a few years before the Council had been challenged by most theologians). In and of itself that may seem unimportant, but it was a source of personal satisfaction to me. Those are only a couple of examples of my expectations and hopes that were in fact realized. Of course the Council treated many other questions in which I was not personally involved.

In a number of interviews in the last few years you have been asked about your assessment of postconciliar developments. On numerous occasions you have stated that the Church has entered upon a "wintry season." What are the reasons for your pessimism?

For lack of time I can scarcely provide a detailed answer to your question. For practical reasons I don't wish to attempt to answer your question with specific examples, as to whether and to what extent in the postconciliar period the Council's mentality and its much heralded "spirit" have remained intact and developed. So, for example, I do not want to treat the question about the extent to which the international bishops' synods in Rome since the Council have corresponded to the intentions and expectations of the Council, or the question whether despite these synods and despite a certain reform of the Roman Curia, centralism has remained or perhaps even increased in the Church.

I won't go into the question whether the new Code of Canon Law corresponds totally or only partially to the Council's "spirit." One can never forget in commenting on such detailed issues that the euphoria in the Church that prevailed during the Council obviously could not have been kept up. Some persons seem to have assumed, didn't they, that with the Council God's everlasting kingdom was practically being inaugurated. Even the Church is subject to various seasons of the year. Consequently, the Church also will continue to experience winters, but precisely in these times believing Christians will be expected to remain fundamentally in and with their Church.

At this point I would like to touch on several points that I consider much more important than certain aspects of church administration and politics. These are points that unfortunately have not been fully appreciated for a long time in the general awareness of the Church. Yet they signify a stage in the overall faith consciousness of the Church from which there can be no turning back. To appreciate properly what I am going to say I have to presuppose an observation which may seem banal at first: it is not the same thing if in many countries public opinion holds a particular opinion as self-evident or if the Church irreformably declares a doctrine as part of its belief system, even if the two seem superficially to be identical.

To get to my point: Fifty years ago when I was studying theology, we assumed that it was clearly grounded doctrine that no person could adhere to positive atheism over a long period of time without personal and grave guilt. At the Council there was no mention of such a doctrine, not even by the most conservative bishops and theologians. The Council stated, without going into any serious discussion about the question: "Nor does divine Providence deny the help necessary for salvation to those who, without blame on their part, have not yet arrived at an explicit knowledge of God, but who strive to live a good life, thanks to His grace" (*Lumen Gentium*, no. 16). The Council goes on to state that "all persons of good will in whose hearts grace works in an unseen way, . . . [are] associated with the paschal mystery in a way known to God" (*Gadium et Spes*, no. 22).

I am convinced that a hundred years ago hardly any Catholic theologian would have dared to defend these statements. To the ordinary citizen in Western society such affirmations must sound completely obvious. For a Church that in season and out of season wants to be and is totally true to divine revelation and to its tradition, such affirmations are signposts along the history of its faith awareness. The faith of the Church cannot retreat from such statements. Although the Church will struggle assiduously to defend its truth against the absence of faith in today's world, it has, by means of such statements, achieved a position for its very own self, on the basis of which there can be undertaken a really lively dialogue with all persons in the world.

Am I correct in saying that this new attitude of the Church has clear implications for the Church's dialogue with non-Christian religions?

Clearly, the answer is yes. According to the old way of looking at things, non-Christian religions symbolized only the frightening darkness of paganism. These religions were regarded as an expression of what human beings, in sin and without grace, could on the basis of their own powers "produce" from below in the form of religion. Today one can recognize as did the Council that non-Christian religions, even as institutions, possess a salvific significance for humankind, without thereby impinging on Christianity's claim and the Church's claim to absolute truth. This seems obvious even to those who share modern liberal values. For the Church, conscious of the Bible's harsh words about pagans, this represents a notable advance in its history of awareness about faith. If one considers the fundamentalistic intolerance of many Muslim governments, one would have to argue that the

Church has irrevocably overcome its stage of attitudinal intolerance. Whether that also is true for the rest of humanity is far from clear.

Does the Church's positive appreciation for non-Christian means of salvation imply a return to the theory, suspect since the time of Origen, with regard to the apokatastasis pantōn *(universal salvation)?*

I would argue that even nowadays it is not possible to assert theoretically the universal salvation of all human beings and, ultimately, the universal salvation of all. That would be like an arrogant appropriation of God's judgment. But I do believe that a universal hope for ultimate salvation for everyone is permissible! If one in the wake of the Council is permitted to formulate such a hope, that would be a further milestone on the Church's way to the awareness of faith, from which there can be no turning back. Such a universal hope (and it is only a hope) is an amazing development for the Church going beyond Augustine's pessimism about salvation.

There was a preconciliar schema that wanted a definition about the existence of limbo for unbaptized infants. This is an astounding development in the Church even if this hope can appeal to the ancient belief in the power of the cross and to God's universal salvific will. This hope for salvation that is found in the Church is something quite distinct from ordinary everyday opinion. All you need do is recall the horrendous history of humankind in this century! This hope pertains to an expression of the folly of the cross which is part of our Christian confession today. For a true realist (despite all hopes for progress and peace, and despite the variety of contemporary life styles) this hope is, in the words of Romans 4:18, "hope against all hope." Ultimately it is hope of eternal life, but for all. The Council encourages this kind of hope. Sober and realistic persons will have trouble believing in this kind of hope, since all progress seems so often to involve naked power. But for us Christians such hope is appropriate. We can no longer expect and maintain in a cold-blooded way, as did our Christian ancestors, that the final and perduring result of world history will for the most part consist in a hellish inferno.

Our universal hope carries with it a burden, of course, since it is heavy and does not dispense us from working so that we do not despair about our society and history. Those who believe that, so to speak, they can rest on the backs of this hope are quite mistaken! This universal hope is one of the perduring gifts of the Council. It's both a consolation and a challenge.

Can you perhaps in summary fashion list some important expectations that Catholics hoped for from Vatican II, but which were not realized, things that might have been important for the future of Christians?

In fact, there are a number of questions and challenges which in the view of many in the Catholic Church were certainly raised by the Council but which have not yet been settled in the post-conciliar Church. One could ask whether women have yet found their rightful role in the Church. One could ask whether the Council's ecumenical "spring" has in fact led to a summer that is producing real fruit. Stated in another way: Have we really come any closer to that unity of the Church for which Jesus prayed? Although there have been many praiseworthy efforts by theologians, one often has the impression that the members of the hierarchy who make the decisions in the different churches have in fact, despite the best of goodwill which nobody will deny, remained up to the present at the level of pure verbal affirmations with their good ecumenical intentions. One could further ask whether in all countries our responsibility for society and for its betterment, as required by *Gaudium et Spes*, is sufficiently vibrant everywhere in the Church. Isn't it the case that too many influential people in the Church are promoting a sheer restoration-like conservatism, inspired more by bourgeois hope than Christian hope, that the foreseeable future will not be as bad as people imagine nowadays?

In light of these open questions would it not be meaningful to propose the calling of a new council as Hans Küng has already proposed?
No, I am not of that opinion. Of course, immediately after the Council, there were voices calling for another, so that the Church might better address its tasks. I do admit that all these questions which I just formulated are open questions and therefore pose difficult and urgent tasks for persons in the Church and for members of the hierarchy. Without a doubt there are expectations that were raised by the Council but which have not yet been fulfilled. But doesn't the Church have responsibilities that transcend everyday political struggles? Do you have to regard each and every issue as so important that it has to be settled today rather than tomorrow? I must admit that my own expectations of the Council have been wonderfully fulfilled. Now I have various tasks to face. I must learn that God's grace is at work even in atheists. I must realize that persons of other Christian confessions are my sisters and brothers from whom very little now separates me. Finally, I must learn that I may and ought to hope for all human beings.

Since the Council, all those teachings are no longer simply my own private and subjective opinions about which I would not nor perhaps should not give much self-critical attention, but they are in fact opportunities and obligations imposed upon me by the holy, catholic Church in the name of God.

Translated by Michael A. Fahey, S.J.
University of Saint Michael's College, Toronto

9•Contemporary Questions

Interview with Alain Woodrow, Paris (1983)

It is said that you have brought theo-logy, speaking about God, back down to earth. "After Rahner" whoever talks about God has to be willing to discover God in every dimension of human life. You are convinced, moreover, that Christian faith can be adapted to all men and women, to all levels of society and to every culture. What are the limits to this kind of "inculturation" of the gospel, given that the formulations of its content seem to be tied to a particular culture and a specific epoch?

In terms of starting point I don't believe that my theology is radically different from traditional theologies. The standard fundamental theology of the last 150 years, when properly understood, attempts with the help of metaphysics and history to provide a rational foundation for faith. In other words, it too begins with aspects of human life. What is distinctive about my own contribution can only be found in the attempt to tie fundamental and dogmatic theology closer together. What I try to do is to rethink the human starting point in regard to the individual questions of dogmatic theology. This is possible because all dimensions of human life already stand under the dispensation of divine grace. A theology that begins with the human person would only represent a false inculturation of the Christian message if it were no longer able to affirm the absolute God and his irrevocable turning to us in Jesus Christ, crucified and risen. Because this fundamental message of Christianity can be understood by all the cultures of the world, there is no reason why a pluriform inculturation of the gospel would undermine the unity of Christian faith and of the Church. This is true even when it is recognized that pluralism in theology and preaching will have to become far more marked than it is at the moment if the message is to be understood by all peoples.

You have offered a series of interpretations in regard to the scope and meaning of particular dogmas. You have thought out loud about structures and office in the Church. If all the churches were to accept your suggestions, Christianity could in fact be reunited. How have the churches received what you have said? How do you see the ecumenical situation today? Do you have the impression that the Catholic Church under the present pope is involved in a restoration of its centralism and dogmatism and of its claim to be the "one true Church"?

I am convinced that the unity of Christian confessions and churches could be brought about more rapidly and more easily than people ordinarily think. A book will soon be coming out in the series *Quaestiones Disputatae* by the fundamental theologian Heinrich Fries and myself entitled *Unity of the*

Churches: An Actual Possibility.[1] I believe that if Rome were to be as tolerant in regard to the non-Catholic churches of the West as it is in regard to the oriental churches, a catholic unity would indeed be possible. Obviously Rome would have to restrain its continuing tendency to centralization and uniformity. In the case of unity with Protestants, Rome ought not to demand more in regard to orthodoxy and the unity of faith than what is demanded in practice of individual believers within the Catholic Church itself.

At the moment there is a great deal of talk about war and peace. In many countries Catholic bishops have taken a position in regard to nuclear weapons. As a theologian what do you think about these issues?

In regard to the question of disarmament and pacifism I share the teaching of Vatican II. Nuclear war is always and in every circumstance morally reprehensible. A Christian, therefore, who begins such a war or who even defends himself or herself with nuclear weapons runs the risk of incurring eternal damnation. Beyond that I personally am convinced that disarmament is absolutely necessary, including taking the first step. It is very possible that without this a nuclear catastrophe is unavoidable. In regard to "taking the first step" there are differences of opinion even among convinced Christians. Although I have no difficulty recognizing that the Christian who rejects it has as much intelligence and Christian sensitivity as I do, I still am of the opinion that in the light of the Sermon on the Mount and in accordance with the true spirit of the gospel we need to have the courage to accept powerlessness and with it, therefore, the courage to take the first step.

Toward the end of this year the Jesuits will be in Rome for their Thirty-Third General Congregation. A successor for the present general of the order, Pedro Arupe, who is seriously ill, will have to be chosen. It is possible that new directives will also be formulated for Jesuits throughout the world. The Thirty-Second General Congregation of 1974 adopted a very liberal approach. Its goal was involvement on behalf of the poor and against injustice in the world. Father Arupe was committed to this. Do you believe that something might be changed in this regard under a new general?

The statement of the 1974 General Congregation of the Society of Jesus on the goal of our work did not reflect a "liberal" perspective. The gospel speaks of an inseparable unity of love of God and love of neighbor. Our involvement on behalf of the poor and of justice in the world flows from this message as heard within the context of contemporary conditions. Pope John Paul II himself, in his speech to Jesuit provincials, and his personal delegate, Paolo Dezza, S.J., affirmed the fundamental approach of the Thirty-Second Gen-

---

1. Trans. Ruth and Eric Gritsch (Philadelphia and Ramsey: Fortress and Paulist, 1985).

eral Congregation. Why should I assume that the statements of the pope and of his delegate were not meant seriously? I, at any rate, hope the line that Father Arupe laid down will continue to be followed in the Society of Jesus. It is, of course, not surprising that the practical application of these principles can lead to differences of opinion among Jesuits and to difficulties between Jesuits and individual bishops.

Translated by Daniel Donovan
University of Saint Michael's College, Toronto

10 • The Peace Movement: A Hope for Many

Interview with Günther Grona, Innsbruck (January 1983)

Professor Rahner, you are one of those Catholic theologians whose voice is heard in German-speaking areas and indeed in much of Europe. What do you think about at a time like this when influential politicians spout words like "war," "military build-up," and "nuclear missiles" as if all these things were to be taken for granted, while people in many countries are fearful about peace and about survival?

Every warlike act that is aimed indiscriminately at the destruction of whole cities or broader areas together with their population is a crime against God and humanity; it must be rejected firmly and decisively. The arms race is one of the most terrible wounds that has been afflicted on humanity. It is enormously harmful to the poor. If no remedial action is taken, it is to be feared that one day it will actually bring about the disaster for which it already provides the means. Warned of catastrophes that humanity itself has made possible today, let us use the time that is still offered us by God responsibly to find ways to overcome the differences that divide us in a manner that is worthy of human beings.

This is also the answer that Vatican II gave in *Gaudium et Spes,* numbers 80 to 82. I believe that if one takes this seriously as a well thought-out teaching of a council of the whole Catholic Church, then I really need add nothing more.

The results of the arms race, of the development of ever more sophisticated weapons, including those of mass destruction, can in many ways already be experienced in peacetime. Public funding, for example, for social needs, education, and culture is being cut back. What do you think should be done?

I consider it frightening and insane that funds for education, culture, and the struggle against poverty as well as contributions to Third World needs are being reduced in order to funnel money into the development of more weapons, including nuclear weapons. This kind of action is particularly insane because it leads to a worsening of the social, cultural, and general human situation which, in turn, increases the possibility that the terrible weapons of war will in fact be used. It is right to struggle against all this with every possible legal means.

In a time like ours with its uncertainty and confusion about the future, the Church itself comes under special pressure. The faithful turn to it and expect that it will take a stand and provide some hope. What should be the position of the Church and its representatives in our time?

The Church as a whole must clearly condemn every nuclear war as a crime against God and humankind. Beyond that the question must seriously be asked why and how one can continue to arm oneself with nuclear weapons even as one declares that such weapons will never be used under any circumstances. Here are contradictions that should make us all think. In this context I would like to refer to a statement by Cardinal Joseph Höffner who recently affirmed that there must be room in the Church for those who defend nuclear weapons as well as for those who attack them. I agree that this possibility must exist. But this does not undermine the fact that those in the Catholic Church who oppose the nuclear build-up not only are in agreement with the teaching of Vatican II but also are clearly affirmed in their position and are encouraged to act on it.

The U.S. Catholic bishops are presently working on a common statement on behalf of peace and the survival of the human race, and against war and the development of missiles. They want to issue a warning to the political leaders of their country. ("The

Challenge of Peace—God's Promise and Our Answer," Pastoral Letter of the U.S. Catholic Conference of Bishops on War and Peace, 1983). How do you judge what they are doing?

From my point of view this effort has to be judged as most welcome. I am sure that the American bishops, who are all knowledgeable and responsible and who have a genuine faith in God and in humankind, have not taken the issue lightly. They know exactly what they are talking about when they condemn nuclear weapons and their devastating consequences and when precisely as bishops they raise their voices in warning. Everywhere in the United States today there is a sense of just how disastrous a nuclear war would be.

Even if from a theological point of view one should not exaggerate the effect of their statement on American political leaders, it will certainly have a considerable impact on the population at large. European and especially German Catholics ought to listen very carefully to what the American bishops have to say in these matters. It can be helpful to them too.

The so-called Old World, contemporary Europe, has been drawn into the wake of the threat of war. This in turn has provoked a response in the form of the peace movement. It has reached a previously unknown intensity and breadth in Germany, England, France, Italy, Spain, the Netherlands, Austria, and Scandinavia. Does this movement represent an opportunity for coming closer to world peace and for giving humankind a future?

The development of this peace movement is for me one of the most gratifying prospects for the future. This kind of commitment and involvement must increase. It is to be hoped that the peace movement will also develop in the various countries of Eastern Europe and that it will be able to express itself there publicly. One must condemn the repeated attempts to bring the goals and the movement itself in Western Europe into disrepute by claiming that it is infiltrated or led by Communists. That is not only dishonest, it is unprincipled and malicious. This kind of charge does an injustice to the dedicated people involved in the movement, people who take its concerns very seriously. These include many practicing Christians. It also trivializes and undermines the legitimate goals and demands of the movement.

The only real dangers threatening the peace movement are internal division and the tendency to divide the world into friends and enemies in the way that we do in our East-West relations. In the coming year differences in regard to the deployment of missiles will intensify and will lead to new levels of conflict over the whole question of nuclear arms. The peace movement, which in our time has become a hope for many people, would do well to continue to

pursue its legitimate goal by legitimate means and to hold fast to its principles
of nonviolent opposition.

Translated by Daniel Donovan
University of Saint Michael's College, Toronto

11 • Marian Devotion Today

Interview with participants in a colloquium on Marian devotion,
Innsbruck (May 1983)

*After a number of years of restraint, we are experiencing today a partial renaissance
of devotion to Mary in the Catholic Church. Protestants in particular wonder about
the meaning of, and the justification for, such devotion. They are especially scandalized
by the idea of Mary's role in the mediation of grace.*

I believe that one can speak in a meaningful way about Mary's role in the
mediation of grace. A pope such as Pius X certainly spoke of it. Obviously
one can be afraid that this kind of language could cloud or endanger the
unique and fundamental mediation of Jesus. Because Protestants on the basis
of their tradition have such fears, Vatican II spoke of the reality of Mary's
involvement in the mediation of grace without using the term.

Many years ago in Rome I once spoke with the Protestant theologian Karl
Barth about devotion to Mary. I asked him, "Can you, may you, should you
perhaps say to another Christian 'Pray for me'?" Barth hesitated because he
knew what I was getting at. Had he simply said yes, then my question would
have been, "Why are you not allowed then to say something like that to
Mary? She is alive, she has been taken up into the life of God. With God she
has not become less than she was but has been brought to fulfillment. Why,
therefore, should I not be able to say 'Pray for me'?" Barth naturally enough

suspected what I would have said and answered, "We would say, 'Let us pray with one another.'" I agreed with his response. When in fact I say, "Mary, let us pray for one another that you might be blessed and that I might be blessed," this formulation still contains a "Pray for me."

To pray for particular people means quite simply to ask for God's grace for them. Why then should one not be able to say that they received the grace *because* I prayed for them? God wills us in our individual uniqueness but also insofar as we are sanctified members of the whole of humanity. God intends a true and authentic social bond, a solidarity, among all people. Each one of us lives with everyone else in a great and mysterious social union; we are all members of the body of Christ. To put it in an overly pointed way, God intends me in my uniqueness so that there will be people like Maximilian Kolbe. Even he was "dependent" on my prayers and on my unity with God.

From this point of view there is no reason to reject the notion of the "mediation of grace." It is of course obvious that, within this great solidarity to which Jesus Christ also belongs, each person does not have the same function for all the others. For all of us Christ has a saving significance that no one else has. That does not mean that other people have no such meaning for others. The idea of the different functions within the one human family applied to Mary means that she, because of her distinct and unique position in the history of salvation, has a role in redemption that is peculiarly hers.

Some claim that neither in the preaching of Jesus nor in the other writings of the New Testament is there any indication that devotion or prayer to Mary was or ought to have been a concern of the first Christians. Do you see the situation any differently?

In Luke you can find the words of Mary "Behold, from now on every generation shall call me blessed" (Luke 1:48b). According to Luke it was the free yes of Mary through which the incarnation of Jesus took place (Luke 1:38). In the Gospel of John, Mary takes on what I would almost call a central role. She is spoken of at the beginning of the public life of Jesus on the occasion of the wedding at Cana (John 2:1–11) and she is there under the cross at the last moment of her son's life (John 19:25–27). These are not simple Johannine anecdotes without significance for theology. Especially when one takes the symbolic nature of the Gospel of John seriously, all these stories cannot be viewed as trivialities without importance for us and for theology.

Moreover, one has to think about what I would call "potentialities" in the content of faith which then develop in the course of time. The fact that the phrase "born of the virgin Mary" is in the Apostles' Creed shows that in the early Church people were already thinking about the role of Mary.

Protestant aversion to a reasonable and meaningful devotion to Mary does not come from Luther. It is a much later development. Luther recognized the virginity of Mary and the fact that she was full of grace. He wrote a wonderful commentary on the Magnificat.

One should not begin with the assumption that things that are not constantly repeated in the Gospels can simply be disregarded by a Christian. Many things have always existed in their roots and in their ultimate premises in the believing consciousness of the Church even though the New Testament bears a rather restrained witness to them.

Let me add another thought about which I have often spoken. Is Christianity just a relationship to an abstract God in his incomprehensibility or does there not belong to it, in contrast to the mysticism of the East, the relationship to Jesus, the saviour and redeemer, as a guarantee of our ultimate relationship to God? If this is so, then we have already accepted a relationship to a human as constitutive for Christian faith and Christian piety. Once we have done that, then the question naturally arises about the place and function of other people and, in particular, about the meaning of Mary within the history of salvation.

The question, however, still remains. To what degree is the status of Mary as taught by Catholic theology contained in, and articulated by, the Acts of the Apostles and the letters of the New Testament?

Why must it be precisely in the Acts of the Apostles? In passing, the Acts are by no means silent about the important role of Mary in the early community. According to Acts 1:14 she belongs along with other disciples to the praying "core community." She is without doubt an important person within the earliest history of Christianity. But, as already said, one has to guard against the expectation that the first Christians had to see and confess in all explicitness everything that belongs to the Christian religion. Much that truly belongs to it only comes to be recognized as such in the course of its concrete historical development. In the light of this development one can legitimately conclude that particular things must have been present from the beginning. Let me take an example. It is impossible to see in an acorn all that an oak will eventually become. And yet it is true to say that the splendor and greatness of the oak are already present in an incipient fashion in the acorn.

Here is another thought. Is it not possible that hidden antifeminine tendencies lie behind aversion to Marian devotion? Should we, precisely as Christians, cultivate such tendencies? In a private conversation Romano Guardini once told me that he really did not know to what degree the fundamental equality of the sexes had found expression in our soteriology, our teaching about salvation and the way it is effected. In saying that, he obviously did not want to suggest that we could, as it were, decree how God should bring about our salvation. But when one thinks of the magnificence of devotion to Mary in the entire Eastern Church, in comparison with which that of even the most "pious" Catholics is restrained, and when one reflects on the plausibility of our modern anthropology, then Guardini's question seems justified.

In saying all this I do not want to deny that there are attitudes and practices in regard to Marian devotion that are incompatible with authentic Christianity. To attempt, for example, through Mary to persuade God and Jesus to see to it that Bolshevism will not triumph is an expression of superstition and godlessness. Or take the story of the man kneeling and praying before a statue of Mary with the child Jesus. Hidden behind a pillar, the caretaker overhears what is said and whispers a few words in response, words that do not please the petitioner. He assumes that the Christ child must have said them and murmurs, "Be quiet, you brat, I am talking with your mother." This is an example of perverted devotion because the role that is here attributed to Mary means that God is no longer the one who acts but the one who is acted upon. Vatican II drew our attention to such pseudo-Marian developments. One should, however, exercise a certain tolerance in regard to harmless excesses in Marian devotion.

In regard to a New Testament foundation for Marian devotion you have referred to a few passages in Luke and John. When one looks at the New Testament as a whole, I do not see that the required biblical basis is there.

Here I have to respond that the New Testament is misunderstood if one thinks of it as some kind of a priori, precisely constructed codex of everything that constitutes Christianity. From a literary point of view it is a collection of occasional writings. This is particularly obvious in regard to the Pauline corpus. Nor do the other writings of the New Testament form a unified whole. Luke thinks and writes in a way that is different from that of Mark and Matthew. John for his part develops an entirely different theology. And so, in my opinion, there is no reason to expect that one is going to find in the individual writings of the New Testament, as in some kind of law book, the same proportion and the same level of explicitness in regard to all that in the course of history has developed out of the New Testament, whether as piety or theology. Let me just add that the spirituality of Protestants—I am thinking for example of Pietists—has developed aspects which are indeed praiseworthy but which have not the kind of New Testament basis that you demand for Marian devotion.

Let me ask a question now, not of the professor, but rather of the priest and Jesuit. Many saintly women and men in the Church were of the opinion that a more profound

devotion to, and greater love of, Mary would bring a believer closer to Jesus. What do
you think of that?

First of all, let me say that every Christian has the right to reject particular
forms of piety as unacceptable for himself or herself. This is also true for
particular forms of Marian devotion. Here are two examples. Grignon de
Monfort who was canonized in 1947 founded a society of Mary. As praiseworthy as his form of devotion to Mary is, I cannot make it my own. The
same is true of that of the saint and martyr Maximilian Kolbe.

Per Mariam ad Jesum ("through Mary to Jesus") is a popular expression in
the context of Marian devotion. I have no difficulty recognizing an authentic
meaning in it, at least if it is properly understood. It is obvious that there can
be no genuine Christian and Catholic devotion to Mary unless one already
knows something in a definitive way about Jesus. And so it is obvious that no
growth can come to Christian faith through Marian devotion unless it is built
on a foundation that affirms Jesus Christ as our unique mediator, savior and
redeemer. If, starting with Christ, individuals were to come to a personal and
intimate appreciation of Marian devotion and if they were to have a psychological affinity for Mary, an affinity that could even be rooted in a special way
in the history of salvation, then it is possible that such people might find in
Marian devotion a way to a more radical, more intimate, more believing
relationship to Jesus.

What I have said about Marian devotion is valid in an analogous way for
devotion to other saints, including Saint Joseph. Take the case of a father of a
family. He worries a great deal about how he is going to provide for his
family. Perhaps for that reason he feels attracted to Saint Joseph. His devotion to the saint, however, plays a secondary role within his total religious
activity. And yet it is imaginable that it might have a wholesome influence on
the whole of his religious life. It could be that he would receive communion
more often, confess more willingly, and perhaps even come to a deeper love
for Mary and Jesus. In his case we would have a *per Josephum ad Jesum* and *ad*
Mariam.

Most Christians, including most Catholics, do not have the kind of relationship to a
saint that you have illustrated with the case of the father of the family.

If you say that Saint Joseph has never interested you, then that fact in itself
does not create a problem. In a similar way, this is also true in regard to Mary.
One should not, however, elevate one's own lack of interest in the saints or in
particular saints to a principle that is binding on all Christians. Especially in
regard to Mary one has to say that she has a significance for salvation in which
a believer should not be fundamentally uninterested. It is not absolutely
necessary to recite the rosary, but one should not refuse on principle to pray

the Hail Mary. "Blessed are you," said Elizabeth to Mary, and "Blessed is she who has believed" (Luke 1:42–45). Every Christian ought to be prepared to say the same thing. Mary's significance for the story of salvation is not simply the same as that of all other members of the body of Christ. As the mother of God, her place and function in saving history are special, unique, and absolutely clear. In regard to them, Christians and especially we Catholics should not be negative in principle.

Let me add one final remark here. It is ultimately a sign of human development when we can admit with gratitude that another person really means something to us. The areas in which this is the case can, naturally, vary considerably. It can even include salvation and grace and our relationship to God. And so as Christians we should truly be able to pray, "Blessed are you among women; holy Mary, pray for us, now and at the hour of our death."

Many young people today say that they do not believe in the virginity of Mary or in the fact that she is the mother of God. For all of us these theological formulations are difficult to grasp in a rational way. We live, moreover, in a social climate in which virginity no longer possesses the same kind of value that it once did. It is in fact often looked upon negatively. What should one do when something that is difficult to grasp intellectually cannot even be approached emotionally?

I admit that the question about the perpetual virginity of Mary is difficult to answer even from the exegetical point of view. I cannot deal with the question in any adequate way in the brief time that we have.

And yet my request remains. Can you not give us at least a hint?

Let's put it this way. I can say quite simply on the basis of my Christian faith that I believe in Jesus crucified and risen, the one who abandoning himself before the incomprehensibility of God allowed himself to fall into the divine abyss and in doing so was saved. It was Jesus of Nazareth who in absolute solidarity with me and with God lived, died, and was brought to fulfillment. Through this faith I have a relationship to the person in whom the eternal and incomprehensible God proclaims that he embraces me in his love and mercy. This Jesus has a mother. In regard to her I know that in freedom she said her yes to the coming of this savior and mediator between God and me. With this basic knowledge I can build a relationship to Mary, one that initially does not require that I go into the question of the virgin birth. When within this already rooted and radical relationship to Jesus and, in dependence on it, to Mary, I subsequently hear from the faith of the Church that Mary bore her son without the involvement of a man, why should I not be in a position humbly to accept this aspect of the Church's faith? It was after all the Church that first proclaimed faith in Christ to me. Why must I have a particularly existential relationship and a special access to precisely this point of faith?

There are a thousand things to which I have no immediate access. Should I therefore sit on the high horse of my self-importance and announce that what I do not understand or appreciate must be nonsense. That would be like someone who enjoys simple folk music but is unable to develop any kind of relationship to Beethoven's Ninth and who therefore rejects it as a stupid and complicated mishmash of noise. One must not make one's own subjectivity the norm for all things.

Or take the example of Maximilian Kolbe. It is possible that hardly any of us will ever experience in our lives the kind of heroic situation that Kolbe experienced in Auschwitz when he was suddenly aware that he was ready to sacrifice himself in the place of the father of a family who had been condemned to death. And yet we must not say, "Such strange stories have absolutely no meaning for us." If we were to say this then we would be as naive as those who angrily throw aside Rilke or Trakl with the comment, "Such rubbish," simply because they find them incomprehensible.

We should rather admit that there are things in life which don't speak to us at the present time but to which, with more experience and greater maturity, we might someday have access. For this reason I would advise a young woman who might turn up her nose at any mention of the virginity of Mary, "Just wait a bit. Let's talk later about all this. It is neither a disgrace nor a sin if you are unable now to understand this teaching of the Church. You should not, however, absolutize your present position, but rather see it as only a moment in your far from completed personal history."

As a final question I would like to come back to the meaning of Mary's intercession. If I have understood you correctly, the doubt about the meaningfulness of prayer to individual saints and to Mary is rooted in the denial of the fundamental capacity of human beings to pray for one another at all. How are we to imagine the mother of the Lord interceding "in heaven" with God for us?

It is obvious that in talking about the intercession of the saints we should not imagine some kind of heavenly office for mediation. It is certainly false to think that Mary would turn directly to Jesus and to God the Father and say something like this: "Fred is not reciting the rosary. I don't want to have anything to do with him. Jack, on the other hand, prays to me everyday. Things really ought to be better for him in his life on earth." We really ought to abandon such primitive and anthropomorphic notions. Let us leave aside all images and simply say that, since every human being is of significance for every other human being, a Christian can prayerfully realize the continuing fundamental significance of the Blessed Virgin when he says, "Pray for me." By doing this he or she becomes more open for the mediation and the intercession of the Virgin. For this to be so, no complicated things have to take place in heaven. When we pray to Mary, we open ourselves to her solidarity with us, the solidarity that flows from her role in the history of salvation and that has been brought to its fulfillment in God.

I would like to say one final thing. When any one of us prays a Hail Mary and does it truly from the heart, then that is certainly much more significant than all our learned talk about it, much more significant than all the theological language that we have used in this conversation.

Translated by Daniel Donovan
University of Saint Michael's College, Toronto

Part III

CONVERSATIONS WITH CONTEMPORARY YOUTH

12 • Contemporary Christian Life

Interview with young women students at the Gymnasium am Anger in Munich (December 1983)

Father Rahner, at age eighteen, right after school, you entered the Jesuit order. Did you really sense that you had a vocation so early?

To be sure, in many ways, young people had an easier time of it sixty years ago compared to you today. Our world has become more complicated, and we ourselves, perhaps, have become more complicated. So, certainly, to make a decision regarding a vocation, especially for a calling to a religious order, is much more difficult today than at that time. In my youth we all sort of took for granted that we were Christians. And as a Catholic Christian one adhered to one's Church with the same sort of taken-for-grantedness. Add to that the fact that my brother, Hugo, who was four years older than I, had become a Jesuit right after World War I, in which he had taken part. My parents certainly had the impression that I wasn't suited for the Jesuits because I was too gruff and too unsocial. Even my religion teacher, Meinrad Vogelbacher, was of this opinion.

But I still entered the Society of Jesus, and things have gone well for me in the past sixty years. If you ask what motives I had, then I would have to say that I was very interested in religious phenomena. At that time, perhaps, I could not imagine that I would become a theology professor; still, I did think that I would become a chaplain to students or something like that. At that time, life in a religious order had attracted me apparently more than the more isolated life of a diocesan priest. But I do not know that for certain anymore.

Your decision, then, did not take place overnight. There was nothing overwhelming, no sudden inspiration or something similar?

That is an interesting and intelligent question. I must confess honestly that I do not recall any such lightninglike illumination, or a sudden, perhaps mystical, experience in my calling. No, in my case it did not happen so dramatically. Of course there are people who feel called in an entirely different way. Think, for example, of George Bernanos, who quite suddenly had the impression of having a definite calling. Or think of Paul Claudel or Blaise Pascal. Such sudden experiences, which come like bolts of lightning, are entirely possible. Whoever has had such experiences is to be congratulated. However, there is another way of being called, in quiet reflection, and in a prolonged process of discernment and making one's way toward a definite decision for one's calling in life.

Father Rahner why did you choose the Jesuit order, and no other?

Let us consider some of the orders specifically. I could not sing, and therefore was certainly not predestined to become a Benedictine, even though, at that time, I did have good connections with the monastery at Beuron. A Capuchin or even a Franciscan lifestyle, for example, did not appeal to me. Perhaps I was too rationalistic for that. Moreover, I did not feel any calling to the goals of any strictly missionary order. If I had, I could have entered the Steyler Missionaries. Certainly I was not interested in working only in schools; otherwise I would have gone to the teaching brothers. In short, my interests were more undefined, broader, and of quite a rational and intellectual kind. And so, I decided to become a Jesuit. But, in the beginning, even this decision was certainly not yet of absolutely fundamental signifi-cance for me. Only later on did I enter into the real spirituality of the Jesuit order, the spirituality of Saint Ignatius of Loyola. Then I was surely very happy to have made this decision, which, perhaps in the beginning, was rather vague.

Father Rahner, the Jesuit order makes an expressed commitment to strict obedience to the pope. How do you reconcile this fact with your critical stance toward the Catholic Church?

First of all, what is demanded of a Jesuit, practically and concretely, in regard to the pope is nothing other than that demanded of other religious orders. In order to be able to establish a great difference in this regard, you would have to develop very subtle "ideologies." And more than that, every Catholic Christian, whether priest or not, should positively affirm in faith the Catholic Church, including the pope.

Now, to turn to the second part of your question. Such a positive rela-tionship is undoubtedly compatible with a simultaneous critical stance to-ward the Church and toward what the pope does, or what his Roman advisers do, for example. No Christian is obliged to a blind, corpselike obedience which only says yes and amen. On the contrary, there is within the Church something which is necessary to its very being, that is, a critical relationship to a specific way of life, to particular rules, and the like, even of this Church. Since this is always the Church of the pope, the bishops, the priests, and the laity, there is an obligation to criticize these specific persons.

Thus there are differences, and it may happen that a critic will be disci-plined; such things have happened to me. As annoying as such censures may be, they should not put in question the ultimate relationship of a Christian to his or her Church. For example, when you have an argument with your parents, you don't stop loving your parents because of it. A family argument belongs within the framework of a positive relationship to your parents. The relationship of individuals to the Church and to specific officials of the Church is similar.

I have a question on the topic of "politics and the Church." You once said that the Church dare not give up its fundamental right to question critically and, under certain circumstances, to designate individual political decisions as anti-Christian. Should the Church as Church address itself to politics, or should it keep its distance for the sake of the gospel?

One must differentiate here. If a state, for example, would demand that a certain number of its existing children be put to death, and only a certain number be allowed to live in order to foster a specific population policy, then it is clear to everyone that the Church must declare that this is against human dignity and the importance of life; such measures contradict God's commandment. Now, can anyone say that this is unjustified interference in politics? On the other hand, one must admit that the Church cannot make decisions in many political questions because it is simply not able, from revelation, to take a position on concrete detailed questions.

For example, the Church can say that there must be taxes in a state and all citizens must be justly taxed. But what that means concretely is another question. Should taxes, for example, be raised directly or indirectly? Those are questions which are answered from the concrete application of basic principles. In these questions the Church cannot reach any single, clear certainty. Thus cases of interference in politics are possible which the Church does insist upon and must insist upon. On the other hand, there are cases of such interferences which the Church must forbid even itself.

Of course, in the history of the Church, this distinction has not always been observed. Thus Pope Pius X declared that he was really against Christian labor unions. Catholic workers should, he thought, try to exercise their rights and possibilities in purely Catholic workers' organizations. Objectively viewed, this was probably an unjustified interference. The pope had gone too far by meddling in a question in which he had no competence.

Conversely, many young Catholics are of the opinion that the pope and the bishops must be much more engaged in the question of peace and disarmament. Possibly the Church is exercising too much restraint in this area. In all such cases the individual Catholic is called to a very special responsibility. Concretely, at the time of Pope Pius X, a member of a Christian labor union might easily have said: "I have all sorts of respect for the pope and his authority, but after mature deliberation, I have come to the conviction that Christian trade unions are justified, because we, with our Catholic workers' organization alone, are too weak."

Another example: a Christian could easily be for more disarmament or even for unilateral disarmament, even if the German bishops or the pope himself were to act much more cautiously.

Let's not make it so easy for ourselves as Catholic Christians to be deeply wounded and cry out if the pope does engage inappropriately in politics, and let's not whine if, in our opinion, in certain cases, he fails to get involved politically.

Abortion and birth control are issues that concern both the politicians and the Church. As a man of the Church, what position do you take in this area?

In these points, I defend, basically, the same position as the official Church. The direct killing of the fetus is objectively against God's law, and against the dignity of the person—a dignity which also cannot be taken away from a fetus. It is an entirely different question whether the state should criminally prosecute such an objective offense against the Christian moral law. I believe that often the bishops have not kept these two questions sufficiently separate. The question of the moral judgment about abortion and the question about penal prosecution of abortion are two entirely different things. Add to this the fact that even according to normal Catholic teaching many cases are conceivable where a person may engage in abortion in good faith. If a doctor, in a certain case, were to perform an abortion in order to save the mother's life; if it would be against his or her better judgment; if the same doctor would have pangs of conscience and feel that he or she would be sinning by not ending the pregnancy prematurely, then, in that case, I would not deny the doctor's good faith. The same can be said of many other moral questions. But abortion and birth control are still two different things that can't simply be lumped together.

In recent years the Sermon on the Mount is on everyone's lips. Do you think that the Sermon on the Mount can be a concrete guide to a new structuring of society?

That's a difficult question. The problem, exegetically, with the interpretation of the Sermon on the Mount is already so complicated that I honestly do not feel competent to apply it in this case. This is a shame, I grant you. Nevertheless, I believe that, from the imperatives of the Sermon on the Mount alone, one cannot derive an actual state, or an actual social order. With all due respect to the Sermon on the Mount, there is no possibility for a Christian to make the Sermon on the Mount the law of the land, as do modern Islamic fundamentalists who make the Koran the official state law.

However, it goes without saying that a Christian must give preference to the imperatives of the Sermon on the Mount over objectively rational arguments. Thus it is possible for a Christian to arrive at conclusions that others would never reach by using purely secular, ethical reasoning.

If, for example, I place the question of concessions made during disarmament negotiations under the cross and under the holy folly of the Sermon on the Mount, then, perhaps, I would come to other results than if I were merely to reflect objectively about the aspect of the balance of power. The question which one must then face is this: May I as a Christian, who has reached a decision under the aspects of the wisdom and the folly of the Sermon on the Mount, force others for whom the Sermon on the Mount has no binding value to follow my decision?

Father Rahner, now an entirely different question. We Catholic students want to celebrate the Eucharist this Christmas together with our Protestant fellow students. Why isn't this permitted? Why may we only have a liturgy of the Word?

This question of so-called interfaith communion is very difficult to answer because, in this matter, one is not operating in a sphere of clearly defined dogmatic teachings. That is to say, theoretically, you can maintain a certain distance from the bishops and the directives of Rome, if you are of the opinion that you have good reasons for doing so. However, that still does not say that practically and concretely speaking you may simply reject the aforementioned directives of the Church. The Catholic Church, represented by the magisterium of the bishops and the pope, teaches that communion is the highest sacramental expression of ecclesial unity. Where this unity does not exist, or does not yet exist, it should not be symbolized by a communal eucharistic celebration. Whoever views the present-day situation of the separated churches as a completely uninteresting and unimportant matter religiously—somewhat comparable to two different department stores selling basically the same goods—cannot understand why interfaith communion is not allowed.

However, if a church, be it Protestant or Catholic, has arrived at the conviction that in itself it has an importance for faith different from other churches, then I find it quite understandable that one simply does not consider the communal celebration of the Eucharist meaningful or even possible.

Right up until most recent times Protestant Christians have made a distinction between Reformed and Lutheran, and they rejected the communal sharing of the Lord's Supper out of the same conviction which moves the Catholic Church today to take a skeptical stand toward interfaith communion.

Naturally the question arises whether conceivably there could be any exceptions to this fundamental position of the Church, and in what circumstances these exceptions would be allowed. Perhaps Rome should actually demonstrate a greater liberality in this regard. I remember that the eminent Cardinal Julius Döpfner, on the occasion of a pilgrimage to Palestine, made it clear to an accompanying Protestant theology professor that he should not go to Holy Communion during the eucharistic liturgy. In my opinion it is a completely open question whether he should have been more generous in such a case.

Once I had to bury a nephew. A few Protestants were also present at the Mass. Of course, as I distributed Holy Communion, I didn't know who was Catholic and who was Protestant. So I gave communion to all who wanted it. However, that does not change my opinion that a communal sharing of the Lord's Supper, which is celebrated everywhere and in all situations in the same way, would ultimately endanger the meaning of the Church and the unity of faith. And I believe that leaders in the Protestant Church are of the same opinion.

Father Rahner, to many today the Church seems to be imprisoned in an ivory tower. One can only guess at how many people are frustrated by theological terminology alone. The purpose of your criticisms was to get the Church out of this ghetto. Please excuse the frank question, but why did you write your Dictionary of Theology[1] *in so complicated a way that hardly a layperson can understand it?*

For example, if you go on to study physics, you will soon formulate and understand sentences that I certainly will not understand. Therefore I believe that if there is a theological science which has to reflect upon, make more precise, and express this or that matter, which the average churchgoer usually is not interested in, nor understands, then it is not something to get upset about.

I presuppose, of course, that the theologian does not suppose that he or she should burden the average Christian with these scholarly things. But certainly there are theological matters that are difficult but must still interest a layperson. Then you cannot spare that person a certain spiritual and personal effort.

Talk of an "ivory tower" is a significant, but also a very obscure way of speaking. Ask yourself: When do you find yourself in an ivory tower, really? For example: I can easily imagine that a Tibetan monk will get into the heaven of my God and of Jesus Christ, presupposing, of course, that he lived according to his conscience, and did all that he could. But does that mean that in spiritual demarcation I must give up the contours of Christianity and the Church, according to the motto "Be Embraced, Oh Millions"? Am I to leave the ivory tower in this way? Certainly not. It would be a poor solution if the

---

1. Karl Rahner and Herbert Vorgrimler, *Dictionary of Theology*, new revised edition, trans. Richard Strachan, David Smith, Robert Nowell, and Sarah Twohig (New York: Crossroad, 1981).

Church were to sink to the level of a worldwide association, into which all human beings could enter, no matter what they thought! Faith, sacraments, Jesus Christ, Holy Spirit, and God belong inextricably to Christianity, even if these beliefs limit our ability to relate to other world religions.

On the other hand, it is obvious that theologians must try much harder than they have until now to see to it that this "ivory tower"—so that it might be up to date—has wide, open "gates," through which modern persons can enter, and so be able to consider the house of God their own home. Only in this way can the Church overcome a ghetto mentality.

The Lutheran Church has had women in pastoral office for a long time. What would you think if the Catholic Church also allowed women into official ministry?

First of all, we must hold onto the fact that the Congregation of the Faith has declared, in an authentic, but nondefined way, that according to the will of Christ women may not be ordained in the Church. I have openly presented my own opposing views. That is, I am not bound to declare the teaching of the Congregation of the Faith, for which I have great formal respect, as absolutely binding and obligatory for me. We must leave open the question of who really is right.

Furthermore, it seems to me that many Christians today suffer from a remarkable schizophrenia. On the one hand, in a sort of demeaning theology, they seem to perceive a priest more or less as a ritualist, as a secondary functionary of a societally constituted Church. On the other hand, these same Christians get all upset if such an office is not allowed to them or to certain groups. Personally I can easily imagine that one day, through a further development in society's thinking, the Catholic Church will acknowledge the ordination of women with eucharistic powers to preside over communities.

Yet I think that for a woman it really isn't crucial to be a sort of church officeholder. What is important is that she be a human being who can make Christianity real in completely different ways than a man or a priest can. Furthermore, there have always been women of fundamental importance for the life of the Church, for example, someone like Hildegard of Bingen, or the doctors of the Church, such as Teresa of Avila. This surely shows that women need not live a merely shabby, shadowy existence in a man's church. As regards the possibility of ordaining women as priests, there is, indeed, the so-called authentic declaration of the Church's teaching office, but it is not a definition. And so one may not consider it as a final and definitive obstacle for further theological discussion, nor for a historical development which might result from such a discussion.

You have often used the concept "anonymous Christian." Could you please explain this term and tell us what kind of "Christian" is meant by this term in our time?

In the tradition of the Church since about the time of Ambrose right up to Vatican II, there is an irreformable teaching which says the following: if persons are true to their conscience, they are living in God's grace and can reach eternal salvation even if they are neither baptized nor members of the Roman Catholic Church. In other words, such persons are justified, made holy, and are temples of the Holy Spirit.

Naturally the question arises whether one should call such a person an "anonymous Christian" or whether one should avoid this expression because of certain misunderstandings. As you said, I myself have often spoken of an "anonymous Christian." Whether one should speak of an "anonymous Christianity" is a further question. Other theologians, such as Hans Urs von Balthasar or Hans Küng have rejected this terminology as absurd. But there can be no disagreement of opinion with regard to what is actually intended.

Father Rahner, for me the promise of living forever is a very strong motive for believing. Now, if every human being, believer or not, Catholic or not, will enjoy eternal life, then I must ask myself, almost of necessity: Why should I believe? Why should I be Catholic, at all?

If God had not encountered you in the concreteness of history, that is, in Jesus Christ and in the Church, then, of course, you could be saved on the basis of a life of fidelity to your conscience and of a true, if rudimentary, faith. Then you would find your eternal salvation "outside" the officially constituted, visible, and organized Church. But the moment it becomes clear to you, in a binding way, that the concreteness of the confession of Jesus Christ is precisely the concreteness of the ultimate relationship to God, then you can no longer say: Christianity does not concern me, I am going to seek my salvation in another way. The "another way" is a part of that way which is obligatory for other people. You, however, must walk the entire way, because you have come to recognize the goal correctly.

Let me give you an example. In view of my merely rudimentary musical understanding it might be enough to be able to whistle the tune "Three Blind Mice." Nevertheless, I am, then, in a certain sense, musical; I am on the way toward an ultimate musical ideal. But, if you, as a highly gifted musician, had a genuine encounter with Mozart, you could not say: I scorn Mozart, and I will stay with "Three Blind Mice." It is similar, if you, as an educated person, recognize certain moral obligations. You cannot ignore these obligations by saying that a less educated person does not recognize them. This means, then: the explicitness and societal nature of the ultimate relationship to God are not simply any old decisions left to a human being.

It follows from this, then, that the person who has concretely encountered Jesus Christ, the Crucified and Risen One, must also confess him in order to reach the salvation which the "anonymous Christian" has reached in a preliminary way, to be sure, but in a form which nonetheless guarantees his or her salvation.

Doesn't this mean, then, that the concept "anonymous Christian" implies the end of all missionary activity and, at the same time, the ultimate salvation of all human beings?

You have raised two different questions. First, to speak of the "anonymous Christian" doesn't, in any way, imply the end of all missionary activity. The task of missionary activity is the further development of the divine life implanted like a seed in "the pagan." Missionary activity should enable persons to make explicit and to verbalize and to institutionalize that which is present in them in a rudimentary way.

Second, I believe that you can answer the question about the salvation of all human beings quite simply: you have the right to hope that there is a universal salvation which encounters every spiritual person. But you do not have the right to assert theoretically that this salvation will take place for everyone. One can interpret the eschatological threats of Jesus as thoroughly vivid and creative warnings of a possible destiny for a free, thinking being. But I, in any case, believe that you do not have to assert definitively and theoretically that these threats will certainly take effect. And this means that you, as a human being who grants to others as much as you grant to yourself, also have the right to hope for everyone that Jesus' threatening discourses will not be fulfilled.

One should also remember that while the Church has determined that relatively many human beings have reached eternal bliss, it has never stated definitively that anyone has failed to attain eternal bliss. At least this proves that one may bravely and happily hope for everything, presupposing that one does not fall into a cheap, secular optimism. After Auschwitz, but also in view of today's horrors, we really need the almost "crazy" optimism of Christianity in order to be able to hope that, ultimately and finally, in some unimaginable way, through the greater power of the love of God, everything will turn out well. Let us guard ourselves, however, against some sort of folksy, secular optimism, according to which God must justify himself before the tribunal of our shameless, pretentious demands.

Father Rahner, are you afraid of death?

When I have to go to the dentist, I can find the treatment terrifying from a purely instinctive point of view, and so, in this sense, be afraid of it. But still I can say to myself with my reason: dental care does not kill anyone. But that means that in this case reasonable calm and instinctive fears are already closely bound together. It is similar with regard to the fear of death. No Christian must say that he or she has no fear. One can admit fear, for even Jesus sweated blood on the Mount of Olives in view of his future. Ernst Bloch once said that we must conduct ourselves like the Sioux Indians who at the stake stoically endured all sorts of tortures, including death. I think that is nonsense. If I hurt horribly, I have the right to scream. And I have the right to be afraid, and consequently the right to be afraid of death. But if you are able to say, as my late Jesuit provincial, Father Augustin Rösch, said on his deathbed: "In the name of the Father, and of the Son, and of the Holy Spirit," and then die, then that is also fitting, to be sure.

Father Rahner, what would you leave as your last will and testament to the youth of today?

It is hard to give a short answer. One could look upon my "Ignatius of Loyola Speaks to a Modern Jesuit" as a sort of last will and testament. I became conscious of this when I read it over, later. But it is less of a last will and testament for youth. It is much more a resumé of my theology, in general, and of how I tried to live.

To the youth of today: I wonder whether we are not really already in a period of decline. But I have the impression that today's young people are very strongly involved in social and political affairs. They should, to be sure, bring this involvement into an inner synthesis with their religious sensitivities. After all, God does exist, and we do have a personal relationship with him, and there is God's personal judgment after each one's death. One cannot dismiss all these things in favor of a sociopolitical and sociocritical involvement. Every age has its danger which consists in the inclination to reduce Christianity to something that may appear precisely at the moment to be absolutely urgent and necessary, but something which, to a certain extent, is also conditioned by what is fashionable.

For this reason I think I am compelled to say to a young person: Don't merely embrace socialism, properly understood, but consider that what is "genuinely Christian" implies a personal relationship with the living God, who is not merely an old-fashioned cipher for "humanity."

I would say: believe in God, pray, try somehow to live out the absurdity of your life. As long as you are cheerful, content and joyous in hope, you need not let a grumbling old man talk you out of your joy in living.

Still, it is true that, to a certain extent, life flows into disappointment, simply because death waits at its end. One of my fellow Jesuits, who lived in the nineteenth-century, had as his life's motto: *J'ai porte la via, desire la mort* ("I have endured life and have desired death"). To us this sounds a bit exaggerated. As young people you do not simply have to endure life; rather, you have the right to find it beautiful and worth living in human and Christian joy. But still, somewhere, the burden, the disappointment, and the end of life do come.

No one escapes having to die with Jesus Christ. Paul once expressed it this way: "If we have died with Christ, we will also live with him" (2 Tim. 2:11).

The whole Christian life consists in weaving together realities for whose structuring one can offer no formula that is really practical. When you are young, perhaps you think that you have a grand, maybe even an ideal, concept into which everything fits. But in time, to a certain extent, such an ideology of life vanishes. And nothing remains for you but to hand over to the eternal God your actions, your disappointments, your sins, your successes— your whole life. Only God can make sense out of this mess.

Today you do not need to busy yourselves too much with such things. But still, even in one's youth, somehow, one must anticipate that which will only become of concern later on, so that one is prepared, to a certain extent, for life with all its shadings.

And so I hope that you, in all your youthfulness, in your courage, and in your lust for life, might learn a little from this old man's wisdom.

Translated by Robert J. Braunreuther, S.J.
Boston College

13 • Contemporary Youth and the Experience of God

Interview with Hubert Biallowons and Ferdinand Herget, Augsburg
(1984)

Father Rahner, what inspired you to enter the Jesuit order?

Well, that was a good sixty years ago, and the world was somewhat more wholesome and better, even if the First World War (1914–18) had just ended.

But in many areas of civil life, of an individual's relationship to the Church, to Christianity in general, and so on, there were nowhere near the problems which press upon us—especially young people—today. To that extent I can actually say very little about my motives for entering the Jesuits. Furthermore, anyone asked about his or her motives sixty or more years ago wouldn't remember them precisely anymore. So, how should I still know them so precisely?

Certainly I had religious motives. Even then the life of a Jesuit was not exactly a spectacular career. I wanted to become a priest and I wanted to be a priest in a community. Furthermore, to be sure, I had certain intellectual and scholarly preferences and so the Jesuit order seemed obvious, even though I knew relatively few Jesuits at that time. People asked me, of course, whether my brother's entrance in 1919, three years before me, essentially influenced my decision; but, with all due love and respect for my older brother, I would like to say that his own entrance had no really important significance for my own decision.

Father Rahner, you once said that Jesus Christ has been the "norm of your life." Does not "Jesus as norm" imply a sort of heteronomy, a being determined by someone else?

I think that every intelligent reflection on the nature of freedom shows that freedom cannot be boundless, arbitrary action. Freedom is the task of accepting and respecting objective norms because of an inner decision. To that extent I see no problem in the fact that Jesus should be the norm of my life. Whether, and to what extent, Jesus has actually become the norm of my life, I believe, is up to the good Lord, who judges human beings, positively or negatively, quite differently than their expectations. But right away I would like to add that back then, more than sixty years ago, one's relationship to Jesus, in the sense of the completely normal orthodox faith of the Church, was naturally a little different than it is for many young people today. They are enthusiastic, perhaps, about Jesus' critical stance toward the civil and religious authorities of his day. Perhaps they rejoice, also, in the love and willingness of Jesus to sacrifice himself. They practice what might be called today a "Jesusism," which does not take into account the whole content of the Catholic faith about Christ which confesses, namely, that Jesus was true God and true man in the unity of the divine person! Perhaps such a formulation is not very intelligible these days. It must be explained precisely. I hope that in my theology I have made a modest contribution toward doing so, especially insofar as it is clearer that Jesus, as man, was also a true man and not just a livery worn by the eternal God.

But, in those days, the confession of the true divinity of Jesus Christ was for me, and perhaps also for many others in the Catholic Church, self-evident. To that extent we clung less perhaps to a Jesusism than to the clear and obvious confession of Catholic Christology, if you would like to phrase it that way. It is obvious that young people today have genuine problems in this regard. For this reason, therefore, the Church must help them much more intensely and openly than is often the case. But the fact remains: Jesus Christ is not just any old ideal figure among human beings, such as Socrates, Buddha, Martin Luther King, or Mother Teresa; rather, he is the ultimate, irrevocable self-expression of God to the human race in history.

You have always worked as a pastor and theologian. Were there not times when you doubted the existence of God?

I would really like to say no! Of course the relationship of a human being to God, that is, faith in the reality of the incomprehensible God who is over and in our existence, must grow according to the usual laws and experiences of development. In this sense my faith in God has not been a rigid, fixed doctrine that was simply repeated over the course of the years. To be sure, the total relationship of a human being to God can change, grow, perhaps become confused, have difficulties. We all experience the feeling of God's nearness or distance, but still I would like to answer your question with a No. These days, perhaps, that sounds dumb, naive, or socially determined. But why should I ever doubt then that a boundless, incomprehensible, eternal mystery, which carries all reality in its origin, has always surrounded me? For me the problem is not with the existence of God, but that we can say and pray "You" to this eternal, incomprehensible, inscrutable, nameless God. Yet that was not a real problem for me in the sense that I thought now one way, now another. It was a genuine problem in the sense that as a human being one must always radically attempt anew, on the one hand, to let God be God, the one before whom one must surrender unconditionally and whose incomprehensibility in one's own life must also be recognized, and on the other, that one can still say lovingly to this God, "You."

Father Rahner, you speak of the problem of worshiping God, of saying "You" to him. Cannot one be religious in a certain sense, and yet just let the question of God alone?

So you mean a religiosity without God? Here I must say you are deceiving yourself about reality. I would even add what I have so often said and preached: if God is only interesting to me as a stopgap and guarantor of my "needs," then I am not speaking of the true God. The true God is the God who must be worshiped and loved for his own sake. He is the enormous and radical, all-supporting and penetrating reality of the most personal kind, toward which I must direct myself and to which I must surrender myself. Only then is God "God." Everything else is subjective emotionality that remains unreal, which seeks comfort, a certain feeling of safety and a feeling of closeness somewhere with a few other human beings, but which is really far from searching for God.

If someone were to declare absolutely: "I have no use for such a God," then I would say: "Fine, let it be for now. But just wait a while and see whether, in the ultimately empty space of your existence, you can be happy and fulfilled in this way."

The ultimate paradox of human existence consists basically in this: one must love selflessly and may not seek one's own happiness, if one would be happy. The true paradox of a genuinely fulfilled human life consists in this: one must adore God for his own sake, unless you want to fall into the emptiness of disillusionment and ultimate nothingness!

Father Rahner, you ascribe a saving effect to the paradoxes of human life. Skeptics could say: "Life in our society is indeed paradoxical. The only person who really has a good life is the person who does not care about others. The pious person gets pushed aside most of the time. Why bother yourself, at all, with the question of God? He does not help at all. Life is tiresome and unjust enough without him."

I grant that human beings rightly concern themselves, first of all, about the concrete future of their lives, about surviving, about questions such as eating and drinking, and so on. Naturally such concerns are not immediately inspired by God, but rather by the immediacy of one's own existence. This seems obvious to me. And it is also correct that God has given no guarantees to the person who loves, worships, seeks, and honors God, that precisely because of this, life will be good and joyful. There are plenty of people who pray, love, keep God's commandments, seek to serve their neighbor selflessly, and still get cancer, and face a hard and miserable end to their lives. God has given human beings no insurance against such heavy blows. Genuine Christians have died with as much difficulty as people for whom God has never been important.

In my opinion, however, a basic characteristic of Christianity is to be found in this surrender in the face of the incomprehensibility of human existence. And it is precisely for this very reason, I believe, that we have the opportunity today to bring youth to the heart of Christianity, because youth senses more clearly than in years past the questionableness of human existence, especially in its societal dimensions.

Father Rahner, your theology is characterized by the attempt to show that human experiences are open to a possible experience of God. Do you, as a theologian, think that there are possibly experiences of young people which you would describe as "experiences of God"? In other words: Is there a special way of leading young people into these experiences of God? Is there a special mystagogy for young people?

Naturally it is impossible that young people simply have completely different experiences from grown-ups or old people. Young people and old people are human beings; they are spiritual persons and people with consciousness, who exist in transcendence, beyond every single imaginable circumstance, toward reality as a whole. To this extent I do not think that the experience of God which young persons might have is radically different from one which they might have later. But, to be sure, at the same time a youthful experience is still a special experience, one which is conditioned by that particular stage of life, perhaps more joyous, perhaps more natural, more spontaneous, and subjectively enthusiastic, in a certain sense. An old man's experience is conditioned by death's approach. It is the experience of the disillusionments of life. It is the experience of perhaps not having accomplished much, despite all one's efforts and ideals. Therefore there are indeed different shapes that this ultimately one and the same experience of God can take.

The real question which we should ask, and which, of course, cannot be answered here in a few minutes is this, I think: How can young persons who have such an experience be brought to reflexive awareness and to learn that what they have experienced in their transcendence as a spiritual and free person, in an unverbalized and unobjectified way, at its deepest level really has to do with God? How, in other words, can persons be brought to realize, to observe reflexively, that they have constantly and unavoidably been dealing with God all along? This brings with it further consequences about how one should pray, about the liturgy of the Church, and so on. How to do this is the real question.

Can you be more precise?

Let me say this: every experience of God consists, in a certain sense, in a yes and a no, in an anonymous unity of yes and no. And perhaps the young person experiences the yes more clearly than the no. I think that the young person experiences more immediately and more matter-of-factly than the adult that everything has an ultimate, positive meaning. They surely fight for their ideals with more enthusiasm; they consider these ideals self-evident. They despise the middle class which, in its consumer world, has no room left for ideals. Young people often attempt to commit themselves to things from which per se they do not hope to gain anything for themselves. All these are spontaneous, indeed positive, joyous, and inspiring experiences. If they are, at the same time, amplified and radicalized into the infinite, then an experience of God is tucked away in them.

An old person would just say: "I can more easily overcome my immediate world with the help of the experience of my disillusionments, of my age, of my faltering, and so on."

This is the way, of course, that a young person's experiences of God distinguish themselves from those of an old person. Not in such a way that they simply have nothing to do with each other. Quite the contrary, spread out over a person's life history, such experiences are actually constantly crossing over into each other. Perhaps even an old person may once again have a splendid experience of the positive, of meaning, of the importance of the beautiful, of truth, of profound love, and so on. And so an old person has a natural access to God coming out of his or her positive experience of the world. But, more often than not, one probably will encounter the negative side in an old person. Generally people do not die in an ecstasy of enthusiasm and joy, but rather with difficulty and apparently in a melancholy draining away of life.

Accordingly, the experiences of God which an old person has, someone who is approaching death, are unavoidably different from those of a young person, who, appropriately, while not pushing such things totally aside, does pay attention above all to the positive realities of beauty, of love, of fidelity, of patience, of success, of creative achievement, and who finds a dialogue with God coming out of these experiences.

"Punkers" and other groups of so-called "dropouts," however, do not have this experience of the meaning of life. What happens to them?

To be sure, many young people today ask: "What does it all mean? Isn't everything, ultimately, senseless? Why do I continually tumble into a gloomy emptiness in which I can no longer really survive?" To this extent, conditioned by the whole mentality of an age, there are surely very sharp deviations from those experiences which I described before as possible places for experiencing God. Nonetheless, the characteristics which I sketched for a possible experience of God do have value. Young people who have a negative attitude obviously propagate their basic attitude in a typically youthful way.

For example, they raise a huge outcry, and precisely by the fact that they deny everything in a massive way, they actually feel themselves affirmed! It is precisely this positive enthusiasm for the negative which an old person can't come up with anymore.

Let's not talk any longer about experiences of God in general, but rather of the experience of God and the Church. It is not just young people who no longer consider the Church as a possible place to encounter God. They plainly see it as an obstacle on the way to such a possible encounter.

In no way would I dispute that the Church in its actual pastoral practice, with its legalism, its ritualism, its concern about itself instead of God can be an obstacle to such an experience of God. To be sure, there are "church officials" (I will not say many, but some, at least) who only call themselves "priests." They maintain the ritual and administrative business of the Church, but they are hardly the persons most suited to uncover such an experience of God out of the depths of human existence and to make it intelligible. But still one must stress that this experience of God is not simply the private affair of a human being in a safe little room. It is this, too, but it is something which must be objectivized socially as well.

Precisely the young have nothing against this! The new, fast-growing sects prove it. But these sects come into being precisely because the traditional churches are experienced as obstacles!

I don't think this is the case. Why should I be hindered by the Church from also praying in my private little room? Where does the Church radically stop me from praying together with others, as at Taizé, for example? Where does the Church stop a priest from celebrating the Lord's Supper with his community in such a way that the social and the individual dimensions come alive together, in an inner, mutual reconciliation? Why should a priest today no longer be able to preach in such a way as to arouse an inner religious experience in his hearers, at least to some extent?

It is true that hustle and bustle predominate in the churches. Socialness, however, is always something other than, or more than, an arbitrary sympathy group of a few young people that soon disintegrates again. And I would really like to know how long today's youth sects will last. Without a doubt they arouse a certain feeling of protection and a strong emotionality. They will very quickly fall apart. Other experiences will come which will cause the young persons in question to leave, provided they have not been completely indoctrinated by the sect.

I do not deny, however, that the Church often makes obstacles for itself in its mission which one could avoid. Still, you have to say that in the sociality of a genuine community of faith certain demands arise automatically; sacrifice and renunciations are expected. And for this reason, for example, I can grant completely to a bishop or a pope that he has a normative, limited, and correctly defined significance for my religious life, even if right now I might not care for him that much personally. Of course I can also seek out in a religious order, or in a small grass-roots community, people who are to my subjective liking in the religious area. But all large societal groupings of human beings demand, in addition to these sympathy groups, much broader and objectively more durable societal groupings. And a religious human being must also be able to come to terms with these.

Not the least of the hard things that the Church's societal nature includes are its sexual norms. How can these be made reasonable precisely for young people?

I have to grant that now you are asking me more than I can answer. I am no teacher of youth. I never was and perhaps because of a certain subjective mentality, I have always been just an old, reflective human being. But I believe that I can say enough so that even the young people of today can understand that sexuality is an area of their freedom, and indeed of their responsible freedom, of their moral duty, and of their destiny. Without a doubt you cannot bracket sexuality out of the area of moral responsibility. That in no way means that sexuality is nothing more than an exercise field for morality and moral self-control. Why shouldn't young persons experience their sexuality in a positive way? It is just that sexuality must be viewed as a partial task which is ultimately drawn into the totality of a human being's life task. This task is essentially a moral one that must answer to God.

Of course I know that young people these days, when they reach the age of sixteen or a little older, take offence at certain norms of sexuality which the Church proclaims. And the plain fact—which no one who knows the history of moral theology will deny any longer—that the Church in earlier times did not always come up with individual norms which were precisely the right ones, or which were genuinely and vitally human, this fact is, of course, a proof that detailed norms are not always above doubt in every instance. For example, I presume that there can be differences of opinion in the Church as to how, in individual instances, premarital sexuality can and should be expressed in a genuinely human way, that is, in a way that is truly according to the will of God. Possibly there are still further traditional attitudes in the Church's moral teaching which are not completely fair to a genuinely human, and hence Christian, sexuality. Since I am no moral theologian, I don't want to go into details.

All Christians find themselves confronting moral questions in a Church, whose moral consciousness is situated in history and must remain situated in history. To be sure, historicity does not mean that one can seriously expect that the Church will proclaim in a future sexual morality precisely the opposite of what it teaches today. Love, sexuality, the binding together of two human beings in a total relationship, fidelity, self-control, among other things as well, obviously will always remain valid. For this reason the Church must proclaim such values even these days. Doesn't a laxness which is fundamentally inhuman rule today precisely in these things? And it is far from proven that everything which the Church has to say in the area of human morality is "old-fashioned," and that it merely belongs to the past history of moral norms. It is thoroughly possible that even very hard demands can be basically freeing for human beings. For this reason they can reasonably be presented as a genuinely human formation of sexuality.

I think that persons must figure out for themselves how they are going to proceed in individual instances. Each person has a personal responsibility which no one can take away. One should be critical not only of the Church but also of oneself. To this extent, each one also has the freedom granted by the German Bishops' Conference in the Königsteiner Declaration with regard, for example, to the teaching of Paul VI in *Humanae Vitae* (1968).

So one need not evaluate Humanae Vitae *as infallibly defined?*

No, no one can claim that Paul VI in *Humanae Vitae* was making an *ex cathedra* decision. One can clearly prove that he did not do that. In the Roman Curia there clearly were efforts to urge Paul VI to do so. But he did not do it. Of course you have to grant, if you are honest, that there can be binding, irreformable teachings which are proclaimed without an explicit *ex cathedra* decision of the pope. Surely there is a consensus of the magisterium that has the quality of a catholic, irreformable dogma independent of such an *ex cathedra* decision. But it has not been proven that the teaching of Paul VI has the character of a dogma in this sense. And I believe that in fact it cannot be proven because the consensus among the entire episcopacy requisite for an absolutely binding *ex cathedra* decision in this question does not exist. I am not saying that this teaching is simply not true and thus could, or should, be rejected by everyone out of hand, with no understanding of the matter, egoistically, simply following one's own way of acting. This teaching contains an authentic declaration, but not more!

There are a number of known cases in this century where the teaching office first took a particular position which it later retracted, either expressly or quietly. Just think of what Pius X, in the fight against modernism, taught authentically and with pressure on a number of Old Testament scholars of that time. Today no exegete would support the view of Pius X that, with few exceptions, Moses himself composed the Pentateuch.

I am not saying that *Humanae Vitae* must await the same fate as the above mentioned papal writings in the battlefield of modernism. No one knows that. We must await history and its further development, and from there receive the results. To that extent the restriction regarding authentic, but not necessarily irreformable, teaching is justified, I think.

Furthermore, this interpretation has never been denied by Rome. The Königsteiner Declaration, then, allows Christians their own decision of conscience in the matter of sexuality. But if persons take upon themselves their own decision of conscience and an independence of moral judgment in this area, then one must also really and truly confess: "I take this responsibility upon myself before God and his unspeakable holiness, and also in the face of his inexorable judgment. That is to say, someday I will have to render an account as to whether I used another human being, in the area of sexuality, only egoistically, or whether I understood this area as an area for the concrete expression of a truly radical selfless love of my neighbor."

You spoke just now of God's judgment and, with that, of the possibility that a human being might fail the test before the divine judgment seat. But in other places in your writings, you confess your hope that there is no "hell" and thus no ultimate damnation.

I do not say that I could state in the form of an apodictic judgment coming out of my own self-understanding or out of a certain concept of God that "hell" may be empty. One can hope, however, that radically forgiving love can ultimately bring it about that all human beings say a final yes to God so that actually no person must be damned in the face of divine judgment. So I may hope. But I cannot make a theoretical statement about it, since in this earthly sphere definite knowledge on this matter eludes the created mind. Yet, if I hope for God's grace and forgiveness for myself, I also have the right and the duty to hope for the same for every human being. So, as a Christian, I don't have to take the position that it is certain that many human beings are damned, and that I have the right to hope for something better, namely, salvation, and not only for myself.

Doesn't this hope for the salvation of everyone imply the abolition of human freedom?

No, absolutely not. Look, Christian theologians have always been convinced—from Paul, through Augustine, through the Council of Trent, through all the Reformers, up to the present day—that the power of God, if God wants, can bring it about that human beings are drawn to the love of God, without destroying freedom. I cannot say: God *has* to do this! But I believe that there is no Christian theologian who would say that God could not do it, because without doubt in many instances God does fail because of our human freedom. Human freedom exists and God does not touch it; but

God can, nonetheless, in the sovereign power of God's grace and love, move freedom, once again, toward a positive yes to him. I don't know whether he does it or not. I do know that he certainly does not *have* to! But I can hope that in the sovereign freedom of his love and grace he does, in fact, do it.

One last question. How do you envision the future of the Church? You spoke once about the Church of tomorrow being a Church of mystics.[1] What do you mean by this?

With this expression I wanted to take a position opposed to an opinion which used to be dominant, according to which knowing about God was thought to be only something indoctrinated from outside a person. According to this point of view, knowing about God is similar to knowing about Australia, which for most of us is simply knowledge conveyed from outside. But, if human beings only know about God in this way, then, of course, as broad a consensus as possible among all human beings is necessary with regard to the question of God.

I think that people must understand that they have an implicit but true knowledge of God perhaps not reflected upon and not verbalized—or better expressed: a genuine experience of God, which is ultimately rooted in their spiritual existence, in their transcendentality, in their personality, or whatever you want to name it. It is not a really important question whether you want to call that "mystical" or not.

People today are surrounded by an atheism of indifference, not even by a positive hostility to theism, but really by an indifference. The God question is taboo and suppressed. And so it is not enough for people to learn about God from outside themselves. Whoever wants to live a convinced and genuine Christian life in the secularized desert where the God question is taboo must, therefore, want to be involved with God in the deepest experience of his or her person.

In the past everyone said: "God exists." Consequently, each individual had to say: "Then I guess it is true!" But from what source does today's person draw an absolutely firm conviction about the existence of God, according to which he or she can live and die? I think the only solution consists in this: one must try to lay bare the wellsprings for such a conviction deep within the human person. In the final analysis it is unimportant whether you call such a personal, genuine experience of God, which occurs in the deepest core of a person, "mystical."

Translated by Robert J. Braunreuther, S.J.
Boston College

---

1. "Christian Living Formerly and Today," in *Theological Investigations 7: Further Theology of the Spiritual Life I*, trans. David Bourke, (New York: Herder and Herder, 1971), p. 15.

14•Dialogue with Youth

Interview with women students at the Blessed Virgin Mary Institute conducted by the School Sisters of Notre Dame, St. Pölten (October 1983)

Father Rahner, you know about the hopelessness in the world. Do you believe that despite so many pressing problems—unemployment is just one of them—there are glimmers of hope?

To be sure, you live in an age that is not exactly delightful. But you should not believe that this is an epoch that cannot be compared to others. Around 1925, when my younger brother wanted to become a doctor, our relatives thought: "For heaven's sake, you want to become a doctor? In that profession you will not even earn enough to pay for the water in your soup." So one would have to say sensibly: "These are bad times, but they don't always have to be so."

Whoever is diligent, works, and does not simply demand too much from life need in no way dread the future. There is no reason to do so. With regard to the economy, many things will of course have to swing to another level. But is that so bad? We make demands on life which were totally unheard of sixty or seventy years ago; but people survived in those days, served God and one another, and were content.

Now if you want to know what the future holds for you, then I must admit that I do not know. I would have to remind you, moreover, that the Christian theology of hope commands us not to surrender prematurely, not "to throw in the towel," but to have some trust in our selves. On the other hand, it gives us no guarantee that our life will unfold in a pleasant way. One can become seriously sick, even while young; one could get cancer, for example, or in some other way head hopelessly toward death. There is no guarantee that such things might not happen. But still one can say: "Ultimately you can even handle such terrible blows." My friend, Alfred Delp, in the prison in Berlin-Plötzensee, had to have hoped up until the end that somehow he would not be hanged. But it turned out differently, and he dealt with it.

You spoke of hope. Perhaps you could tell us a bit more about what you mean by that?

You could say that the human person is a being which exists stretched in time, out of the past, through the present, into the future. This future which one strives for, however, is not simply something we create. Some things, perhaps, you can control—for example, your graduation. But many things, health, the choice of the right marriage partner, and so on, are not able to be produced, and in no way are simply within a person's disposal. Still, one must will and strive. And one cannot say: "I am only interested in what I myself can fabricate through my own strength and my own planning." Human beings live, after all, by striving after things which they need and which they still cannot simply fetch for themselves. And so the "Principal of Hope," as Ernst Bloch called it, is, to some extent, an essential, basic structure and fundamental function of humankind. Then from a Christian and theological point of view the question arises: What can I hope? Not: What can I myself produce? But what can I really hope for, for myself?

For example, not every one of you can reasonably expect to have the best grades in all subjects on your course transcript. There are things for which one cannot reasonably hope at all. Because of my first infarct a long time ago, I cannot expect to have the heart of a twenty-five year old. The Christian teaching about hope certainly says that, while there are many things for which I cannot reasonably hope, I can still hope in the Absolute, the Infinite and the All-embracing. According to the Christian view, this hope in God is not justified because I could reach him on my own, but rather because the infinite God has moved toward me in ultimate love, self-donation, and communication.

Now you will ask: "What can I do with such theoretical stuff?" Well, I can only urge you to turn inward and to ask yourself: "What do I make of my concrete, real situation which I cannot blame on anyone else? I am constantly on the way toward others and toward future things. And yet the question persists: Are all these future things just a stage heading toward final emptiness, toward collapse, into nothingness, into absurdity? Or, do I have the right, and possibly even the duty, to hope beyond all stages, and so to hope precisely for everything?"

Even though you are young you should not just say: "I would like to graduate, take some dancing lessons, marry my boyfriend, study, pass my university courses with flying colors, and earn lots of money." That is all well and good, and yet the question persists: What happens next, and what is behind all this? Ultimately, again and again, you come up against the one question: "all or nothing?" The Christian, however, should be the one who has the courage to hope for everything and not nothing. Ultimately the Christian is obligated to an absolute optimism, and this despite all negative experiences inclining a person toward pessimism. In the words of Blaise Pascal: Christians must risk everything and wager that they will not be eternally disappointed.

Do you believe that only Christians have the courage "to risk everything"? Don't you think that a non-Christian, say, a Muslim, could also have the courage to risk everything?

I didn't say that other people couldn't do this. The Second Vatican Council has declared that God and his salvation are not far from those who are true to God according to their conscience. This already answers your question. When Muslims worship God in their way, say, reciting the Koran, then they have hope, to be sure! These Muslims hope that the eternal God will be ultimately reached beyond death.

In the past the Christian faith was so formulated as if the Christian way were the only true way and all other ways allegedly led into nothingness. Today, however, putting it simply, even an orthodox Catholic would have to say that anyone who lives according to his or her conscience is on the same road as the Christian. Only the reflexive knowledge of the truth is, if I may say so, more clearly expressed in the Christian.

Now, you could object: "Alright then, I'll become a Muslim, and spare myself any further development of my religious knowledge regarding my relationship to God." But one may not argue like that; when, and to the extent that, the ultimate self-expression of God in Jesus Christ has encountered you explicitly, you may not say: "That does not interest me!" On the contrary, you must affirm everything that is explicit, reflexive, and differentiated in your ultimate relationship to God, because you would deny your ultimate relationship with God if you were to dispose of it indifferently. You as a Christian can't pretend that you didn't know more explicitly, in a more developed and more radical way than a non-Christian, about the ultimate meaning of life. You have this knowledge precisely because of your encounter with Jesus Christ through the message of the gospel and through the Church.

Yet I hope that all human beings somewhere in their lifetime, at least before they die, have an ultimate, positive tendency toward God in hope, faith, and love. And even if they are unable to verbalize and formulate their hope, I hope that they will be saved as "anonymous Christians." That is to say, wherever persons truly, radically hope, God is present, the experience of his Spirit is present, and everlasting life.

What do you understand by the words "experience of his Spirit"?

That is difficult to explain in the short time that we have. I could refer you to my reflections on the topic in "Experiencing the Spirit,"[1] but I do not want to recommend my own books.

Let us try a few examples. Think of a psychotherapist. He brings his patients to the point where they admit to themselves, reflexively and expressly, what they themselves have somehow repressed. In this consists their healing. What was repressed was not simply utterly absent from their consciousness; it was present in a repressed way. There are such phenomena. There are things which are present in the consciousness of a human being.

1. *The Spirit in the Church*, trans. John Griffiths (New York: Seabury, 1979), pp. 1–31.

The person knows them and at the same time does not know them; that is, the person is aware of them, and yet this awareness remains unreflexive.

Another example: you go to the market and you want to buy two heads of cabbage. The woman in the marketplace tells you: "If you want to take home two heads of cabbage, you must pay twice as much as for one." This calculation is clear to you. You could say that the entire logic of Aristotle is basically present in an unreflective but real way to the person who understands the calculation.

So much for preliminary remarks. Now, if someone comes to me and says: "What do you think you're saying about the experience of the Holy Spirit? I've never noticed anything like that," then I'd answer: "Slowly, my friend, whether you really didn't notice anything is precisely the question. You may have been completely conscious of the experience but, to a certain extent, unable to put a name to it."

The problem for me would be to attempt a sort of spiritual psychotherapy, or a therapy of grace, with the skeptic. Thus I would have to make that person aware that he or she has by all means experienced absolute transcendence in a repressed way, and in so doing has also experienced what we Christians call "grace," "supernatural experiences of faith, hope, and love," in a word, "experiences of the Spirit."

Where could that person have had in actuality such experiences of the Spirit? Perhaps in the situation of absolute loneliness. Everything becomes unreal. You are totally alone. The narrow-minded person would then say to himself or herself: "I'll drink a glass of beer, I'll go dancing, then these dumb impulses will go away by themselves." But the Christian who has learned to pray can endure this seemingly silent, horrible emptiness. The Christian is able to surrender to it and thus experience that what we call "God" is already present in it. It is just that the average person—sometimes correctly, sometimes incorrectly—overlooks, drowns out, and represses this spiritual experience of the Spirit. Granted, a mother who must feed her child can't pray explicitly and expressly. She is right when she ignores for a while her own often enormously deep and ultimately mystical experiences. But one shouldn't go through one's whole life keeping God's silent presence out of the limitless breadth of one's existence because of one's profession, pleasures, or these days, because of drugs. There are people, of course, who cannot endure the loneliness and so believe that they must numb themselves with drugs and, in this way, seek a cheap and sensational experience of human transcendence, of the constant getting out of one's self. But this is a false road.

If I have understood you correctly, on the one hand, you hope that ultimately all human beings will be saved. I even had the feeling, judging from your words, that you firmly believed this. That sounds very optimistic. On the other hand, you point to the danger of the many false and humanly harmful ways to God. In the examples which you gave I had the feeling that you take these dangers very seriously, and that sounded much less optimistic. And so I ask myself: How can God allow these dangers? Why are there drugs which harm human beings physically as well? If God wants to save us all, why does he allow evil?

If you are asking me, "Why does God allow so much evil in the world?" then I must admit: I don't know. I only know that an infinitely good and holy God does exist. But I don't know how the fact of evil in the world, how Auschwitz and other things are compatible with this. But one thing I do know. If out of protest against the evil in the world you want to eliminate God from your life, the story gets much worse because then you have nothing but an abysmally bad and absurd world. If in the name of love for others you can really answer for that—fine. But I don't think that you can. To the person who asks as, for example, Milan Machoveč did: "After Auschwitz, how can you believe in God?" one can rightly answer that at least some of these unfortunate human beings went into the gas chambers praying and believing in God.

So I would like to say that I do not have a final reconciliation of these apparently contradictory experiences that is intelligible to me; nonetheless, I believe that one can and must live with both of these experiences, even though one can't bring them together into a higher synthesis.

Of course there are also people who say that there is no serious evil. For them evil is simply an unavoidable appearance of friction in evolution. As Christians, surely we can't take it that lightly at all. We are the ones who must take evil with more radical seriousness than all others. Despite this we must hold fast to belief in the one, living, eternal, holy, and good God, and we must hope that this synthesis will dawn for us someday. Walter Dirks narrates in his memoir of Romano Guardini that the eighty-year-old theologian once said toward the end of his life: "When I enter eternity, it is not only I who must give an account before God, but then I, too, will ask the angels how there can be so much suffering, pain, death, and senselessness in the world," and then the angels and God will have to answer him. Let us do as Guardini. Let us wait.

One question which is a bit marginal, but which for me, too, has to do with evil. You mentioned Alfred Delp, who underwent the death sentence in Berlin. Must not I as a Christian be absolutely against the death penalty?

I'm personally against it. But I think that in each case it is the level of development of a society that makes it legitimate that at different times a capital offense is treated in different ways. So one should not condemn earlier times presumptuously, when one or another society took the death penalty for granted. But one can probably say that the death penalty is not a sociopolitically effective means for checking serious crimes in our day. So society and the state should have the requisite respect for the human person and human life that they will renounce the death penalty. Still, in this matter there is no univocal opinion among Christians; for this reason, one should put up with a difference of opinion in the Church on this matter and not "scratch each other's eyes out." If you want to be against the death penalty, from a Christian viewpoint, this is by all means allowed.

If you will permit it, let us take another jump from the theme "death penalty" to the theme "Christian role models."

Saint Francis has always been one of the great models for Christian living. He is very attractive to today's youth. Perhaps especially because he lived very simply, because, to a certain extent, he lived like the birds of the air and the lilies of the field. How can today's youth follow its ideals without, at the same time, becoming separated from the world?

Too subtly formulated: It is clear, of course, that you can't become birds or lilies. But you can't live like a Nicolas of Samos or a Catherine of Siena either. You must become what you ought to become. To this extent you can't simply draw from Francis of Assisi a literal recipe for your life, according to which you would just live and become the happiest and most free human being, feeling as good as the lilies of the field or the birds of heaven.

But you could let Francis of Assisi ask you: "Don't you put too much value on something that is basically unimportant and insignificant—things, pleasures, successes, money, and so on? Are you possibly on the way toward absolutely identifying your self with this 'thing'? Are you perhaps already so narrow-minded that you've convinced yourself that you can't be happy without certain things?"

You don't have to take off your last garment and give it back to your father, as Francis did. Finally, in the course of his later life, Francis did have to clothe himself once again. He did have to eat and drink, and he developed a good friendship with Clare of Assisi. But he was someone who had a radical experience of how little a person needed to be happy, who had an inner and ultimate relationship to God and to Jesus Christ, the Crucified One. Every human being must try something similar in his or her own way. Often in life it will happen that one must give up much, less out of one's own choice and decision than from the fact that the ultimate thing, the decisive thing, will be taken away, perhaps because the person becomes sick, or is unhappily married, has little success in one's profession, is left behind by one's associates, and so on. Then it will depend on whether the person can finally let go of what has been taken away from him or her. In this regard, Francis of Assisi is a sublime role model for a Christian.

Young people like to get excited about the fact that he spoke with the birds, for example. Meanwhile don't forget that Francis of Assisi experienced the bitterness and disappointments of life. He was sick. He had to experience disappointments even in his own religious order; he died quite young. To be sure, his greatest problems were those with his order. He must have realized that things couldn't go on the way he thought they would in his first burst of spiritual enthusiasm. Later on "bourgeois" and "more reasonable" brethren came along and said: "He must allow us to have our own possessions. For example, we need at least a few books. If one wants to preach, then one must at least prepare oneself accordingly." Francis came to be at peace with these disappointments, with this pain and also with the inevitability of dying. In his Canticle of the Sun he not only praised the water, the sun, and the moon, but also "Brother Death."

Saint Francis is one of those people who tried out of their relationship with God to come to terms with the incomprehensibility of their situation. To be sure, Francis was a marvelous romantic, full of love for the earth, but he was essentially more. Often he prayed through the night and experienced himself in the following of the poor and crucified Jesus. He received the stigmata, that is, the wounds of the Crucified. You should be enthusiastic about Francis of Assisi, but you must see the whole person and not just a few aspects of his life.

What fascinates you about Ignatius?

Ignatius of Loyola is the father of my religious order. Perhaps one or the other of you may have read my essay, "Ignatius of Loyola Speaks to a Modern Jesuit." By and large, what inspires me about him and what he can say to us today are stated there. The School Sisters of Notre Dame are spiritually related to Ignatius. For Mary Ward was a woman who allowed herself to be inspired by him.

We were just speaking of Francis of Assisi. It occurs to me that these two saints, as drastically different as they were in temperament and uniqueness of calling, were alike in many ways. Thus Ignatius once said that he was ecstatic when he contemplated the starry heavens. And he danced a Basque dance for a diplomat to whom he gave the Spiritual Exercises at Monte Cassino because the man was melancholy. Both Ignatius and Francis of Assisi were men for whom the following of Jesus, indeed the poor and crucified Jesus, had become the decisive norm of their lives. They lived a few hundred years apart. Although that makes a difference with regard to the history of culture and spirituality, still they are more related than one often thinks.

Translated by Robert J. Braunreuther, S.J.
Boston College

Part IV

THE CHURCH
TO COME

15 • In Dialogue with Atheists

Interview with László Zeley, Budapest (December 1983)

Professor, in your Foundations of Christian Faith *you wrote that "as theologians today we must necessarily enter into dialogue with a pluralism of historical, sociological, and natural sciences, a dialogue no longer mediated by philosophy" (p. 8). Does this mean that theology, and so the Church, must react more directly to the facts, the events of the world?*

To be sure, theology's real and central task is the interpretation of the statements which this theology considers to be God's revelation. But the Christian message necessarily contains not only a metaphysical and transcendental component but also an expression of the historical saving event in Jesus Christ. To this extent, theology certainly has, from the outset, an orientation toward history and cannot separate or dispense itself from it.

In addition, theology has precisely the task of explaining, interpreting, and making intelligible divine revelation for the concrete human beings of its time. For this reason, theology must of course know something about the persons it will address. Thus it is absolutely essential for theology to pay attention to a person's individual and social situation. Certainly every theology itself is a theology of real and poor human beings. For this reason, theology must always consider itself to be lagging behind its task, and so failing, to some extent.

You are known as one of the most important humanistic and "optimistic" thinkers of the twentieth century. To what extent and how can you possibly have such a point of view, given the economic, social, and ideological changes of the 1980s?

Of course I can't respond to the compliment which you just gave me. But I would like to say, in answer to your question, something which I've never expressly said before. Without doubt, during the 1950s and 1960s right up to the Second Vatican Council, we represented and lived an optimism that has been only partially fulfilled in the developments of the last decades. So the Council's decree *Gaudium et Spes* can be blamed, despite all that is right in it, for underestimating sin, the social consequences of human guilt, the horrible possibilities of running into historical dead-ends, and so on. If we theologians, despite all this, hope for universal salvation, then it is because this optimism belongs precisely to the absurdity of the cross, to which we are bound as messengers of hope in God over against the hopelessness of humankind.

125

The political opposition between the two great power blocs has become sharper. In your opinion is it time for the two philosophical systems behind these power blocs, namely, idealism and materialism, to be on the lookout for an understanding?

Realistically one must grant that the two superpowers are much more sharply opposed to each other than they were, perhaps, ten years ago. So the danger of an atomic war is likewise much greater, and more real today than it was a few years ago. I don't have the competence to decide who is mainly responsible for this development, but we must reckon with the possibility of a catastrophe. But in my opinion it is a completely different question as to what extent the political opposition actually rests on metaphysical systems. I think that while the great powers proclaim philosophical reasons for their politics, in actual fact they act out of much more primitive power considerations for which philosophical systems then provide an ideological robe. Since this is the way it is, we ordinary mortals—little people who bear the pain of this horrible history—have, all the more, the primary duty and task of speaking with each other in open, fraternal dialogue and of discovering points of mutual agreement, which may not be clearly visible at first but ultimately are present.

If a serious humanism is present on both sides, then certainly the ideological systems can also speak with each other; they can come closer together; they can gain a greater understanding of each other, and influence the political elite of their nations away from primitive power politics, and ultimately toward taking the peace of the human race more seriously than their own banal power interests.

In your book mentioned above you write: "Wherever human history is lived and suffered in freedom, the history of salvation and its opposite are also taking place, and hence not merely where this history is actualized in an explicitly religious way in word and in cult and in religious societies" (p. 144). What does this mean for people who do not believe in God?

I would like to say two things in answer to your question. First of all, it is self-evident for a Christian, especially for a Catholic Christian, not only that the relationship of human beings to God is made up of expressly religious acts and accomplishments but also that, according to our viewpoint, all of human life lived in freedom has meaning for the relationship of human beings to God, and so for human salvation. We are on the way to God not only when we go to church—which, in my opinion, we should do—but also when we encounter our neighbor with an attitude of service, love, and justice. Paul once formulated it this way: whoever loves his or her neighbor has fulfilled the law.

Second, today, especially in view of the insights of depth psychology, it is evident to us that the ultimate frame of mind of human beings and their own reflexive self-interpretation are not necessarily identical. In other words, it is almost banal to have to say that in the depths of our being we all are other than we interpret ourselves to be. Consequently, it is nothing special at all if I add that there are very many people who think that they are atheists, based on the reflexive interpretation of their own person, but who, in the really existential decisions of their lives, actually affirm what we Christians call "God," and our relatedness to him.

To put it concretely: when someone, in an absolute, selfless way goes against his or her own egoism in making an ultimate decision and chooses that which is good and true and just, then that person—whether he or she knows it or not—has affirmed the existence of God. So it is simply obvious to me that there are people who consider themselves to be atheists but who, in the concrete living out of their lives, actualize an ultimate, unreflected, and, to a certain extent, wordless affirmation of God.

For me it is a foregone conclusion that I, as a Christian, a Catholic, and a priest, must desire and work toward achieving that what these so-called atheists realize in their lives will also become clear in their reflexive, verbalized consciousness. But before these human beings have achieved that, they can, in the ultimate, fundamental decisions of their lives already be what I, poor sinner, hope to be.

Translated by Robert J. Braunreuther, S.J.
Boston College

16•Marxists and Believers for Peace

Interview with Julia Koch, Budapest (March 1984)

On March 1, 1984, in Budapest, a three-day conference came to an end. It had the title: "The Responsibility of Human Beings in the Contemporary World." Approximately one hundred prominent representatives of the intellectual life from fifteen nations—Marixst philosophers and religious thinkers, theologians—presented their points of view about peace and nuclear war. You gave a lecture at this conference on the topic of "realistic humanism." What do you mean by this concept?

I tried to summarize something with that phrase. If I say that there are philosphical differences, for example, between Marxists and Christians, still there can be a great many mutually agreed upon opinions. Some examples: the fact that human beings are obligated to a common dialogue; are responsible for seeing to it that the world is not destroyed; that no atomic war breaks out; that we must live in peace with each other; that each must respect each other's freedom. To a certain extent, different world views can come together in such common human convictions. This, then, is what I call "realistic humanism."

How can the "masses" and the scientists influence the politics of arms control today? How can they secure peace?

I don't have a pat answer for that, but I think that the more the "masses" take an interest in such things, the more they form public opinion, the more as clear and genuine a conviction as possible exists among the majority of human beings, the less possible it will be for governments to execute criminal plans.

In your opinion what is the real meaning of such a conference as this? What can such a small group of intellectuals accomplish?

I believe that we can estimate our importance and effectiveness very modestly, and still feel obliged to participate in such a meeting. After all, every one of the world views represented here began very small and first existed in the heads and hearts of very few. Every one of the world views represented here—whether Christianity or Marxist-Leninism—must be convinced then that a few thoughts in a few heads and hearts can still be of immense importance if they form and change humanity and its world in some significant measure according to their own self-understanding and in conjunction with other causes. What I mean is this. It makes sense to speak with other people. Our situation, which is one of immeasurable menace in every regard, forces us to do so. And such a dialogue is possible because, despite all the distinct philosophical differences that separate us, and which we must each judge very radically from our own position, it is still possible for us to talk with one another. As strange as it may seem, the possibility of dialogue itself ultimately belongs integrally to all world views which contradict each other.

Translated by Robert J. Braunreuther, S.J.
Boston College

17 • Atheists and Believers

Interview with the editors of *Vigila*, Budapest (March 1984)

Professor Rahner, an international conference of Marxist and Christian philosophers took place from February 28 until March 1, 1984, in Budapest. What was your own impression? Was anything at all important discussed? Were people at least honest and frank with each other? And in your opinion is a genuine dialogue possible at all?

First, I would like to say something very abstract and general. Dialogue must be possible because we must live with one another, after all, and because human beings cannot do this merely on a material or biological basis. Genuine freedom and the ability to make decisions are really only possible when people talk with one another. This absolutely necessary dialogue—basically identical to the entire intellectual, cultural, social, and community life—can be concretized and organized in different ways. That small and modest event which took place here is an example of this. Of course one can't say that, without this dialogue, without this event, there would be no dialogue among humankind. But one can't say as well that, because there is a universal dialogue anyway, we do not need such an event. The need for all people to talk with all people must be concretely objectified. In addition, every human group of any kind—be it a socialist society or the Church—is in danger of isolating itself and of walling itself into some sort of ghetto. In this basically false way one tries to avoid conflicts and differences of opinion. A counterbalance to such temptations is an event such as this, where Marxists and Christians talk with one another.

I would like to voice, however, a few slight misgivings. Although I have never said it this way, still I would like to express it now. I am somewhat skeptical about dividing the participants in the conference into two "flocks"— believers and Marxists. Perhaps such a differentiation is unavoidable. Perhaps it is even a question of honesty to make it clear from the very beginning into which group of people each person wants to count the other. But this, of course, causes difficulties.

For example, we Christians had the impression that a French Marxist was clearly distinguishing himself from many other Marxists, who were represented here with equal legitimacy, and who presented their positions with equal legitimacy. I have the same misgivings when we Christians are herded together, as it were, into one pen. For example, would not a Reformed theologian offer a completely different theory about the relationship of the Christian to the state than I would?

A second misgiving. This morning there was talk of the "representatives" of the different opinions. I objected because I'm not an official representative of Christianity. And I presume that many Marxists, too, attach no great importance to such representation. Furthermore, much of what I or what some Marxists—each speaking from his or her own deepest conviction—have declared here could be thoroughly disavowed and disclaimed as unorthodox by the pope or some central committee.

Do you think that the intellectual ghettos, which you mentioned, have been opened up by this dialogue, or not?

That's a question certainly worth going into in detail. You can certainly say that when someone with patience and goodwill allows the position of a philosophical opponent to be presented and explained to him or her, then a certain opening up has already taken place on both sides. As an old schoolmaster of theology, I know that in the past within the Catholic Church we used to set up certain theses in order to identify Mister X or Theologian Y, this heretic or that non-Christian philosopher, as an opponent of such and such a thesis. With that the matter seemed sufficiently clarified. One did not take the trouble to reflect upon what this "bad opponent" actually meant, how he came to his opinion, and what was correct under certain circumstances in his position. One held back from a genuine opening up, and so also from confrontation with one's theological opponent.

Today, in the Church, one still hears such things: this or that person is a Marxist, and so I hold the opposite opinion. Thus one possibly blocks out the experience that this is by no means necessarily so.

Can you be more precise?
Yes. For example, I was surprised with the matter-of-factness with which József Lukács spoke about responsibility, fairness, truth, and similar ethical principles. I thought at once: How can a materialistic philosopher speak about such realities with that kind of matter-of-factness? Putting it plainly and simply, I was delighted that one could talk with the "opponent." Perhaps in this way we will actually make progress. Certainly further self-criticism is needed on the part of Christians.

Where do you think the probable starting points are for such breakthroughs between Christians and Marxists?
To begin with, the most important. During this conference, when people were labeled "believers," it was assumed that one understood faith to mean faith in God. When one speaks about faith in God, I'm afraid that a Marxist might have notions about which I would say: "For goodness sake, of course I don't believe in such nonsense!" The customary use of the term "believers" makes me feel forced into a category with which I simply have nothing to do. Naturally the question follows: Am I then an unbeliever, or am I perhaps even the real believer? I do not want to find fault, but it occurred to me that during the entire meeting not a single word was said about the meaning of the word "God." It was simply assumed that this was clear. But obviously this is not one hundred percent clear. Many a time during this meeting I would have loved to say: You, my dear Marxist, why don't you question me at least once about what I mean by the word "God"? But then I would like to ask you, the Marxist, precisely what you really think when you say there is no God. I would ask further: "Does your world view have room for the conviction that all reality actually somehow holds together instead of falling apart into an absolute disparity?" His answer could possibly be yes, and I would continue: "Can you have something to do with this ultimate, real unity of all reality?" Only then, when one addresses these and similar problems, can you determine whether a Marxist believes in God or not.

And what if the Marxist, nonetheless, rejects belief in God?
Then one would have to investigate whether he or she is rejecting something that really has nothing to do with my belief in God. For example, Erich Fromm visited me once in Innsbruck and told me that he was a talmudic Jew until he was twenty-eight years old. Since then he has been an atheist. But as

soon as you "scratched around" a little at this denial of God, it came out that Fromm wanted, as he almost said directly, to have the "throne of God" empty, because of panic and fear that God would be confused with an idol. That means, Fromm actually believes in God!

But if atheism, even if it is only that of Fromm, is so easy to explain, then how it is that Christianity, at least in many parts of the highly civilized world, is in a state of crisis?

Allow me, first of all, to state one thing: it is an absolute certainty for me that there exists an ultimate unifying ground of all reality. Now, of course, the problem just begins for me. How can I, although I am just a tiny little piece of the world, have a serious, so-called religious relationship, a relationship of love, of trust, and of adoration with this ultimate, primordial ground of all reality? In other words, the real point for me is this: my relationship to this absolute and ultimate, and, of course, personal primordial ground of the world can be, in the true sense of the word, religious. Or, putting it still another way: for me, the truly incomprehensible reality is to be found less in the fact that such an immense and primordial reality which is behind me, under me, above me, permeating all reality, exists, and more in the fact that I can say to this reality: "Our Father in heaven, hallowed be Thy name." And I would like to add right away: I can only believe that this is possible if I trust that God himself has taken this initiative—God as this Absolute who accomplishes becoming so small that God even has become human. But why do I trust that God can do such a miracle? Because I build on the fact that he is greater than, but can become smaller than, all my metaphysical concepts of him, and because I have had the experience that such arrogance on the part of the tiny creature "delights" the Absolute. That is, I pray, and I have the impression that my prayer reaches God.

If I have understood you correctly, you have just spoken about "anonymous Christianity"?

Yes, Let me add right away that I don't care whether one finds this terminology helpful or confusing. By no means does the expression "anonymous Christian" mean that a Christian can give up explicitly being a Christian. In no way does it also mean that explicit, even ecclesial Christianity is superfluous. Well then, what does it mean? Basically, precisely what the Second Vatican Council clearly assumes and teaches without embarrassment, namely: there are human beings who are not Christians, sociologically, sacramentally, and confessionally, and still they are justified and ordered by God's grace toward eternal life in the immediate presence of God. This is true for members of any religion whatsoever, and also for atheists who follow their conscience—that is what the Council says.

Thus far the presuppositions. Moving out from these, one could be asked: First, what sort of terminology should one use for this fact described by the magisterium, and, second, how can one explain this fact theologically? Or how can one make it clear that such human beings, who have no immediate and explicit relationship to historical Christianity, and so no such relationship with Jesus of Nazareth either, are still saved and redeemed in the way expressed in Christian faith, and can come to eternal life? One must make the dilemma clear: the Catholic Christian cannot avoid believing that all human beings who yearn for salvation will be saved through Jesus Christ, and through divine grace be united with him. But billions of human beings have no explicit, believing relationship with Jesus Christ. They haven't even heard of him. For example, a boy who has grown up in an almost thoroughly atheistic society has perhaps heard that Catholics and Orthodox Christians exist, but that is of as much interest to him as the Dalai Lama and his religious background probably is for you.

In years past this theological problem was not treated with such sharp focus or urgency. I even believe that Christians in earlier days worried too little about it. Augustine also knew that in the southern part of his African homeland there were people who were "untouched" by Christianity. But he just consigned these to the *massa damnata*, to the damned masses—too cold-blooded for my feelings. Of course we cannot think like that anymore. For example, in a socialist society—"socialist" understood in a positive, in a metaphysical sense—I cannot perceive myself as someone saved and re-deemed by God if, from the very outset, I don't care whether God finds, saves, and brings all others to eternal life. In perhaps one hundred years Christianity may be just as skeptical regarding the future of the world as it is today. But with regard to the salvation of humankind, at least, I believe that one's basic hope will be for the salvation of all, even of those who do not belong to the outward and visible Church. Marxism should recognize these and other positive developments. After all, Marxism does not possess pure truth.

What do you mean by that?

I mean that significant differences even exist in Marxist teaching. On the one hand, Marx believes in a radical development of humankind. On the other, he sets up the Marxist teaching office, as if Marxist-Leninism is already in possession of pure truth. For example, why can't one say that, strictly speaking, belief in the steady progress of humankind is basically an illusion, because humankind will be as extinct as the dinosaurs of the Cretaceous period in at most two million years?

Humankind will die out? Is that really your opinion?
Yes, that humankind will someday biologically die out seems to me to be quite probable. But of course I have no way of knowing when this will happen. Humankind has been in existence for perhaps two to two-and-a-half million years. Measured against the age of the earth that is an incredibly small span of time. If the earth is perhaps twelve billion years old—or whenever the Big Bang happened—then the existence of human beings is comparable to the last lines in a thick book. Soon the last letters in this line will be written—apart from the fact that humankind today is intent on destroying itself.

Unfortunately it looks that way. But why shouldn't the Marxist assume that humankind will still be able to summon up the strength to stop this insanity?
Because in the atheistic world the question arises: How are ultimate values absolutely binding? Here is an example which comes from Albert Görres. Imagine you are sitting in front of a piece of equipment and you know: if I press this button, my enemy who has insulted me dies and I know with absolute certainty that no one will be able to prove that I killed him. Ask the Marxist: "What keeps you ultimately from pressing the button?" He could respond that his humanitarianism commands it. But then I would ask: "Why must one act humanely?" I don't know how a Marxist would answer now. His reason must be realistic, of course, and not idealistic. And yet the reality which he or she presents would have to be able to ground the absolute demand of the postulate.

I don't see any difficulty. The absolute reality which you demand is, for the Marxist, life in this world, because he or she knows no other. In other words, one does not press the button because life and life in this world represent an ultimate and absolute value.
To what extent can they represent an absolute value? After all, the Marxist ultimately grants that this entire human life, which is like a gleam on a small planet in a world made up of billions of galaxies, is really nothing.

A Marxist could object: "But the human spirit is still the most beautiful blossom of matter." Somehow this is true, too. And for this reason it would be wanton for someone to want to wipe out humanity.
But humanity will either unite or, as it were, wipe itself out one day, in at most a few million years. . . .

But that is not the fault of humankind. . . .
But it comes out the same. . . .

How so?
Because a reality that is heading toward destruction on its own can't come up with the demand for absolute respect, on its own.

But it is happening!
This just raises the question as to why. If one really knew that human beings are only a biological reality, then one could not do it. But why, on the other hand, should one not grant explicitly that human beings from the outset have a real relatedness to an absolute reality?

That is what I also think. Otherwise one is inconsistent. For to set up absolute demands, without naming a truly absolute basis for these demands, leads to unsolvable problems.
I see no problem in the fact that this false theory is not realized by people in practice. Rather, I would be afraid that I, as a sinner and a Christian, wouldn't live out my correct theory in practice. I, the theist, can lose God; but the atheist can find God. To be sure, the atheist doesn't say "God," but "I may never destroy humankind; I **may** not be so egotistic that another person has no place, and so on." In **making** this norm absolute, the atheist has basically affirmed God, even if he or she denies God in reflexive, conceptual, and articulated theory.

But this does not mean that the entire theory doesn't really matter. A Marxist would say: "With the absolute necessity of the dialectic movement of the world my worldview will prevail all by itself. Nonetheless, one must objectify it and transform it into a moral postulate in the face of others." A Marxist just doesn't state that the world will become socialist, but demands that we must make it so.

But this is the case just since the twentieth Party meeting. Until then, there was no official theoretical ethic. According to Lenin there was not supposed to be one, because people thought—just as you said—that everything would proceed automatically or dialectically. It was only twenty-five years ago that people saw that it would not happen all by itself, and consequently people began to formulate a sort of theoretical ethic.
As our conversation winds down let us again return to the possibilities for understanding between Christians and Marxists, theists and atheists. It seems helpful to me not just simply and stereotypically to say "God," as long

as it is unclear just what one means by the word, and all the more so as long as it is unclear what others are thinking when they use the word. To be sure, one can overdo being careful in the use of the word. In this regard there is a very pertinent story by Heinrich Böll ("The Collected Silences of Dr. Murkes"). In the story a learned man wants to avoid using the word "God" in a radio lecture. Instead of this word he uses excessively the phrase "that higher being that we all worship."

I would like to say that it is a fundamental event in intellectual history that the consciousness of, or knowledge about, God in modern times—let us say, since the Enlightenment—has become more difficult. This means, however, that because of this difficulty, a more genuine conception of God occurs than before. Traditional Christian theology, the doctrine about God, knew, for example, that God is infinitely simple but nonetheless omnipresent. This theology was aware that the entire history of the world was not just set in motion at the beginning, but that it can proceed steadily only because of the immediate dynamism of God—God's cooperation, preservation, and "concurrence," as it is called. That was the meaning of the concepts: *creatio continua, conservatio,* and *concursus divinus.* To this extent one may not consider the traditional theology "dumber" than it in fact was. But it must be made much clearer in sermons, in the history of the proclamation of God, and in the struggle with atheism that God is not a particular reality in the usual sense, about which one can have knowledge, as one can have about Australia, for example, so that at the end of some sort of consideration one could state that God was, so to speak, the ultimate spring which powers the world's clock.

Allow me to ask you one more time as we conclude. In your opinion what is new in the Christian concept of God?

It is not a matter of something radically new. I already said that. For example, every neoscholastic, no matter how old-fashioned, knew that the world and God could not be counted together so that God plus world would be more than God. And yet this obvious insight in the field of the philosophy of religion seems, strikingly, to have played no role in the average religious sense of people. Another example: one says against every form of pantheism that human beings can resist God through their freedom. Correct. And yet one almost instinctively and almost unavoidably understands such a proposition incorrectly by thinking of a human being as a reality which, granted, was at some earlier time created by God, but now stands, to a certain extent, over against God as his or her own absolute. But that is false. Up to now, traditional Christian life and piety have ignored thousands of factors in the relationship between God and the world—things that I believe are extraordinarily important for a contemporary relationship to God. For example, what does this really mean: God, in whom we live, and move, and have our being (Acts 17:28)? The answer to this is not to be found on a piece of paper in some drawer of our dogmatic theology. So let us ask ourselves: Do we perceive ourselves, to some extent, as that moment which leaps out of the living, primordial will of God? If I am honest I have to admit: no, I must think expressly about it. But I know that my religious life must be more and more permeated by the theoretical foregone conclusion that I can't move toward God only when I want to, but rather that I myself always rise up out of God's creative will. That has nothing to do with pantheism, although it is often perceived as such.

And so there are and there will continue to be many more developments in Christianity which are important for a rapprochement with other world views, and which in no way lead away from Christian faith; on the contrary, they only make it clearer.

Translated by Robert J. Braunreuther, S.J.
Boston College

18 • Realistic Humanism

Interview with the editorial staff of the German language program of the Hungarian radio network, Budapest (March 1984)

At the last international meeting in Budapest of Marxist and religious philosophers, your presentation, Professor Rahner, was listened to with lively interest. You expressed the hope that between both great philosophical systems, between Marxists and "believers," there could be a basic agreement in regard to the truly existential questions of

*humanity. What are the issues that have to be addressed if such a "realistic humanism,"
as you call it, is to become a reality?*

I suspect that the discussion in such an interdisciplinary or, if I might put it
this way, inter-world view symposium would have to focus on the following
question: What general human and moral presuppositions must exist if
humanity is to have any hope of dealing with the worldwide and total threat
that is facing it? No one will deny that the fundamental anthropological
questions and especially the ethical ones are taking on in the present situation
a radically new seriousness and urgency. It is even possible that the enormous
gravity of the situation is drawing us closer to one another in regard to our
anthropologies and perhaps even leading us to new positions, or at least to a
partial consensus, which could not be achieved apart from the present
situation. I believe that partial agreements are possible prior to any general
understanding at the level of world views. Such agreements would have
meaning and significance for the overcoming of our present crisis. This
presupposes, of course, that they are clearly and forcefully articulated and
that they are acknowledged by as many as possible. If such were to be the
case, they could really have an influence on the collective decisions of humanity.

Could you tell us where in your opinion such agreements might be possible?

We say, for example, that we are free, historical subjects, and that therefore
we have responsibility for what we do. This means that our future cannot
simply be accepted as the product of subhuman forces. The future is also our
responsible act; it cannot be passed off on anyone or anything else.

Each one must be ready to open up a space for freedom for everyone else
without first determining the nature of this space, and therefore with the
danger that it will be filled in a way that goes against one's own wishes and
expectations. Tolerance in this sense must be a rule and an accepted obligation. Much that affects us in common should be dealt with in an open
discussion in which the participants do not simply attempt to force the others
to accept their will, and this even in the case where such pressure might be
successfully applied. Power is not simply to be identified with justice, and
justice must triumph and be respected even when it cannot be enforced by
power. With these statements we have already formulated a series of common
principles which one might call "realistic humanism," whether the term itself
is a good one or not. The principles that I have evoked and that are recognized
by all of us clearly lie this side of the ultimate philosophical differences that
divide us.

*But does the laying down of such a formal frame of reference help to overcome the
serious and very real differences that exist?*

First of all, it would be foolish to deny that there are such differences. One can certainly argue whether Ronald Reagan is pursuing a peace policy that is simply unclear or whether he is involved in dangerous arms development. When we turn to the question about the ultimate meaning of reality, the differences of opinion are much more marked. There will always remain a chasm between Christians and Marxists in regard to whether there is an infinite ground of all that is, which we call "God" and with which believers affirm they can have a relationship. In spite of this I believe that one can and must put oneself into the other's position. Everyone has to admit that we are fallible and short-sighted, and not well informed about everything. If, on the contrary, one tries to give the impression that one's own "party" is made up of ideal people endowed with pure truth and selflessness, and that the opposition are all villains, who want slyly and cruelly to unleash war, then as a human being and a Christian I would say: no, that is not the case. Just as people are not one hundred percent evil, they are not one hundred percent good either. And so we have to begin with a realistic concept of humanity precisely when we want to remain in conversation with one another, despite profound differences.

Allow me now, Professor Rahner, to ask some questions relating to the concrete situation in Hungary. What possibilities do you see for cooperation between Catholics and the rest of Hungarian society, given that this latter is rooted in Marxist principles?

You are asking me more than I can answer. I know far too little of the general situation in Hungary, the precise structures of its society, and above all of the state. And so I can offer no recipes for cooperation between Christians and Marxists. What is certain is that they must live together. That means, to put it crudely, that they cannot be satisfied with simply not killing one another. Rather, they must to some degree cooperate positively. A Christian, moreover, has an obvious duty to serve an organized society—called a "state"—in everything that is required for the well-being of that state and its society. From this perspective an objective and reasonable collaboration on the part of Christians and more particularly of Catholics presents in reality no fundamental problem. Where I see difficulties is whether and to what degree the state, organized as it is along socialist and Marxist lines, will provide Christians with the opportunity to participate, and whether they will be allowed to do so spontaneously and with freedom of conscience. I can only work with those who allow me to work with them. That is obvious, but in practice a great deal depends on it. To the extent that Marxist and Christian fundamental views of reality remain in conflict with one another, it is clear that a struggle of ideas and convictions cannot completely be avoided. According to Vatican II both parties have the right to live out of and to proclaim their convictions. To a certain extent this is self-evident, so long at least as people are not all obliged to have the same opinion or so long as they have not all arrived at absolute truth. The issue finally is whether there will be such a struggle and in what form it will be conducted.

Could we perhaps formulate your idea in a somewhat different way by saying that there must be a kind of pluralism involving Marxism and other world views?

Yes, I would not hesitate to underline and to stress that. Thank God that we can and may say this in Hungary. I hope and certainly do not deny that there is a pluralism here that is understood as more than the coexistence of an absolutely victorious world view and a radically primitive one that is condemned to extinction. This probably manifests that Hungarians themselves are convinced that in the final analysis every country is best served by an authentic pluralism.

The activity of Professor Tomás Nyíri, one of your best Hungarian friends, is an example of such a pluralism. For six years now he has been directing a theological correspondence course and has recently defended his postdoctoral dissertation (Habilitation) *before the Hungarian Academy of Sciences.*

To put it simply, I don't have the competence to claim in a kind of canonization process that my dear and respected friend Nyíri always and everywhere hits the nail on the head. But if this theological correspondence course is a sign of real freedom of opinion in Hungary, then I am delighted. I am equally delighted that Nyíri has been accepted into the Academy of Sciences. Such a decision seems to me to be a hopeful indication that people in Hungary intend to accept freedom of conscience and freedom of conviction.

Translated by Daniel Donovan
University of Saint Michael's College, Toronto

19•Our Relationship to the Church

Interview with the Catholic student community of Munich, Munich
(November 1983)

*Father Rahner, most of those who are taking part in this conversation are Christians.
All are university students, and many, indeed, are studying theology. Each of us has a
particular relationship to the Church; in some cases it is very intense and in others much
less so. Each one could give good reasons for his or her position. We all, however,
experience a certain dissatisfaction. As a man of the Church, what can you say about
the relationship that a Catholic should have to the Church?*

What your question is inviting us to do is to reflect together as baptized
Catholic Christians on our relationship to the Church. Presupposed in what I
am going to say is that we do have some kind of relationship to it even if it is
problematical. We relate to it in quite a different way from, for example, a
Tibetan monk beating his prayer drum. Most of us grew up in Christian
families. We were baptized. We received some kind of religious instruction
and have had experiences with the Church's liturgy. To put it simply, we can
presuppose in our conversaton a concrete relationship to the Church. What
you are rightly asking yourselves as intelligent and educated people who feel a
personal responsibility for your life is: "What about my relationship to this
Church? What could and should it be?"

According to quite standard reflections and principles in Catholic theology,
it is to be taken for granted that the relationship of Christians to the Church
can vary considerably. People can, as it were, be born into the Church; they
can be educated or "trained" in its way of life; they might perhaps pay church
taxes and occasionally even visit a church. Such a relationship, which itself
can exist in a wide variety of forms, can be described as the kind of relationship that persons have to social institutions within their sphere of life. In
this context it could even appear to be normal and natural. Catholic Christianity, however, would say that such a relationship is not at all the kind
desired or required in regard to the Church.

When does such a "desired" relationship become a reality?

It exists when, first of all, the message of the Church, that is, what it has to
say about the world, humankind, and God, is accepted in faith and truly
understood. This has to be more than some kind of vague infantile memory in
the head of an educated woman or man. For the moment, the exact content of
the Church's radical saving message can be left open.

As a second requirement, the Church itself must be affirmed as an inner, necessary, and valid moment in my Christian faith. That is a statement that is not widely accepted as self-evident. And I am thinking here not just of Christians in general, but of a great number of Catholics. If I experience the Church only as a more or less reasonable, sociological, factually given element of my total situation as a human being, if I understand it only as a more or less well-structured organization for mediating religious expectations and experiences, then for me, in spite of its objective presence and the way it impinges upon my consciousness, it has no real religious or theological significance. For myself, I hope that to some degree I truly realize what I am saying when I affirm that "I believe in the one, holy, catholic and apostolic Church." By this I mean that the reality "Church," in itself and in its relationship to me, has a saving significance which has been willed by God. It belongs to the very stuff of my existence, my conduct, my faith, in a word, my life.

For obvious reasons Christians who are somewhat alienated often find precisely the affirmation of faith in the "holy" Church impossibly difficult. What is to be said to this?

There are certainly many Catholics who feel what you suggest. They really do not believe in the Church as a reality in which God makes his final and definitive promise of himself to us. To me what is important here is to remember that too often we confuse cause and effect. For the person for whom the Church constitutes an inner moment of final existential decision and attitude, that is to say, an inner moment of faith, it is not surprising that in relation to it we can have all kinds of experiences that are unfortunate, annoying, and nerve-wracking, and that provoke us to protest. For such a person all offenses caused by the Church are and remain provisional and, in the last analysis, secondary.

I believe that I can say that I have experienced more scandals in the Church than perhaps any dozen of you together. That is not so surprising, because I am after all eighty years old and I have had a great deal more to do with the Church than you will probably have in the course of your life. But for me all the anger is in the end secondary. When I affirm that, in what in the strict sense is called "Church," I hear in a believable way the absolute promise of God in which he says to me in Jesus Christ, crucified and risen, "In the absolute power of my love I communicate myself to you and that for all eternity," then measured by that everything else is secondary. Then I experience my life as a waiting for the fulfillment of this absolute promise in which God guarantees not this or that but himself, the absolute God, the incomprehensible one, and forever. Given this, is it difficult to understand that for me everything of a negative nature that I experience and suffer in the Church is of secondary concern? Whoever has not, or has not yet, been able to realize how profoundly the Church belongs to the event itself of salvation, naturally has a quite different relationship to it. In the face of negative experiences the question is very quickly asked: Shall I still remain in the Church? The question drives me "crazy." For me as a believer it is in the last analysis meaningless. What can the word "still" mean here? It is like asking whether I will "still" be a human being, or whether I will "still" live in this pitiable twentieth century. With such basic realities of life, there is really only one alternative: either a radical protest that carried to its extreme would have to end in suicide, or an acceptance and living through of life with all its negative aspects.

The point for me is that Christians remain in the Church in spite of all the anger that they might feel about it.

If Christians are thus obliged to remain in the Church no matter what happens, are they not forced into some kind of blind obedience? Would this not be the case when the Church gives orders that go directly against their views?

Let me begin with a preliminary remark of a fundamental nature. If someone were to come to the conviction that fulfilling a particular ecclesial requirement would be against conscience and therefore sinful, then before God that person would have the responsibility and duty to say no. That is obvious. In regard to your question we have to begin by distinguishing between doctrinal and other decisions. An example of the latter would be the following: if as an assistant pastor I were assigned to Timbuktu rather than to a place of my own choice, that would not pertain to doctrine but to the area of ecclesial administration and law. But you were certainly not referring to these sorts of decisions when you spoke about "blind obedience."

Let me therefore talk about doctrinal decisions. As a first point, the following should be kept in mind: whoever has come in faith to the realization that the Church in principle can teach in particular cases by means of a final and defining *ex cathedra* decision, must when such a case occurs accept in faith any teaching defined in this way. According to official ecclesial statements, however, there are very many teachings even of the magisterium which in the Church's own interpretation do not enjoy this kind of certainty. To put it another way, there are teachings in regard to which the Church can err; there are, to use the common terminology, declarations which are reformable.

Here is an example. In a recent interview Cardinal Ratzinger declared for all intents and purposes that the book *Unity of the Churches* that I wrote with Heinrich Fries is utter nonsense. He said that it contains more acrobatics than logic, that it has little to do with reality, that I am turning the Church into a barrack-square, and so on. That such an opinion of a cardinal, even if he happens to be a former theologian, obliges me to absolutely nothing is obvious. If Cardinal Ratzinger had made his statement as head of the Roman Congregation for the Doctrine of the Faith, which was not the case, then I would have the obligation to read, understand, and test it in an unprejudiced and self-critical way. If, after doing this, I came to the conclusion that the cardinal's argument was a weak one, then I could say: "I am very sorry but I have a different opinion than you do and I am going to stick to it." That, too, is self-evident. It should also be obvious that in such and similar cases there are various levels that have to be clearly distinguished.

When the pope, for example, proclaims that we ought to gain an indulgence during the Holy Year, then such a statement has much less weight than a decision taken by the Congregation for the Faith after year-long reflection and discussion. This, of course, could still be wrong. Nevertheless, if we want to be reasonable, we should not approach the Roman magisterium with the current quite common mentality that affirms that all Roman declarations are to be opposed unless they contain a strict proof of the falsity of one's own opinion. Such an attitude that a priori rejects everything that even the Holy Father might say is wrong. It is as if, as a cancer patient, you were to say: "What doctors diagnose is nonsense. I know everything much better."

It is no disgrace to experience oneself as incompetent in some things. If after mature reflection I believe I have every right to reject a nondefined teaching of the Roman magisterium, then in such a case I regard myself as not bound in faith to accept it. If, for example, you had been of the opinion in 1920 that the letter to the Hebrews had not been written by Paul, even though Rome, around 1910, had affirmed this to be the case, then with a good conscience you could have disagreed with the Roman magisterium.

But what about church regulations and commandments, above all those that affect everybody like the Sunday obligation? Am I obliged in such cases to absolute obedience?

There you have me. What church regulations still exist that seriously affect the layperson? You might say, a father ought to have his children baptized at an early age. Laws in regard to fasting hardly exist anymore in a practical sense. You mentioned the Sunday obligation, but today this is interpreted by theologians differently and with considerable nuance. You might also refer to the fact that Cardinal Ratzinger has declared in the name of the pope that it is still forbidden to belong to a Masonic lodge even though this is no longer mentioned in the new Code of Canon Law. Church authority can of course make laws that are not in the Code. If someone were to insist on joining a lodge, I would ask: "Why do you want to join? You can be happy and even successful in your work without belonging to a lodge." If he, however, were to defend the view that Freemasons represent something acceptable from both a human and Christian point of view, then I would not want to stop him.

The cleric, as in a certain sense a subordinate official in the Church, receives many more orders in regard to which he might ask himself: "Must I obey?" In this area there is a considerable body of casuistry. I would say once again: if after mature and conscientious reflection you have come to the conviction that following a particular command would make you guilty before God's judgment, then you have the right and indeed the duty not to obey it. Saint Thomas would have said that if in such a case you were to be excommunicated, you would still have to follow your conscience.

To be quite honest, I don't believe there are many such situations in the life of a priest. Naturally there are problems, as in the case where one believes that a church could have been built for less money, thus making possible the construction of a home for young people. In such and similar cases you can become angry, even furious, over the decisions of a bishop. You might even regard him as narrow-minded and out of date, but you surely will not be able to say: "If I help to build this church with this money and thus fail to provide a home for youth, I will be guilty of a serious sin before God and my conscience." And so in such cases one must obey.

Many older Catholics like to compare their relationship to the Church with their relationship to, and love for, their parents. Some of us wonder, how can one come to love the Church?

Let me ask a question in return. Are you able to love Christ? Can you say that you stake your life and death on the fact that through faith in Jesus Christ, crucified and risen, you are redeemed and made holy? If you can affirm this and if in fact you truly entrust your ultimate existence to him, then it could be said that you already have this positive relation to the Church. This is true because and insofar as it is the concrete appearance of this message of Jesus, and because it is the community of those who believe in Christ and who entrust their existence in its entirety to him. If the comparison between the relation of a Christian to the Church and that of a child to its parents still bothers you, then disregard it. Ecclesial language often refers to "Mother" Church. It is a custom that goes back to earliest Christianity. What it affirms is something that really makes sense: the Church is the mediator and guarantor of my life in unity and solidarity with God. To this degree I can call the Church my mother. Obviously this has nothing to do with infantile attachment to the Church or with a clerical identification with all that goes on in it.

Let's take an example. If (and I underline the if three times) someone were to say: "The trips of John Paul II get on my nerves," then I would counter: "Be prudent, take your time, reflect well on what you're saying. But whatever judgment you come to, in the final analysis it does not touch your real, theological-religious relationship to the Church." Or if someone says that the German Church has too much money and that it ought to do much more for the Third World, then such a person has made a judgment that objectively is at least questionable because too sweeping. I myself once had a real row with Bishop Franz Hengsbach in his episcopal residence in Essen because, with others, I disapproved of the way he had handled himself in Central America. Even that, however, was not able to distort my vision during a meeting with Ernesto Cardenal in Frankfurt. With all modesty, although he embraced me warmly, I found what he said from both political and theological points of view to be a fair amount of nonsense. He affirmed that with the Sandinistas in Nicaragua the kingdom of God had finally broken in. We heard ideological fantasy such as that there were no more prisons and that everyone loved one another. In terms of such experiences I would say that if a bishop or the pope is a little more careful in regard to some developments in the Third World than some of their critics, it is by no means a priori certain that their position is unreasonable. We must examine issues individually and be self-critical and critical in regard to others, critical even of the criticism that is often legitimately brought against the institutional Church. But no matter how all this works out, such problems for me do not touch my final relationship to the authentic and substantial nature of the Church.

I know, of course, that my friend Johann Baptist Metz would probably say: "Karl, I tell you, you must, precisely as a Christian, be far more radical, upset, and angry about many things in the Church." To a certain point I can understand that a person who believes that the world from beginning to end is a rather messy place is not surprised that it is much the same in the Church. When, however, one is convinced that it is a community that is loved by God, the community of those who are baptized in the Holy Spirit and in whom his charisms are alive, then one would also insist that it involve itself on behalf of peace, justice, and the struggle against sinful structures in a more radical way than all other communities. When we Christians fail to do this, it is a greater scandal than when others fail to do it. We who are baptized and endowed with light and grace by the Holy Spirit, we who have our final hope in eternal life with God, we must be much more sensitive to the scandals, the pitiful behavior, and the petty-bourgeois mentality in our Church. But even here we should exercise a certain calmness and patience. After all, we are all sinners.

Father Rahner, excuse me for interrupting. What I had in mind with my question was something else, the well-known modern alternative "Christ, yes; the Church, no."

Let us imagine that ten people were to say: "This 'stupid' institutional Church is of no interest to us; let's separate from it and found a charismatic and enthusiastic fellowship." At some point someone is going to have to announce: "We are meeting next Tuesday at 5 o'clock, and you my Spirit-inspired brothers and sisters must all be there." Then the problem will arise where to get the chairs and where to find the money. Finally, someone will have to be chosen treasurer just as it was with Jesus' community. In other words, it won't be very long before you have an institutional Church, that is, an organized Church with legal structures. It might well be that things will be run in a more familial and charismatic way in the one case and in a more bureaucratic one in the other. Fundamentally, however, there is no difference between them. From this point of view, in spite of anger and irritation in particular instances, I have no difficulty in accepting the existing institutional Church as the concrete form of the charismatic Church.

Father Rahner, may I interrupt again? I did not want to separate the Church of faith from the institutional Church and perhaps plead for a Church of pure faith. What interests me is the question to what degree what we call the institutional Church is really only an organization or association like any other. It certainly claims to be more than that, namely, a bringer of salvation.

You are of course right. In the case of the Church we have a social reality which presents itself as the legitimate embodiment of the pneumatic; it claims to serve the Spirit that is in it. Such a society obviously has a different character from, for example, an association of rabbit breeders. This has implications for the organization of its legal structures. Their character must ultimately be determined from their task. To this degree, the external structures of the Church are different from those of a profane society. Here is an example. A sacrament is, on the one hand, an external ritual action which as such can be regulated; on the other, we understand it as the appearance and effective symbolization of an event of grace. The same theory holds, although at different levels, for the other legal realities in the Church that appear to be purely profane.

Another, frequently formulated argument against the institutional Church runs as follows: in order to fulfill the most important concern of the Church, love of neighbor, it is not necessary to belong to the institutional Church. How can this be answered?

One would have to ask first what is understood here by love of neighbor. If, for example, I believe that the most magnificent and radical act of love of neighbor is not simply to provide food and clothing but rather to see to it that the absolute and incomprehensible God takes this person into his own inner life; if, in other words, I consider the bringing of the good news the highest act of human love, then it is obvious how such a broad notion of love of neighbor automatically leads into the realm of the Church. Persons who love themselves in God, who see themselves as not just biological living things, which, although a little crazier than "rational animals," are destined like everything else in the world to end in nothingness, these persons, I say, who respect and love the other as someone addressed by the message of eternal life, they have already established the foundation for the Church. A private love of neighbor that remains, in a certain sense, intimate is no full and total love at all. As an old man, I belong to an individualistic epoch in the history of ideas. I wonder, however, how it is that a slogan like "socialism" can be so plausible to the younger generation when in their relation to the Church they remain critical individualists. Something here clearly does not quite fit together.

Let me add an example from my own life. Most of you surely know Roger Garaudy, the former "chief ideologist" of the French Communist party. Later, as I understand it, he was thrown out of the party. I met him once at Chiemsee where we discussed the possibility of founding a journal for dialogue between Christians and Marxists. I said that I had nothing against it; he agreed but added that he would have to consult the central administration of his party. At the time I wondered what typical Catholic theologian today, wanting to be enlightened, liberal, and critical in regard to the Church, would say that he would first have to ask his bishop. He would consider such a thing as beneath his dignity as a free and critical human being. Garaudy, on the other hand, did not feel that at all because as a socialist he understood the social implications of even the smallest questions and decisions.

You advise us not to allow our relation to the Church to be disturbed by outward forms. I wonder why the Church constantly acts in such a way that almost inevitably it is misunderstood precisely in regard to outer appearances. To be concrete, why is there apparently a law according to which the further up in the hierarchy the clergy are, the finer and more splendid their robes have to be? Or why does the Church deck itself out in this period before Christmas with so much glitter and splendor? Would it not be more credible and less open to misunderstanding if it were to present itself differently?

It could well be, but if it were done differently, is it not possible that then the Church would glory in its very modesty?

But the fact is that the higher clergy does incline very strongly to outward show. Many symbols of secular life have been taken over into the world of the Church. Is that inevitable? Should the Church not seek to present itself in another way?

Let me stress once again that in questions like these we all have the right to our own opinion. We can even try to win acceptance for it in the public forum of the Church. But this kind of thing should not threaten our ultimate relationship to the Church. Tell the bishops and the pope that they ought to be more simple. I have nothing against that. But don't go too far in your criticism. Why should an important liturgical function of which I feel myself very much a part not have a certain splendor? Should all churches look like miserable dumps? Are churches like those at Ottobeuron or Ettal or the Wieskirche with all their liturgical pomp and splendor bad a priori? If someone like myself has little appreciation for this kind of thing, he need not take part in it but can choose instead a small and simple eucharistic celebration. Why should I take such things amiss and forbid them to those who enjoy the pomp and who experience it as an expression and embodied celebration of their inner Christian life?

I don't want to undermine justifiable traditions. I would just like to ask whether some things could not be done in a more simple and more relevant way today.

In regard to this question people disagree. I myself have no strong opinion about it. If the bishops, for example, were to stop wearing their mitres, that would be perfectly fine with me. To be quite honest, I found it a rather dreadful sight at the synod in Würzburg to see a whole swarm of bishops tottering forward one after the other, each with a mitre. But then again I am not the *arbiter elegantiarum* (the judge of taste) in the Church. Things don't have to be done according to my standards. If the bishops take delight in their robes, if they find them beautiful, sacred, and bathed in an aura of the eternal and the definitive, then that is their right.

You yourself have said that what is special about the Church in comparison to other social institutions is rooted in its understanding of itself as a universal bringer of salvation. Father Rahner, how does this understanding and the claim to absoluteness that is tied up with it relate to the social pluralism for which you have repeatedly called?

In order to answer this I would have to go over the 450 pages of my *Foundations of Christian Faith.* Your question simply raises too many other questions. There are religious, philosophical, and fundamental theological questions such as: How can I believe in God? Is there a God? Can he reveal himself? There are exegetical questions, too, like: What can we know about Jesus Christ? What kind of claim did he make? Given the complexity of the issues, permit me to formulate something in a rather provocative way. In the case where someone is unable to accept the claim of Jesus and of Christianity as truly binding on himself or herself, then he or she is in no way obliged to accept it. That is to be taken for granted. In regard to the objective side of the situation, this of course says nothing. It could be that there are people who really think that they ought to poison me. If they are truly convinced of this, then they ought in God's name to do it. To put it into a theological formulation: if someone were convinced in conscience and before God that he or she ought to kill me, then I would say: "For God's sake, do it, for if you don't you won't be able after death to stand before the judgment of God." Objectively seen, such a proposal would be crazy, but that is quite a different issue.

I have a question that is less complex. What do you think of the German bishops' paper on the arms race?

Your question is no simpler. First of all, I can't presuppose that I alone am intelligent and that all the bishops are dumb. If, however, after serious and self-critical examination I were to come to the conviction that the statement is not sufficiently pacifist in its orientation, then I, as indeed everyone else, may reject it. And in spite of that one can be and remain a good Christian. With my nephew, the Heidelberg medical doctor, Thomas Cremer, I wrote something for the book *Atomic Weapons—Can They Be Justified from a Christian Standpoint?* (Düsseldorf, 1982, pp. 98–115). I argued there for prior concessions in regard to disarmament. No church authority ever criticized me for doing so. This was probably not simply because someone thought: let Karl talk; the less fuss we make the better. I have the impression that the above-mentioned paper reveals a greater capacity on the part of the German bishops to learn than I personally had expected. In this they offer a contrast to the Central Committee of German Catholics.

You say that one could reject what the German bishops say and still remain a good Christian. In the New Testament it says: "Who hears you, hears me"(Luke 10:16).

Even according to the official teaching of the Church this phrase doesn't mean that everything that church authorities declare to be the case is necessarily right. Since 1967 we have had in our possession a pastoral letter of the German bishops about the magisterium (Letter of the German Bishops to All those Entrusted by the Church with the Preaching of the Faith, September 22, 1967). It is explicitly stated there that the Church can err and has often erred in matters that are not defined *ex cathedra*. The letter also says that where someone comes to the conviction that he or she is more knowledgeable about an issue than the bishops, then in theory and practice he or she can deviate from the authoritative but noninfallible teaching of the magisterium. That is the explicit teaching of the German bishops, and Rome has never protested against it. One can therefore read the phrase, "Who hears you, hears me," with a certain reservation.

The Italian Archibishop A. Pangrazio, during Vatican II, brought into the discussion of the ecumenical decree the notion of the "hierarchy of truths." Is that, as

Hans Küng has suggested, an attempt by the institutional Church to break free of "irreformable" doctrines?

In my opinion Küng here clearly contradicts teaching that is obligatory for a Catholic. And I have often said this directly to him. Along with others, I twice wrote on Küng's behalf to Cardinal Agostino Casaroli, and I have received a letter from Cardinal Ratzinger. I have in no sense any personal animosity for Küng. After all, we did found together the journal *Concilium*. That, however, doesn't change the fact that Küng rejects a binding teaching of Vatican I and, independently of it, in my opinion, is wrong when he affirms that the Church can err even in those cases where in its own understanding it makes a judgment in a definitive and irreformable way. From a historical point of view no proofs can be brought for Küng's thesis. Whoever refers to *Humanae Vitae* has to be told plainly that, quite consciously on the part of Paul VI, no *ex cathedra* decision was given in it.

One has to admit that there have been and that there are authentic non-defined magisterial teachings that are de facto erroneous and which nevertheless have had an unfortunate influence on the life of the Church. That, however, doesn't change the basic principle. Hans Küng objects: "You keep on interpreting magisterial decisions until you are in agreement with them. This success is achieved only at the price of the original meaning of the defined doctrine." My answer is that of course I have to interpret if I am even to understand what I am supposed to believe. I cannot simply repeat a statement whose concepts I have never understood. Such credulity is nonsense and unchristian. To put it differently, it is my responsibility to deal in a personal way with church teaching. I have to ask what it means and what it doesn't mean. There is no magisterial teaching—including no defined teaching—that doesn't require a subjective appropriation and therefore an interpretation. It can of course happen that my interpretation is totally false or at least partially so. It is up to the Church to tell me if that is the case. So long, however, as I honestly and openly maintain an interpretation which the institutional Church doesn't reject, I have the right in this reasonable fashion to make my peace with such a definition. At least I take this kind of approach for granted.

But what then is the meaning of the teaching about the "hierarchy of truths"?

If you read the statement of the Italian bishop who was named earlier, it is obvious that what he wanted to do first of all was to defend the existence of the hierarchy of truths. In fact its existence is self-evident. That there is a God is a hundred thousand times more important than that there are indulgences or a specific number of sacraments. Archbishop Pangrazio expressly stated, moreover, that this does not imply that those truths that are not at the top of the pyramid can simply be rejected. If you don't accept the affirmation that the letter to the Hebrews was written by Paul, then, although rejecting a church teaching that was held right into the twentieth century, you are not rejecting a defined truth. Such a proposition is not even contained in the hierarchy of binding truths of faith. But even among those truths that are in fact required to be believed, there is a considerable gradation in regard to their significance. As already stated, this doesn't at all mean that I can reject any such truth. What is open to question is the degree to which I must positively affirm it.

Take the case of a Protestant historian of dogma who says that he can't understand how, from the point of view of history, it can be shown that there are precisely seven and not eight or six sacraments. To such a person I would say: "If you want to be a Catholic, you are not permitted to deny, as some kind of godless error, the claim that there are seven sacraments. You can, however, more or less disregard it as relatively secondary in the hierarchy of truths."

Or, to take another example, if I were to ask you to explain to me the meaning of the Trinity, I suspect that a good number would end up talking nonsense. In this case, too, I would say that you can be good Christians without worrying about such subtle questions.

As we come to a close, permit me to ask about the reforms that you would like to see in the Church. What in your opinion most needs to be reformed?

This year a book on the papacy is being brought out by the Südwest publishing house. The editor of the book, Bruno Moser, asked me to describe how I might imagine a pope of the future. What I wrote is a letter of Paul VII in the year 2000 to his friend Peppino.[1] In it he presents his understanding of his office. I am against a certain kind of Roman bureaucratic centralism. When the Congregation for the Faith declared that the nonordination of women is a matter of doctrine, I wrote an article against its position. I know that for the time being nothing is going to change in regard to this question. We will simply have to wait until it gradually seeps into the consciousness of the Church. Unfortunately that will take a very long time. It took four hundred years before we had a liturgy in the vernacular.

It seems to me, Father Rahner, that your answer doesn't take seriously enough certain aspects of the question. To put it concretely, what about the situation where the Church, which I love, not only limits my possibility of serving in the way that I would like to, for example, as a priest, but prevents it in principle simply because I am a woman?

1. See "Die unvergängliche Aktualität des Papstums," *Schriften zur Theologie 16* (Zurich-Einsiedeln-Koln: Benziger, 1984), pp. 249–70.

Let me ask you a question in return. Do you have, on the basis of a personal inclination, the right to demand an official function in the Church?

There is always the possibility of changing one's denomination. . . .
If you are convinced that the Catholic Church is simply one of many conditioned and arbitrary religious groupings, all having the same worth and validity, then naturally you can convert to a Protestant church in order to became a pastor. A serious Catholic would have to say: "I would like very much to be ordained; not only that, but I am convinced that in two or three hundred years there will be no laws against it in the Catholic Church. For now, however, I simply have to accept this restriction on my life." Who doesn't experience curtailments, limitations, and disappointments in regard to subjective and totally legitimate life plans? What does someone say who finally finds another person with whom he or she expects to achieve the radical fulfillment of his or her personality for time and eternity when the beloved is suddenly killed by lightning? Is the situation of such a person any easier than that of a woman in the Catholic Church whose lifelong dream of becoming a priest comes to naught because of the regulations of church law?

Translated by Daniel Donovan
University of Saint Michael's College, Toronto

20•The Future of the World and of the Church
Interview with Giancarlo Zizola, Rome (1982)

In the course of your life, Father Rahner, you have worked with many theological committees. You were a peritus at Vatican II, an advisor to the German Bishops'

Conference, and so on. You also belonged to the International Theological Commission. Why did you leave it?

Because it had become superfluous. It had lost its function. The Congregation for the Doctrine of the Faith no longer took the suggestions of the commission seriously. One can have an academic discussion among theologians without a commission set up by Rome.

Were you disappointed about it?

Despite everything, I haven't lost any sleep over it.

Could we say that a conservative wind is blowing again in the Church?

Some distinctions are called for. A conservative tendency is certainly perceptible in Rome. That, however, is probably often a result of the fact that some Catholic theologians defend positions that are objectively incompatible with the teachings of the magisterium. Dangers for the continued handing on of the content of the Catholic faith do exist, dangers which are in part provoked by so-called progressive Catholic theologians. The magisterium thus has legitimate grounds for imposing sanctions and for examining positions that are to be found in Catholic theology. On the other hand, it is also true that there are from a church point of view reactionary positions in the strict sense of the word, like those of Archbishop Marcel Lefèbvre.

Do you have the impression that these reactionary positions have met with excessive toleration?

I don't believe that they are accepted by Rome or by the pope. There is, of course, a certain tolerance for reactionary tendencies, but perhaps even more for progressive theologians. One should not overlook the developments that have taken place in the life of the Church in the course of this century. If a Catholic exegete under Pius X dared to cite modern authors, he was simply thrown out. Today it is normal, for example, in hermeneutics to consider the results of the natural sciences.

Is it true to say that in recent years the very identity of theology has undergone modification?

In comparison with the period from Pius X to Pius XII, there is a greater freedom and a greater critical distance over against traditional neoscholastic formulations. Today dogmatic theologians are more inclined to accept the results of modern exegesis, both Protestant and Catholic. Dialogue among theologians of different denominations has become more open and fraternal. Catholic theologians no longer work in a Catholic ghetto, but rather in a continuing encounter with modern culture. This is in striking contrast with the past.

What should a theologian be, a mouthpiece for the consensus of the Church or a prophet?
The theologian is certainly no prophet. . . .

Never?
If a theologian has a prophetic charism, then he or she will naturally use it and will know how to do so. Certainly there are currents in theology today that may be prophetic or which, at least, claim to be. One of my students, Johann Baptist Metz, personifies such a form of theology. He has developed the claims and essentials of a political theology. There are other prophetic-theological trends as well that desire to influence the future of the Church or of the whole world.

And how would you define Karl Rahner?
I am a Catholic theologian who attempts in absolute loyalty to the magisterium of the Church to rethink Catholic teaching. This I can say in all modesty. There are, of course, positions of the magisterium that are not definitive. It can err and issue a statement that can be criticized or reformulated. I consider myself a sincere and profound friend of Saint Thomas. I do not, however, agree with those Thomists who are so locked into traditionalism that they can't imagine that any progress can be made independently of traditional Thomism. Catholic theologians not only can, but must criticize nondefinitive statements of the magisterium and develop ever more profound interpretations of the dogmas that have already been defined. Here there is a great deal of freedom, and it must remain so.

Should theologians also involve themselves with the problems of society?
That is an obligation for all citizens and therefore also for theologians. Their proper object of research is in fact Christian and Catholic revelation, but this has a great deal to say that is absolutely essential for the salvation of the world.

One of the greatest problems of modern society is the whole issue of atomic weapons. What do you make of the fact that Catholics hold different positions about it?
Christians can have varying opinions about this kind of social problem and they do in fact have them in regard to atomic weapons. Both sides appeal to

the Bible and to Jesus Christ. In doing this, one side or the other might be right, or perhaps neither. As far as I am concerned, atomic war of any kind is unacceptable. I regard as wrong not only the deployment of nuclear weapons but also the existence of all atomic arms. I say this even though I don't hold both of these positions with equal certainty.

If you could speak to President Ronald Reagan, what would you say to him?
I would say that I do not agree with the way he talks about atomic weapons. He speaks about them without shame and as if they were something natural and self-evident. I would repeat to him what the American bishops are saying; I would remind him that one of them has refused to pay half of his taxes and that another encourages workers to leave nuclear arms plants, and so on.

Would you encourage Catholics to a general attitude of conscientious objection in regard to atomic politics?
On the one hand, it has to be simply accepted that some Catholics declare such things to be absolutely incompatible with their conscience; on the other, one has to be patient with and love those Christians who hold the opposite view. The affirmation is certainly true that atomic weapons offend the conscience of Christians and that therefore collaboration with politics of this kind is simply not allowed. We must, however, presuppose honesty and intelligence on the part of those who see this differently than we do. We have to live with the situation.

What is the task of theology in regard to the question of peace?
It must by all possible means sensitize the conscience of society to the fact that an atomic war, under whatever conditions, is absolutely immoral.

Could the magisterium address this issue more clearly?
I would rather say that Christians could do more. The contemporary Christian is no longer someone who simply waits for decisions from above. He or she must act according to Christian principles without waiting for the authority of the Church.

But have these principles been made sufficiently clear?
The Church has declared the absolute immorality of atomic war. It has not yet declared the absolute immorality of every kind of atomic weapon. It doesn't yet see which of the two positions is in every case right from a moral

point of view. The individual Christian, however, can on the basis of Christian principles opt for a decision in favor of unilateral and absolute nuclear disarmament. For such a decision no declaration of the institutional Church is required.

Would that not ultimately mean that Christians could appeal to Christianity itself in order to justify atomic weapons which, by their very nature, are destined to bring about worldwide catastrophe?

I must simply affirm the fact that some Christians are for, while others are against, such weapons and that both sides appeal to principles of Christian morality. The magisterium, moreover, is not in a position to come out in an absolute way for one **or** the other side. This, however, doesn't mean that individuals have a right to remain neutral. In keeping with their conscience they must come to a definite position in regard to this problem. Not only that, but according to the norms of social morality they have the right to speak out on behalf of a particular view and work to see that it has an impact on public opinion and on decisions of state.

It is essential that I begin with the presupposition that others, even when they have a different and perhaps opposite opinion, are no worse and no less intelligent than I am. There are two principles here that have to be respected: we must state our own opinion and defend it with conviction, and at the same time accept and bear with the standpoint of our opponents, assuming that they too have made their judgment according to Christian principles. This dialectical situation can't be avoided. It can educate Christians with different views in the art of dialogue and thus further the cause of peace.

What do you think will be the fate of our world?

I am no prophet. I hope that there will be no absolute disaster, but I am afraid that it will come to that.

Are the conditions for such an outcome already present?

As far as I can see, there are no conditions that have the capacity at the moment to force the other side to act in such a way that a catastrophe will be avoided.

Do we not need a "spiritual deterrent" based on a total and powerless witness?

Yes. If Christians were humble, believed in the beatitudes, were able to do without material riches, did not in pride think themselves better than others, then a climate and mentality would be created that could foster the prevention of the final catastrophe.

Can we hope that the "great wall" of atomic weapons will be torn down and that the threatening danger will compel us to think of the future of the human race in radically new ways?
I believe that God will triumph over the stupidity and malice of humankind. God will not abandon us.

Does beginning with the human person create an awkward situation for the theologian?
Not at all. For the theologian there is a God-man: Jesus the Christ. Only those who are able to find themselves can find God. The alternative "theology or anthropology" is false.

How then do you explain the concern of the leadership of the Catholic Church about the "temptation to anthropologism"?
Because there are many today, even priests, who think only in terms of this world.

And how do you evaluate the pressure from Rome on clerics and members of religious orders, especially in South America, to eschew politics?
When the clergy forget in an obvious way the spiritual task of priests and focus exclusively on social criticism, Rome is right in insisting on their spiritual and religious responsibilities. Clearly there is a danger that this stance of the Curia, legitimate in itself, could foster a bourgeois and conservative mentality. The pope explicitly admits that under certain conditions and in certain circumstances a priest can exercise political functions. The question of course is: When does there exist in a concrete case the kind of "extraordinary" situation that would permit this kind of political involvement? The issue, for example, in regard to Ernesto Cardenal, who is both priest and minister of culture in Nicaragua, is whether the situation there fulfills the required conditions. About this people can disagree.

What do you think of political theology? Or perhaps putting it better, do you believe that there can be a theology that isn't in some way political?
Every theology is historically conditioned. That is why there are constant "shifts" between theology and history. Changes are constantly taking place in society which have repercussions on theology. And so it is that social ques-

tions have a greater significance today than ever before. In a stable society where there was little change in the short term, social problems were not dealt with in theology. But now, in a world that is constantly changing, social questions have become relevant even for theology. With this new emphasis, however, there is a real danger of anthropological egoism. I believe it would be better for people to think more about God and less about themselves.

Are human rights theologically significant?
Yes. We can even say that those who disregard the rights of others will one day be condemned.

In public as well as private discussions there is frequent mention of the "signs of the time" and of the need to discern them. What for you are the most significant signs of our time?
Ours is a culture dominated by technology and rationality. In spite of all the rationality, however, people don't know what decisions to take in regard to the most important things in their life. Clearly the concrete ideals of our society and traditional ideologies no longer hold sway.

Have all moral systems also lost their validity?
That has to be admitted in regard to many of them. I believe, however, that the principle, love your neighbor as yourself, and the principles of the beatitudes in general are still valid today. They seem to correspond to the deepest needs of humankind, even when in fact they are often disregarded.

That would mean that Christianity still has something essential to say.
Of course it does. One should rather affirm that Christianity has everything to say. When Christianity proclaims the infinite God as the attainable goal or end of humankind, it offers humanity a unique promise. Whatever Christians today do on the basis of false criteria, that will never justify the conclusion that Christianity has nothing more to say.

Do you think that it is possible that we are going in the direction of a higher form of religion?
Obviously Christianity must continue to develop. It is, however, neither dead nor surpassed. It remains the absolute religion.

But was it not you who developed the teaching about the saving function of non-Christian religions?

It is a teaching of Vatican II. The Council affirms that those who are true to their conscience can obtain salvation. It also says that Christianity is a religion for all people. Both points of view are thoroughly compatible.

Are we moving toward an entirely new religious language?
Since language depends on the historical context, it is always in a process of development. It is therefore self-evident that religious language in the year 2000 will be different from that of the past. In the midst of all changes, however, the fact of continuity must not be overlooked. I read Plato, for example, and I understand him quite well. History knows no moments of absolute discontinuity. In the final analysis we are not able to estimate adequately just how much religious language will change.

Your own religious language, in comparison with that of an average Christian, already seems to have undergone a change. Rahner the theologian rarely uses the concept "God." You often speak in your work of the "mystery" that human beings come upon in the everyday situations of their life. What do you mean by the word "mystery"? What constitutes the mysterium *of human life?*
That is very difficult to answer. Perhaps it could be put briefly this way: ultimately, for me, the mystery consists in being able to grasp rationally that the incomprehensible really exists. This is the highest act of human understanding.

Was that not at times a drama for you?
Yes, it often was. But the pressure lessened once my reason grasped that it stands before the absolutely incomprehensible mystery. There is, you know, a form of Christian agnosticism, the acknowledgment of the absolute mystery. Doesn't even Paul speak of the *theos agnostos*, the unknown God?

Did such an idea of God, rejecting as it does all images and concepts, never lead you into doubt?
Christian faith, when it is truly serious, is always exposed to doubt. Faith and doubt belong together. But that doesn't mean that one is an unbeliever.

Then what is unbelief today?
Twenty years ago, Erich Fromm said that he was an atheist. In doing so he was anxious not to confuse God with an idol. It was this concern that drove him to atheistic formulations. It often happens that Christians exchange God for some idol that they have made with their own hands. In fact there are

people who believe in quite precise concepts but who in the midst of their existence are profoundly unbelieving. In the same way it is possible for someone to be a radically believing person and yet reject certain words and formulations.

At the present time, what, in your judgment, is the most dangerous heresy?
To believe in God only when he helps us, or rather when he should help us.

That would mean that a Christian can learn from non-Christians and even from so-called unbelievers.
It is possible. As a Christian one can certainly learn a more radical Christianity from those whom I like to call "anonymous Christians."

What are the most important theological problems today?
The oldest ones, which are in fact always the most relevant: How is an authentic experience of God possible? How can I truly experience that in Jesus Christ God has communicated himself to us in an absolute and irreversible way?

Can one say that contemporary theology is coming to a more radical formulation of its questions?
It is quite apparent that the formulation of basic questions is being carried out today in a more radical way. It is imperative that this process continue. The number of important theological questions is legion. Here is but one. How can I show people that God is more significant than their stomach? Issues related to ecumenism would also have to be included among pressing contemporary theological concerns.

Are you referring in this last comment to the papacy?
In a number of particular areas relating to ecumenism there are already agreements among theologians. Other issues remain unresolved, especially those that touch on the function of the pope. This is a point that remains difficult. The one Church of the future will not be the Roman Catholic Church in the form that it exists today. It will be marked by a legitimate pluralism, a much greater pluralism than that which has existed in Roman Catholicism. From the point of view of the greater pluralism to come, the existing pluralism among Christian denominations is not so far from the one Church of the future as one might think.

What would be the most striking changes?
Let me take an idea from Walter Bühlmann. The Church will be made up of a network of small basic communities with some kind of organized inter-relationship. This commonality will be assured by the bishops. There will have to be a pope, but much else will be different.

For example?
Present Roman centralism will no longer exist. It will not be allowed to exist. This opinion is quite compatible with the conviction that Rome will, from many points of view, have a greater significance throughout the world than it does today.

Could you imagine that the center of the Christian world might no longer be Rome and the Vatican?
If the pope were to live somewhere else, yes. Walter Bühlmann has said that he could go, for example, to the Philippines.

Do you think that another ecumenical council could be useful?
If and to the degree that the Church understands itself as *ecclesia semper reformanda* (a Church always in need of reform), then it must constantly address the problem of change. I am obviously not satisfied with the present state of the Church. Nor is the pope. The question is: What are the most pressing things that need to be improved? It has to be asked, for example, whether African marriage ethics are to continue to be modeled on those of Europe. The problem of our understanding of the nature of marriage must be dealt with, together with other questions, as, for example, whether all forms of African polygamy are truly incompatible with Christianity. Absolutely imperative would be an authentic and legitimate decentralization of the Church, with all the consequences that would entail. Can there, for example, on the basis of Catholic teaching, be ways other than the present ones for choosing episcopal candidates and for naming bishops?

What do you think of Pope John Paul II and his style?
First, a preliminary remark. In my opinion it is one thing to obey and another to applaud. Christian obedience isn't to be confused with mere conformism which shies away from personal opinion which itself is always open to modification. To address your question more specifically, I believe that the pope's trips are not what the Church today really needs. It would be better if the Holy Father remained in Rome and exercised his leadership in the Church from there.

Doesn't the question about the priesthood of women also belong to the pressing issues of the modern period?

Certainly. And when the Congregation for the Faith declares that it is impossible to admit women to the priesthood, then I have to argue against it and affirm from a dogmatic point of view that the priesthood of women is not impossible.

Alongside the many problems of modern theology that you have evoked, is there one question that seems to you as a theologian to be perhaps the most important?

Yes, there is such a question. It runs like this: Is human existence absurd or does it have an ultimate meaning? If it is absurd, why do human beings have an unquenchable hunger for meaning? Is it not a consequence of God's existence? For if God really doesn't exist, then the hunger for meaning is absurd.

A final question. Looking at the great range of your publications, one wonders whether theological creativity isn't a form of prayer and worship for you.

I at least hope that it is.

Translated by Daniel Donovan
University of Saint Michael's College, Toronto

21•Christianity, A Religion for the Whole of Humanity?

Interview with Gwendoline Jarczyk, Paris (April 1983)

It was always a major concern of yours to relate systematic reflections to concrete situations, to bring together dogmatic and pastoral theology. What is the real basis for this apparently necessary combining of theological thought and action?

There are two different reasons for the close relationship between systematic and pastoral theology. The first is a practical and obvious one. Theology is intended to serve preaching, and preaching addresses people where they are, so that they will be able to bind themselves more intensely to God in their own concrete situations. And so systematic theology, which is no "art for art's sake," has a pastoral task. The second reason is related to the ecclesial nature of theology. It is a reflection on the Church's proclamation of the gospel. In addition to this, there is today a particular task and difficulty for systematic theology.

In the first fifteen hundred years of Western culture everything that the Church and faith affirmed was regarded as quite self-evident and certain; it was firmly accepted in the public life of society. Today we live in a secularized world, a world in which atheism is taken for granted. In such a situation, preaching must deal in a totally new, more precise and more intensive way with the person to whom one wants to bring the gospel message. Theology has to reflect in a much more profound way on the human person as hearer of the Word. It must consult modern anthropological sciences which simply did not exist earlier. It has to know and respect what the modern natural sciences reveal about humankind. To a certain degree theology today must also become political theology. It wasn't I but my student Johann Baptist Metz who developed political theology. In spite of controversy in regard to questions of detail, there exists between the two of us a common fundamental conviction: today, in order to serve the preaching of the gospel, the social sciences have to be drawn into the work of theology. In addition, a great deal more thought than in the past must be given to the social presuppositions of earlier forms of preaching. One ought, for example, to question whether our understanding of the relationship between office and the individual believer has been influenced by a sociopolitical view that might have been molded decisively by the feudal systems of the past. Nor is it necessary that guilt be involved in such a phenomenon. In a similar way, one could ask whether the role of women that at one time was taken for granted from a sociological point of view has not continued to be operative in theology in a way that is no longer acceptable today, and so on.

164

The contemporary world is disintegrating into a multiplicity of cultures. How can a message of salvation be formulated for such a world so that it can be understood and accepted by all cultures?

Contemporary theology must be theology of a world-Church. The question about the possibility of an authentic inculturation of Christianity in Africa, South America, and above all East Asia is very difficult to answer. The problem has certainly not been reflected on adequately in theology.

With the exception of the relatively small Eastern churches and Orthodoxy, which themselves are influenced by the West, it can be said that down to the middle of the twentieth century there only existed a European theology with "exports" around the globe. These exports were only possible in conjunction with the wave of European colonialism. Today this is no longer operative. The plausibility of Christianity for other cultures can no longer be grounded in the superiority of Europe and the West. We must come to a Christianity that has genuinely achieved an inner and essential synthesis with other cultures. There are signs that this is beginning to happen.

Because Vatican II, in comparison with Vatican I, wasn't a council of European bishops and of missionary bishops of European extraction, but to a marked degree a council of an authentic world episcopate, the beginnings of a theology have been provided that will no longer be simply European, but inculturated in a variety of traditions. Obviously, with this, the problems haven't been solved. On the contrary, the impression is that Rome is very hesitant in this area. It has, for example, reacted in a distrustful fashion to South American liberation theology. This is perhaps a sign that the Vatican has not yet understood that an East Asian or African Christianity ought to have a very different appearance from its European counterpart. To take another example: it is clear that Rome has not yet sufficiently understood that, in regard to the structure and interpretation of marriage in Africa, there are quite other presuppositions at work than in the Western world. Or take the fact that even today liturgical texts used in non-Western countries are simply translations into local languages of our European versions. But is that enough? It has to be asked why Rome balks at efforts to carry the process of inculturation any further. It surely has to do with an understandable desire to reinforce unity in matters of faith and Christian morality. At the same time, from the point of view of universal human history, the contemporary situation of Christianity is something radically new.

One must reflect on the fact that right down to the present day there has never been in the entire history of the world a religion that wasn't just the religion of a single cultural area. It could of course be said that if religion were to take on the form of an abstract humanism, then it could become the belief of the whole world. Christianity cannot, however, provide a model for such a humanism. It is essentially a religion which, as a historical product of the revelation of God, developed, first in Israel and then in the Western cultural world, into what it is today. How such a religion, the very essence of which is rooted in history, can become a religion for all cultures without losing its identity is a still unresolved problem for Church and theology.

Another issue relevant here is the confrontation with worldwide atheism. Christianity thus stands before a twofold difficulty. Perhaps, however, both these aspects are, even in a positive sense, more closely allied than we know. But this too, in my judgment, has not yet really been thought about in the official Church. That is why I recently expressed the wish that the pope might write a substantial encyclical on atheism. I am quite willing, however, to admit that he has had understandable reasons for not doing it up to now. The task is in fact enormously difficult. And yet to the degree that I can expect of all people—in spite of cultural and existential differences—that they are related to the absolute mystery of the one and eternal God and to the degree that everyone can understand that death can be undergone in communion with the one Jesus crucified and risen, an ultimate unity of faith is possible for all humanity. To everyone I can say: "The one incomprehensible mystery of God is a reality and you must die into it. At the same time you have in Jesus, who by the way was not a European, the promise that this leap into the incomprehensibility of God can really succeed." Starting from this point and in spite of all the problems that have been touched on, we can have a calm assurance that the Church has a message that can be understood around the globe. The extent to which this message will be heard or not is an open question for the future. This is finally very much tied up with the question whether the Church as the fundamental sacrament of salvation for the whole world and for all people must have a certain numerical and historical significance or whether it can abandon this without automatically undermining its roll of being a universal sign of salvation.

You constantly stress that all people have an experience of transcendence whether they know about God and revelation or not. In this context your statement comes to mind that among unbelievers there can be found many "anonymous Christians." What do you understand by this concept?

I am not at all certain whether I or someone else first came up with the concept of the "anonymous Christian" or of the related but distinct concept of "anonymous Christianity." What is correct is that my theology has been closely related to these notions. First of all, I would like to say that I am quite indifferent to the word itself. If for religious, pedagogical, or other significant reasons it is found to be dangerous or open to misunderstanding, then simply drop it. What I affirm is that, at least since Vatican II, there can be no doubt that those who have been divinized by God's grace in faith, hope, and love are not identical in number with those who explicitly believe in Jesus Christ and are baptized. The number of the "justified," to use the scholastic term, or of those "justified in the grace of God," to speak with the Council of Trent, is not identical with those who have been baptized and who belong to the Church or to the Christian churches. There are, as Augustine already knew, a great many who seem to be inside but who in reality are outside, and many others who seem to be outside but who in fact belong to the invisible Church of those who are graced. In this sense it is self-evident and certain that there are "anonymous Christians." How many there are; how many become such in the moment when through death their existence takes on its definitive state; how such people who do not belong to the visible Church and perhaps have no explicit faith in a specifically Christian sense can be believers—such questions are obviously difficult. They are by no means as yet adequately clarified by theology.

We don't know, but today we are permitted to hope that, in spite of all ideological differences and in spite of so much horror in the profane history of the world, many, perhaps even all human beings, belong to those in whom the free, gratuitous, and overflowing grace of God is victorious. This is a conviction that one can and, indeed, must have.

A traditional Lutheran might say: "I do not claim that only the baptized will be saved but I know absolutely nothing about the eternal salvation of the unbaptized." Earlier scholastic theology would probably have answered in the same way. Since the time of Saint Augustine and practically right down until today there has been a mentality in the Church that regarded salvation by God's free grace as an exception. Being lost, remaining in the *massa damnata*, in the Augustinian phrase, was more or less thought to be the norm. At the very best it was among the baptized that a better balance between the damned and the saved was thought to exist. Today, however, we have to say that we hope that the definitive outcome of world history will not leave behind for all eternity the "trash heap" which traditional theology has called hell.

Naturally I do not presume to know how in the last analysis the infinite mercy of God, which the present pope has so praised, can coexist with his justice and with the possibility that a person can through free decision be lost. I do not claim to be able to offer a comprehensible synthesis in this regard. I say, as an average Catholic and theologian, that a person must reckon with the possibility of eternal damnation. Nothing, however, obliges me to affirm that I know with certainty that this unquestionable possibility will ever become a realized fact. I can say that I hope for the one and fear the other. I fear eternal damnation in particular cases and yet I hope for the possibility of a final *apokatastasis pantōn* (salvation of all), in spite of the fact that this hope is constantly being undermined by our empirical experience.

With all respect to Saint Augustine, he must be asked: "How can you believe in the victory of the cross of the eternal Son of God and at the same time see no problem in the fact that apparently enormous numbers of people are damned? Does this not testify to an indescribable coldness in your heart?"

Naturally, after Auschwitz and all the horrors of the present time, we can't simply embrace a Christian-liberal optimism. We can't say that the history of the world will end in wonderful and blessed harmony. Yet it is also true that I am not entitled to abandon my hope for everyone.

I have great respect for the genial theology of Thomas Aquinas. There is, however, a saying of his to which I can't subscribe. Thomas says that a person can only hope for himself or herself but not for others. To that I can only respond that, as a human being who is obliged to love others to the end, I have the holy duty of hoping for everyone and only subsequently do I have the right to hope for myself, poor sinner that I am.

Translated by Daniel Donovan
University of Saint Michael's College, Toronto

22 • The Unity of the Church to Come

Interview with Eduard Kopp, Hamburg (February 3, 1984)

The euphoria we were experiencing ten years ago in exchanges between the confessions seems to have disappeared? Why is that?

Not everybody shares your assessment. For instance, my friend Karl Lehmann just recently criticized the opinion that ecumenism is at a standstill.

My own opinion, however, is that we are at a standstill. One could even argue that what we have seen is that the initiatives and goals of the Council will need a much longer time to achieve palpable results than perhaps we thought earlier. My own view is that, despite the "Lima Document" and despite the agreement between Anglican and Catholic theologians, in fact nothing is progressing at a proper pace.

There are two reasons for this: one, we are trying to achieve dogmatic consensus that is not attainable concretely, and even in another ten to fifteen years cannot be attained; second, from a canonical point of view, that is to say, in its new Code of Canon Law, Rome has never clearly stated that an actual church reunion will not mean nor need it mean a radical elimination of any distinctiveness of those churches united with Rome.

I assume that the Roman officials—among whom I would mention Cardinal Ratzinger and Cardinal Willebrands—know and support that fact. But I am puzzled why this is not clearly stated. Because only then can one concretely negotiate; one can determine what Rome holds absolutely as its faith position and what Canon Law requires. I mean that Rome should clarify that its relationship to the other churches should be comparable to its relationship with the Eastern churches in communion with Rome. Uniform and absolute consensus, or one that tolerates absolutely no difference of opinion in theological matters, cannot be achieved. Nor is it necessary!

Are you arguing for "Unity in Plurality"?
That's the expression of my friend Heinrich Fries. It is related, however, more to the plurality of individual churches (*Teilkirchen* as I prefer to call them), which would include even the Roman Catholic Church in its present structure and ways of proceeding.

Still, the pope would likewise belong to the one Church taken as a whole, since he exercises a specific, essential function vis-à-vis the worldwide Church. Just as an Eastern church in communion with Rome possesses its own tradition, its own way of life, its own liturgy and theology, accepted to be sure by Rome, so something similar must exist for the Protestant churches.

Would the Protestants be open to the Petrine ministry of the bishop of Rome? Is this in any way conceivable?
First of all, I have to say that for me as a Roman Catholic theologian the idea of a whole unified Church without the function of a Petrine office for the worldwide Church, and so for all particular churches, would be unthinkable. Whether or not there is an openness for this, and what kinds of modification in the Petrine office would be required, are questions that Protestant bishops would have to address. The Anglican/Roman Catholic *Final Report* published a year ago completely accepts for Anglicans a role for the pope provided it is properly understood, and that it has careful, theological and dogmatic safe-

guards. Of course the question is always asked whether what theologians have treated favorably and intelligently will in fact be accepted subsequently by a majority of the church leaders and the faithful.

And for us Catholics the question we need to pose to our Protestant counterparts is: "Who on your side is the authoritative spokesman in favor of such a union of churches? Could one assume that in such a case a large number of pastors and faithful would go along with the decision?" These are troubling questions to which no one person can give an exact answer. Still, I am not pessimistic because, amid all that Protestant mutual consultation and freedom, it is still the case that the majority of pious and churchgoing Christians will do what their theological experts and ecclesiastical leaders say.

In the book Unity of the Churches: An Actual Possibility, *published by Heinrich Fries and yourself, you write: "All partner churches acknowledge the meaning and right of the Petrine service of the Roman pope to be the concrete guarantor of the unity of the Church in truth and love" (p. 59). You also state: "The pope, for his part, explicitly commits himself to acknowledge and to respect the thus agreed-upon independence of the partner churches. He declares* (jure humano, *by human right) that he will make use of his highest teaching authority* (ex cathedra), *granted to him in conformity with Catholic principles by the First Vatican Council, only in a manner that conforms juridically or in substance to a general council of the whole Church, just as his previous* ex cathedra *decisions have been issued in agreement and close contact with the whole Catholic episcopate" (p. 83). What exactly do you mean by this thesis?*

Our point is this. Looked at practically and reasonably, in the next twenty to one hundred years, there are no grounds for expecting that the pope would make use of his ability to pronounce *ex cathedra* definitions as was done by Pope Pius XII with the declaration of the dogma of the bodily Assumption of Mary into heaven. As you can read in the statement of the 1967 German bishops regarding the ecclesiastical magisterium, the other Roman decisions are not infallible. Consequently, dissent about such a declaration does not threaten the unity of the Church.

Let us take, for example, the 1981 apostolic exhortation of Pope John Paul II, the *Familiaris Consortio* ("The Role of the Family in the Modern World"). I presume that not every Protestant bishop would agree completely with each and every one of its statements. Such an agreement would be very difficult. But a Protestant bishop would have to show respect for such a statement. And why not? It is clearly not the case that such declarations should a priori be seen as nonsensical. On the contrary.

Theologically there would be difficulties in a unified world-Church. But if you take a good look you can see that these kinds of difficulties exist in the present-day Roman Catholic Church. Do you really think that each American bishop agreed with every affirmation in Pope Paul VI's encyclical *Humanae Vitae* (1968)?

What stands out very specifically among the theses concerns the election of the pope. Not stated in the book, but what follows as a logical consequence of your view, is this question: Could it not come to a situation whereby even the once Protestant but now united bishops would have a passive right to vote in a papal election?

We proceeded from the following fact: among the bishops and faithful of different particular churches there exists a fundamental, real, true consensus in faith which springs from within. Of course we would have to assume that the pope would call an electoral college to represent these churches also. These churches are "catholic" inasmuch as they recognize the Petrine office. They regard the Petrine office not as something conceded grudgingly, but as a completely positive meaning and challenge. So my answer to your question: if the pope in this one Church were to constitute an electoral college appropriately representing the totality of the particular churches, then clearly the church leaders from the Protestant side would also have to possess a passive right to vote just as others.

Have you received a response from Protestants concerning the Petrine ministry of the bishop of Rome toward all particular churches?

Among the more important responses was one by Eberhard Jüngel that appeared in the *Süddeutsche Zeitung* (October 1–2, 1983). I also received a very, very fine letter from the (Protestant) chancellery office. But that letter doesn't go into any details.

Many Protestant pastors think that they are perceived by Catholic bishops as "laypersons in disguise." The question about ordained ministries is at the center of a number of conflicts.

One has to distinguish. Regarding Protestant Christians one should leave the theological interpretation of their previous ministry to further discussion. In regard to Anglicans, a Catholic in good standing can certainly hold the opinion that the declaration of Pope Leo XIII concerning the presumed invalidity of Anglican orders (1896) is incorrect, even according to Catholic understanding of the sacraments. Regarding Lutherans the problem is more complex from a Catholic perspective. But I hold it as self-evident from a Catholic viewpoint that even an ordination conferred by someone who is not a bishop is not simply nothing.

How has the Catholic hierarchy reacted to your new book?

Nobody condemns an old fool like me for something he says. You just let him say his piece. I am convinced that I will receive no reaction or only a passing reaction to this new book, just as was the case with my earlier book on the question of ordination that appeared in the series *Quaestiones Disputatae* under the title *Vorfragen zu einenem ökumenischen Amstsverständnis* [*Preliminary Questions for an Ecumenical Understanding of Office*] (Freiburg, 1974). They bury the issues by silence.

Bishop Lohse stated that selection of a bishop as it is practiced by Rome would not be acceptable for the Protestant churches of West Germany. For these and similar examples of clear positions I would like to have Rome respond and say: "This is not at all what we intend." What is lacking are clear statements by Rome regarding what the Catholic Church intends to retain at all cost and what it does not intend to retain.

Rome could say for instance: "Of course we do not require the application of the new Code of Canon Law for you, just as this Code is designed only for Western Catholics and not for Eastern churches in union with Rome," as it states on page one of the new Code.

We come now to the notion "eucharistic hospitality." Here church fellowship and eucharistic fellowship meet. Sacraments are not only signs of sharing but also their causes. Could not eucharistic hospitality be allowed more frequently, as at least one way, if not the only way, of coming together within the Christian confessions?

The chapter in our book that treats this question was written by Heinrich Fries. The question of eucharistic sharing *before* unification of churches is not a theme of *this* book. Eucharistic sharing would obviously be possible among united churches.

Of course Protestants in Germany consistently express the wish that the Roman Church should allow eucharistic hospitality as a partial cause of future unity. They can't take offense, however, if Rome asserts that participation of a Protestant Christian at a Catholic Eucharist is a separate question from the participation of a Catholic at a Protestant Eucharist. There the question of the validity of a specific person's ordination plays a role. If I make this distinction here it does not mean that I am answering one question with a yes and the other question with a no.

In earlier days Catholic moral theologians used to argue that participation of a Catholic in a Protestant Eucharist was participation in a heterodox worship service. According to Catholic principles this is a sin. Nowadays they are surely more generous in this matter. The pope himself in Rome participated in a Bible worship service in a Lutheran parish and he preached there. Thirty years ago this would have been absolutely unthinkable. If Rome thereby is "putting the brakes" on eucharistic sharing, everyone who doesn't want a priori to trivialize the still existing doctrinal differences can understand that. The Eucharist is, to be sure, an expression of an existing unity of faith, and not its cause!

The Protestant churches obviously have problems with the structure of the Church. Will that soon be the case for Catholics?

Alfred Lorenzer raised the objection that Vatican II was a council of bookkeepers, as is expressed in the title of his book *The Council of Bookkeepers: The Disruption of Meaning, A Critique of Religion* (Frankfurt, 1981). These "bookkeepers," according to his view, proved that they didn't understand the existential roots of religious experience. I admit that in fact there is a very real danger and that at the Council, to be sure, there was a certain "rationalism" which was not at all necessary given the purpose of the Council. But what is false in his thesis is that the concrete life of the Church is essentially threatened by that.

Is it true that in the Catholic Church that fundamental consensus which previously existed among rather different theologians and viewpoints has disappeared? Aren't you facing stiffer opposition nowadays than you did even ten years ago? Earlier people crossed swords, but no walls were erected. Nowadays disagreement often leads to suspicions and to exclusions.

I don't think that fundamental theological consensus has disappeared. Earlier there was of course, say between the years 1850 to 1950, a style of life that was in its main lines Catholic. The unified way of living and thinking was never so thoroughly noticeable in the Catholic Church than it was between the time of Napoleon and the reign of Pope Pius XII. Nonetheless, characteristic of this uniformity was that it was realized only by means of stringent measures. Think about the modernist controversy. This style of uniformity cannot survive in a world-Church or in the Church of the twenty-first century unless this Church wants to live on the defensive as a ghetto Church.

A person like yourself can look back on some four thousand publications. The question one is led to ask: Does this work bring you closer to the heart of faith or does one have more questions than ever before? Have you achieved greater assuredness about your faith? Or to put it more baldly: Do you have a good grasp of God?

A theologian who has any brains would never have the impression that he's got God in the palm of his hand. That's obvious. The question is: Does a person do theology because the very core of the material is of interest existentially, profoundly? Or is theology only an intellectual language, just as a philosopher might philosophize without any commitment?

I am convinced that in my case what predominates are religiously existential concerns. For me, my so-called pious books are just as important, I'd say even more important, than my theological publications. One example would be *The Practice of Faith*.[1] Very soon there will be published a collection of prayers I composed, *Prayers for a Lifetime*.[2] Even earlier I always stressed that in point of fact by profession I never claimed to be a scientific researcher either in philosophy or in theology. I never practiced theology as a sort of art for art's sake. I think I can say that my publications usually grew out of pastoral concern. But in comparison to professional scholars I have remained a theological dilettante.

When you started your work as a theologian did you have fewer or more questions than you have today?

There are so many questions in theology; you have to formulate them in ever new ways. Just think of the problems confronting present-day moral theology. In general it must be admitted, just from its starting points and its perspectives, that contemporary theology is by no means such that a modern person can feel at home in the Church without difficulties.

Many people argue that the Church is faced with the following alternatives: either it can exist as a closed society and thereby remain strong, powerful, and self-confident, or the Church can open itself toward a kind of world humanism and thereby has to renounce certain Christian religious practices. In themselves neither possibility offers any satisfactory alternative. Still, where does the proper solution lie?

Right now the present pope [John Paul II] seems to prefer a vision of the Church which resembles that of a closed society. I won't say that this is a priori unacceptable or without meaning. Christianity which lacks self-understanding of a particular and courageous sort and which fails to differentiate itself from the rest of the world can "close up shop." However, on the other hand, if you batten down the shutters, vaunt your orthodoxy, and try to respond to all the problems of moral theology without time for reflection, that accomplishes nothing. If the Church preaches the properly central features of Christianity in a thoroughly orthodox way, but at the same time in a completely modern way, then it avoids the danger that the Church is living for itself, instead of being a sign of salvation for all.

Translated by Michael A. Fahey, S.J.
University of Saint Michael's College, Toronto

1. Ed. Karl Lehmann and Albert Raffelt (New York: Crossroad, 1983).
2. Ed. Albert Raffelt (New York: Crossroad, 1984).

23•Church and Faith

Interview with Erich Gutheinz, Salzburg (March 4, 1984)

Among a large part of our church members there is a growing discrepancy between what we call "faith" and institutional Church. There is often talk about so many people "leaving" the Church.

Of course for some people this "leaving" is fundamentally false and needs to be fought against by the official Church, by its priests and religion teachers; for others, our regret about "leaving" has nothing to do with a condemnation of specific persons, because such "leaving" often occurs for sociological reasons without any personal guilt. But I would want to say that this phenomenon of silently leaving the Church should be a much greater incentive for the Church, the bishops, the religion teachers, priests, and theologians to present the Christian message and the Christian way of life in newer and more attractive ways.

What would you give as some of the possible reasons for this "leaving"?

We shouldn't always blame God and his "representatives" for the large number of people leaving. It isn't as though one can say a priori: this happened because the Church did something wrong. There are even families in which the parents are marvelous human beings who properly raise their children and yet experience terrible setbacks in raising them. So a good number of withdrawals from the Church are practically quite unavoidable.

We shouldn't think that every priest, bishop, or pope, when he preaches the gospel, is always a 100 percent on target. Sometimes it's simply boring. Things are often opposed in the Church which could be encouraged to make the Church an obvious home for people. These are external matters that have nothing to do with Catholic dogma.

Could you list a few concrete examples?

Even today we could organize the liturgy to make it much more accessible to people and far less removed from ordinary persons than is in fact the case. We could preach the real heart of the Christian message in a much more lively, joyful, and courageous way. We shouldn't abandon or pass over moral imperatives in silence, but we should place them in proper perspective. To achieve that we need to communicate what Jesus preached about the powerful coming of the reign of God, or God's self-communication in his glory in more lively, joyful, I might even say, lighter fashion than we often do in our sourpuss pastoral ministry.

Let's be honest. Priests today are still regarded by ordinary people as a breed of police in the service of the Lord. In fact they are not, and they don't want to be. But why don't people regard us priests as persons who possess, teach, and exemplify that absurd optimism which claims that this awful world is going to have a happy ending? That they have a paradoxical optimism which allows them to laugh despite all, to hope despite all, to know despite all their own misery that they are loved by a God who is eternal and holy?

Has the vision of Church elaborated at Vatican II caught on with persons who, to a greater or lesser degree, are involved in the Church's life?

Vatican II raised many expectations, and in general we are far from having seen them realized. We need to learn to combine, for example, in a lively and unabashed way the fact that Christians should not underestimate their Christianity on one hand and yet be willing to admit on the other that God's grace is so powerful and strong that it will presumably save others too. How can these two aspects be combined, radical commitment to an open and ecclesial Christianity on the one hand and universal optimism toward the whole world on the other? More precisely, how can Christians combine these two convictions so as to be public, historical, cultural, social, visible representatives of this universal optimism about salvation, which allows them to dare to hope for others without at the same time downplaying Christianity? This is an issue that hasn't been thought through clearly enough by today's average Christian.

Another real experience is the conflict between what perhaps might be called "people's Church" (Volkskirche) *and "basic Christian communities."*

We shouldn't have any illusions. We have to admit that even in our once Christian countries there does exist a respectable number of Christians, but it is a small minority of persons, when you take a closer look, who are truly and profoundly convinced practicing and churchgoing Christians. Still, because of our optimism about salvation which we've mentioned, we ought not be too frightened by that fact. Doesn't God have to save I don't know how many members of the human race without the Church and even without Christianity? When you keep that in mind, concepts such as "Church from below" or basic Christian communities and "people's Church" *(Volkskirche)* are not strictly speaking contradictory or rival entities. I also think that in our present concrete situation we ought to stress the formation of lively basic Christian communities, not in opposition to normal parishes, but as lively, missionary-oriented communities from below that reach out beyond the purely ritual.

To express this by a comparison, I would say that it is better there be flowering oases in a seemingly sandy desert, that it is more important to have these flowering, lively oases that are not afraid of protecting themselves from the heat of the day, rather than trying to sprinkle the whole desert only superficially with the little water we have at our disposal.

Of course it is difficult because you can't proclaim or practice simply one or the other in isolation.

Are you urging us then to have the courage to face up to our diaspora situation?

Today Christianity is present throughout the whole world in different levels of intensity. In my opinion, in a specific area you can't expect anymore to have a 100 percent closed, homogenous Christianity. The diaspora situation of the Church taken as a whole, which Jesus accepted as something obvious, is now even the fate of particular Christian regions. If the Church as a whole can and must face up to this global situation, then it must also use the same motives and the same methods even for specific regions.

Can you say something about "Church and Politics"?

I don't think that where a serious, acceptable Christian form of politics is practiced it ought to be abandoned. Why shouldn't it be possible, for instance, to have religion classes in public schools? But certain positions we can't really maintain anymore ought to be abandoned without any anxiety and fear. Of course we should also try, in dealing with those who strictly speaking are not Christians, to speak in a very humane, honest, and disinterested way so that, even if there no longer remains a strictly ecclesial-Christian consensus, there can still be in effect a certain human, fundamental consensus.

Are you working on a specific project right now?

If I have the time and energy, I would still like to write a small book in Herder's paperback collection called *Why I am a Catholic*. This isn't the same question as "Why I am a Christian." Despite all my ecumenical openness and willingness to be reconciled, the fact still remains that I must be and want to be a Catholic, a Roman Catholic. This decision is not optional, as, for example, deciding to buy things in one store rather than in another. Even today I still consider religious indifferentism as something completely erroneous, despite my conviction that the Christian confessions can and must do more than what they have done to unite in the one Church of Christ.

Translated by Michael A. Fahey, S.J.
University of Saint Michael's College, Toronto

24 • The Future of the Church—The Future of Belief

Interview with Fridolin Marxer, Basel (January 23, 1981)

Nowadays many are trying to come up with a short formula of the faith, a kind of a minicredo. Father Rahner, you yourself once formulated a short credo of your hopes for the future and for the Church. In such brief formulations of an individual aren't there certain tensions as regards the faith of the Church taken as a whole?

Let me say first of all that obviously you can be a normal, authentic, lively Christian committed to finding eternal life without being a first-class, professionally trained theologian. In earlier times people weren't theologians and they don't need to be so now. It's fine and appropriate if there are lively and alert Christians interested in certain details about the official doctrine of the Church. But when they believe in God, when they hope for eternal life, when they realize this with all the strength of their hearts in their commitment to Jesus Christ, the Crucified and Risen One, then they are Christians, even in the ecclesiastical sense of the word.

It is possible that such "simple" Christians might object and say: "Yes, but to be honest, I have the feeling that I don't know or understand many important teachings of the Church. I no longer know, for example, how many sacraments there are. And, to be honest, I also don't really know what the First Vatican Council said about the pope's authority in the Church. I don't mean to imply in any way that I reject it, but basically I just don't comprehend it. I really can't begin to deal with all that mass of data. I have the feeling that it's not very important for my life and death." To such Christians I can say only that they are completely normal, good, and lively Christians.

But the question, then, where the door is through which they can still enter the totality of Christianity without getting stuck, must be answered in a more nuanced way. Still, I maintain that an intelligent, well-educated, intellectual, Catholic Christian can affirm: "To a certain degree I understand Christianity's fundamental substance. I consider it the real scaffolding of my existence. I treasure it, of course, not as an old-fashioned individualist for myself alone, but in the Church's entire reality. And this precisely because as a modern person the social dimension plays an important role. But as for all those other theological subtleties, I can't and won't agonize over them. That's the job of you professionals."

Once persons have admitted this, then clearly they are sufficiently self-critical to apply the historical and social conditioning of human knowledge not only to their dealings with others but also with themselves. They will not vaunt and declare from on high their own infallibility, or that they know with absolute assuredness, even to the point of being prepared to shed their blood, that the pope is not infallible. Such a thing they cannot know absolutely. If therefore, in what is ultimately a secondary question, they cannot decide something with absolute assuredness, then they would be well advised, knowing their limits and in all modesty, to leave that question aside and to focus instead on the really substantial matters of Christian life in the Church: the celebration of the Eucharist, the baptism of their children, and so on.

Father Rahner, you often speak of questions that are central, substantial, important, and proper. How do you explain that persons can live with precisely a minimum of evidence, on the basis of which faith becomes possible? Does this come from experience? Is there such a thing as an experience of God? Is there knowledge about ultimate preservation or knowledge about eternal life? And what is the relationship between faith and experience, especially in regard to the future, or to the future of belief?

From your own lived experience you certainly know that even the "normal" self-critical and well-disposed person of today (in contrast to somebody of fifty, sixty, or a hundred years ago) is far less ready to accept as self-evident any indoctrination from outside about the meaning of life. In those days pastors and teachers came into school and told children what was what. The students were, by and large, convinced that the pastor or the teacher was right, and so, according to the same norm, they justified the religious instruction and world view taught to them from outside. Possibly here and there they made minor omissions, possibly some in their lives did ignore one or another ecclesiastical commandment (but they did so with a bad conscience). But by and large it was clear how the world was structured and what one was to do and not to do.

Today things are not quite that simple. There exists that well-known, much heralded pluralism of world views. The result is that if Christians really want to be Christians, they have to assume direct personal responsibility for building Christianity anew from within, more independently than used to be the case. Fundamentally included in that is what other people and I call the "experience of God."

In your view, why is that so important?
Let me give you an example. Probably like myself you haven't been to Australia. You've heard that there is such a country where kangaroos jump around. If in the same way, purely externally, you'd heard that there is a God, then you would not have attained the thoroughly, absolutely necessary foundation of your own belief. That God *exists*, human beings don't experience only through indoctrination from outside, which is not to say that we should completely abandon such instruction.

If I had to give to a young married couple a first-rate, edifying, and emotionally moving talk, I could perhaps describe the magnificence, depth, glory, the humanly fulfilling dimension of personal love between a man and a woman. The couple would then say: "What he's talking about is basically just what the two of us long ago experienced interiorly." Still, this external indoctrination of a marriage instruction could of course have meaning. They would, for example, note the fact that they, when they totally and radically admit the love that they have experienced internally, must also behave externally in a certain way. They may not be unfaithful to one another, they may not imagine a priori that they could get divorced tomorrow, and so on. So the external instruction is capable of leading to a clearer and more consistent understanding of an inner experience.

In a similar way, one can speak of the experience of the Holy Spirit. Sacred Scripture is the written expression of such a Christian and ecclesial experience of the Spirit. And the question follows: Is this external indoctrination successful in having an impact on the inner, personal experience of a human being?

Surely we must admit that such mystagogical catechesis will succeed or not according to the condition of individual persons and peoples. Contemporary preaching in the Church must take this fact into much greater consideration. Recently, in a lecture I gave in Rome, I said that the popes write a lot of encyclicals on, for example, the rosary, devotion to the Sacred Heart, indulgences, the sacrament of reconciliation, and so on. But where is the encyclical on modern atheism? I don't know of one. Such a text would be much more important. In such an encylical people would have to be made aware of the possibilities of having an inner experience of God. It isn't the case that persons who say they never had such an experience have in fact never had one. There are surely many people who profess Freud's materialism. In the last analysis they must affirm that responsibility and lack of imputability, love and hate, and so on are fundamentally only simple psychic occurrences. Those who argue such a thesis can nonetheless in practice have experiences that stand in total opposition to what they affirm. If they state: "I have never had the experience of true responsibility for which I'm accountable. I don't know what joy is and real longing is something foreign to me," then I would have to say to them: "Either you are not human and only look like a human being, or you are deceived."

That means that when you say: "God, what's that? And what is an experience of God?" then I wouldn't have to say: "Too bad," but rather: "Relax, maybe you have given other labels to your experiences of God. Perhaps what I say about them in my words and my rules of the game is completely unintelligible to you. Still you have had the experiences that I'm talking about."

Another example. If a Tyrolian farm boy loves a girl, I can probably give him an existential, philosophical lecture on love, about which he'll understand absolutely nothing. Nonetheless, he has had the experience of love, about which I am speaking, and perhaps has experienced love in a much more profound, radical, honest, pure, selfless way than I have, even though I can rattle on brilliantly about it as though I were a Max Scheler.

We come now to another question. Your theory about "anonymous Christianity" has been criticized by several well-known theologians. . . .

Yes, I know. I have been attacked sometimes vigorously, for example, by Hans Küng for quite specific reasons, and by Hans Urs von Balthasar again for different reasons. The term "anonymous Christianity" isn't what really matters. The important thing is that if somebody comes up to me and says: "You assume don't you, with the entire Christian tradition, that, for instance, a Tibetan who has never heard anything about Christianity, possesses an immortal soul," I would answer him: "If you prescind from the question whether the concept 'immortal soul' is appropriate or not, then one can't deny what you say. And were I to try to deny that, I'm sure the pope would jump in to help me."

The person asking the question could then continue: "If this Tibetan dies without having ever looked at the New Testament and without ever having received a Christian sacrament, without baptism, Eucharist, or anointing of the sick, what happens to him then? According to Augustine's view, this person would have to go to 'hell' because of his original sin." At that moment as a Catholic I would have to say no. I would have to answer: "If the Tibetan remained true to his conscience, then he would enter heaven, the same heaven that even I as a poor sinner hope to get to, the heaven of the immediate vision of God, the heaven of eternal life."

The questioner could continue: "Why does a Tibetan get to heaven?" A Christian theologian could answer: "He gets to heaven because God allows him in without demanding all those requirements that God has imposed upon me through my Christian faith." Here I would have to object and offer some precisions based on Vatican II; namely, that the Tibetan gets to heaven because he ultimately experienced that personal, spiritual, grace-filled event that we call "faith," without which neither he nor I can attain eternity. That our two forms of faith are different as regards their content, I don't deny in any way.

Furthermore, even Hans Urs von Balthasar and Hans Küng wouldn't deny that, for example, John Doe, as a baptized and pious Christian, could get into heaven even though what he thought about the Blessed Trinity was "just plain rubbish." In other words, no reasonable Christian can deny that, in the case of a poor and simple fellow Christian, despite every imaginable deficiency in the content of one's faith, the essential nature of salvific faith indispensable for salvation can be realized.

In connection with our example this means: the Tibetan gets into heaven, as Catholic teaching has it, because of supernatural, revelatory faith. Any more than that the Church can't say. Of course this forces me to attempt to articulate theologically, in a somewhat satisfactory way, how in the case under consideration that faith which leads to salvation is given at least *in nuce* (or, if you wish, in a "homeopathic dosage") and how it saves me and the "pagan." Well now, you could of course take the view that God in his mercy and in the power of his grace could already prepare everything in the innermost and ultimate substance of a person, even if I don't know how this is achieved. Sure you can think that, but that doesn't mean that I'm not allowed to explore more profoundly how this Tibetan possesses faith that brings salvation through which he receives God's personal revelation.

To conclude, let me say: Even Hans Küng can't say simply: "That's none of your business." Furthermore, he can't presuppose that this Tibetan who gets into the heaven of Christians can do that without the ultimate substance of faith. And he cannot and may not deny that the salvific will of God truly extends to all human beings, something that Augustine, when you come right down to it, denied. Finally, one may not and cannot deny that the appropriation of God's self-communication by someone who is outside explicit Christianity certainly bears intrinsically upon the ultimate basic structure of Christianity. Otherwise we would have two kinds of human beings: those who achieve salvation through Christ and those who achieve eternal salvation independently of Christ. Again I couldn't accept that. So (even if this is very hard to see) I call this availability of grace and the grace-inspired acceptance of salvation in the case of a human being who is not an explicit Christian "anonymous Christianity."

Translated by Michael A. Fahey, S.J.
University of Saint Michael's College, Toronto

25 • The Church's Situation

Interview with Detlef Drewes, Augsburg (March 1984)

Father Rahner, you have worked your entire life in the Church, you have tried to contribute to its shape. Do you feel comfortable in this Church today?

I am not in the Church to feel comfortable, but only because in it Jesus' call is perceived. Still, that doesn't change the fact that I have reservations about the concrete shape of this Church, or that, if necessary, I might even express my critical reservations openly.

For that you were once censured by Rome. You were forbidden to publish.

That all happened a very long time ago. Since then much has changed. Nowadays in the Church there is space to exercise even public criticism. Let's take the example of the new Code of Canon Law. I don't think that it is especially well suited to the future or even properly designed for the world-Church. I'm free to say that. There is a whole series of things within the Church which to me don't seem to be what they could be or perhaps even what they should be.

For example?

Rome could initiate new, courageous, surprising moves in ecumenical matters. When, for example, the chairman of the Evangelical Church of Germany, Bishop Lohse, states that Protestants could not accept appointments of bishops as they now occur in the Catholic Church, then Rome could say without any trouble at all that this is not a matter required for unity. For not even conservative Christians can maintain that this particular, concrete way of naming a Catholic bishop can only be done the way that Canon Law presently requires. There could be a much broader scope for mutual interaction.

Many Christians would like to have answers from the Church to other questions: What about the Church's position on the remarriage of divorced persons, what about a broader participation of laymen and women in church ministries? Does the Church have the capacity in these matters to act differently than it has up to now?

Yes, it has the capacity. In every question they should look at the matter individually to see whether there is such scope and to what extent. Of course not only permanent dogma but also many other things should not be changed. But they have to have the courage to make meaningful changes.

To whom are you referring when you say "they"?

Among others, the German bishops. I think that they take too few initiatives even in dealing with Rome. I wonder, for instance: Are the bishops happy about the practice of the Holy Father toward priests who left the ministry and have gotten married? As far as the problem of remarriage for divorced Catholics, the Church naturally can't simply accept a second marriage. But a concept is one thing and the reality designated by a concept is something else. Concepts only imperfectly reflect reality. Sometimes there is much more behind a concept (in human affairs) than one finds in reality itself, and often the opposite is also true.

For instance, in recent times you have decisions by ecclesiastical courts regarding declarations of nullity in marriages, to the effect that many "marriages" in the ecclesiastical sense are not real marriages at all, although they were regarded as such. And many commitments between persons that are not recognized as marriages still participate, in certain circumstances, more in the human and ethical reality of marriage than many that are recognized as officially valid. This shows that there are certainly many problems in the Church's theory and practice regarding marriage that have not yet been satisfactorily resolved. These things need to be thought about in a humane, generous way, without the constraints of a rigid way of thinking, even if the Church will never align itself with permissive attitudes about marriage. The Church declares, for example, that the divorced and remarried are to be treated with understanding. But in the concrete what does that mean if this is not just cheap talk? Are there not marriages in many cases that are performed nowadays in church and by civic officials that are not marriages in an ecclesiastical and theological sense? Fidelity to principles and real situations must always be brought together in new ways.

How much responsibility does the Church have in social and political matters? Should the Church not express itself even more strongly than it has up to now about current political questions, as, for instance, they have done about abortion or peace?

To begin with, there exist eternal, indispensable truths which the Church must proclaim first and foremost. That is its task, even if this or that person finds them boring. Objectively the question about the existence of God is much more important than a position paper on a political theme. This shouldn't, however, lead the Church to neglect the political dimension of its task. The Church should speak forthrightly on matters relating to peace, abortion, reduction of work-hours, and other similar topics. But it must beware at the same time that it doesn't allow itself to have its agenda set by the secular world alone.

May I raise another topic. You contributed to Vatican II as a theological adviser for Vienna's cardinal, Franz König. This Council is often described as a new breakthrough for the Church. Up to now what has become of this Council, what has happened to this new breakthrough?

Of course the initial euphoria has died down, and everyday life has resumed. But there have been lasting effects, in liturgy, in theology, in Canon Law, in pastoral care for persons, even though certain restoration tendencies have in the meantime caused me headaches. Much more decisive than the question what is different in the Federal Republic of Germany is the fact that the Church officially acted at the Council as a world-Church for the first time. It broke out of its European and Western limits. This must find clearer expression even in the way we do theology. The cultural and philosophical particularities of many nations need to be incorporated in the theological elaboration of Christian truths which, to be sure, remain unchanged. This is one of the reasons why I am not quite happy about the new Code of Canon Law. It reflects only the Western Church and consequently doesn't sufficiently capture the reality of Catholic Christians in Africa or China. I would like to see the multiple character of the world-Church better expressed in theology, pastoral care, and liturgy.

Translated by Michael A. Fahey, S.J.
University of Saint Michael's College, Toronto

26 • Tasks Facing the Church

Interview with Paolo Ghezzi, Turin (April 1983)

Which among the new insights of the last Council have further matured in the Church and which ones have been abandoned or misunderstood?

Although the Council is not to blame for it, obviously since then there have arisen ambiguities, misapprehensions, erroneous tendencies in theology, practical decisions, and in the life of the Church. It's meaningless to complain about that, and even more so to think that these things can be changed by a simple return to the old preconciliar Church, by a return, let's be blunt, to the days when we had popes named Pius.

The erroneous positions which result from the present-day spiritual and political situation are to be overcome through a positive engagement with today's reality and not through a restorationlike or reactionary flight into the past.

Do you think then that the Church is at all capable of speaking to men and women of today?

The Church must speak with the men and women of today. That is its sacred, God-given task. The pastors and the leaders of the Church would have to bear a very serious guilt before God if they were not to try with all their strength to preach the gospel so that people could at least hear and understand it, without simultaneously creating new difficulties beyond those which are clearly unavoidable.

The Church's task is preaching the gospel, preaching things that are not easy or self-evident, but that are divine mysteries. These mysteries, however, can be preached in such a way today that those difficulties can be avoided which originated in old-time preaching or theology, in a theology that unjustifiably considered itself to be the only orthodox way of speaking about God.

What role can today's Church play in defense of peace as we face the threat of atomic self-destruction?

It's good to make some distinctions. First of all, one should note that Vatican II stated unambiguously that an atomic war in any situation, even when it is a matter of a so-called "defensive war," is absolutely immoral, that is, something reprehensible before God. But it is a completely different question to ask how nuclear war can be avoided and how disarmament can be achieved. On these matters Christians are entitled to different opinions. And so I don't find fault with Rome's preference to show a certain caution and reluctance in these matters, avoiding an unequivocal pronouncement binding on all Christians. This shouldn't prevent Christians, however, from committing themselves out of their own personal responsibility and through concrete measures to total disarmament.

If another Christian disagrees with me on this, I can't assert that he or she lacks any sense of the necessary or is malicious or a bad Christian. But I may say, on the basis of my personal views inspired by my Christian convictions, that he or she is doing nothing to prevent the danger of an atomic war.

How do you see the future of the Church in the year 2000?

I could list fears of what the Church in the year 2000 might conceivably look like. Of course I could also talk about what the Church should look like in my view. If the Church is an *ecclesia semper reformanda* (a church always to be reformed), as Vatican II emphasized, then it is quite clear that it is never exactly what it should be. I can therefore wish what the Church should be and at the same time fear that it will fail to be that sufficiently.

The Church in the year 2000 cannot be a European Church exported to every imaginable country. It must be a Church in which Christianity has been inculturated according to the specific traits of each culture. So this Church must be decentralized to a much greater extent than the Roman officials now imagine. Speaking to Italians, I would say that that does not mean that the influence of the papacy in the world should disappear, only that the pope's important role (which can become even more important) cannot be developed according to the criteria of Roman centralism.

Canon Law too must be decentralized much more. Freedom must be given to the great churches of Latin America, Africa, and Asia to formulate their own canonical regulations in their own way. That requires much greater freedom than what is envisioned in the new Code of Canon Law. That Code, despite some definitely praiseworthy modifications, has fundamentally only restored the old Canon Law.

The liturgy too must be much more decentralized. And finally, there are questions that are, strictly speaking, ethical ones for which answers must be formulated in a new way. To give an example: How in the context of Africa is marriage to be understood, if one is to remain faithful to the will of God and Christ? Such a question will certainly not be answered by those "poor Africans," if we try to impose upon them a pure and simple repetition of European moral teaching about marriage.

How could Christians be led back to the sacrament of confession? Its practice appears now to be stuck in a serious crisis.

Certainly it is desirable that the sacrament of confession be more widely practiced again. The question is, of course, how. The simple exhortation to go to confession more frequently has to confront nowadays the argument (and the magisterium has to face up to this) that, according to the teaching of the Council of Trent, auricular confession is only necessary when a Christian has objectively and subjectively committed a really grave sin. And here the old practice of confession, which imposed on everyone the obligation to confess at least once a year, was based on a hasty and quite scandalous assumption that the ordinary Christian committed each year at least one mortal sin. Such an allegation is quite untenable. And if you reject that, then the problem is: How can the average person be encouraged to go to confession? The Church has to find a new answer. It can't insist upon its old methods, because that wouldn't work.

The Church must rather cultivate and convey a sense of sin and guilt which is new, authentic, and meaningful to persons of our day and age. It might improve the specific methods that are used for confession. That doesn't mean transforming the confessional into a psychiatrist's couch. But for modern men and women who are quite prepared to divulge their innermost miseries to the psychiatrist, couldn't one describe confession in a way that would be intelligible for the general public: "Here is a place where I can express myself. Here in the darkness of my existential situation, for which I am certainly not lacking in guilt, I can experience God's forgiveness, not only in the subjective interiority of my self, but quite concretely in my personal history."

Among the younger generation there seems to have emerged a reappearance of religious awareness. Is this only a flight into the irrational, or is it really a true search for God?

You're quite right, there are young people who give evidence of a real religious rebirth. You only have to go to Taizé and participate in its communal evening prayer to comprehend that there does exist an authentic and profound religious awareness. Which is not to deny that there are also forms of pseudoreligiosity observable in the increase of various sects. I do think that the official pastoral care of the Church needs to develop a much more conscious plan that responds to the often still confused religious longings of the younger generation.

There are young people who say: "I don't need a Church in order to believe in God." How can one respond to such a statement?

Of course there are people who love God without in fact being in the Church. Nobody denies that. But where love for God has achieved its profound perfection and its highest level, it must also be of necessity love of neighbor. And love of neighbor which is truly perfect necessarily implies in the last analysis (unless it wants to remain at the level of a vague idealism) a mutual participation and union in the form of love bestowed upon us by Christ, and that implies union with the Church, life in the Church.

As the year 2000 approaches human beings seem to be marked with anxiety and resignation. What's happened to hope?

Allow me to answer by appealing to a paradox. The men and women of today should especially not "forget" their apparently hopeless situation, but they must also have the courage to confront this explicitly. Then they might conceivably experience how Jesus Christ, the Crucified and Risen One, has given them the possibility, the duty, the right to have an absolute hope for an eternal future with God.

This hope is especially an eschatological reality, that is to say, something other than the human, natural hope for the future. Whoever hopes in truth for that absolute future, called "God," can also have the courage not to settle for such situations which (judged from a purely "natural" perspective) appear to be completely hopeless. Let me express my idea starkly: whoever knows that for him in the final accounting nothing can go wrong for him or her because he or she trusts in God, will be able to muster the courage to avoid becoming resigned too quickly and to flee all problems. Such a person can if necessary dare all, even at the risk of one's own life.

Translated by Michael A. Fahey, S.J.
University of Saint Michael's College, Toronto

27 • A "Wintry" Church and the Opportunities for Christianity

Interview with David Seeber, Freiburg (1984)

Father Rahner, in these last years you've been speaking quite a bit about the "wintry Church." Does this description apply to the present situation of the Church and to Christians living in a secular environment?

I don't know exactly who thought up that expression. Certainly I've used it often. It applies not only to the Church and the kind of impression that the Church makes throughout the whole world. It attempts to characterize our Central European Church and the impression that it makes. I don't know how to evaluate the situation of the Church in South America or in specific countries of Africa. I can imagine that there you're dealing with a more lively form of Christianity and a Church that is much more open to the future than, in my opinion, is the case here in Central Europe. You only need to take a look at the statistics. For instance, what is the situation here in regard to vocations to religious life? How many children in our larger cities are not even baptized anymore? Aren't there some baptized Catholics who accept divorce as something that is quite natural? What is the attitude about even having a church wedding, and so on? In Europe the Church as such is on the defensive.

But adhering to Church and adhering to Christianity are presumably here in Europe not exactly the same. . . .

Of course not. It doesn't really follow that our ordinary human, social milieu is really so unchristian, as the statistics about church attendance seem to imply. People very often experience quite a strong, religious attitude, an ethical responsibility even before God in their lives, but regular church "business," such as attendance at Sunday Mass, reception of the sacraments, and a more discriminating consideration of ecclesiastical regulations on ethical matters, is regarded as much less important or even as old-fashioned.

Even if you can imagine Christianity as more lively in Africa or South America, isn't it quite an illusory escapism to point in hope to the upsurge of churches in the Third World while bemoaning the European situation?

In any case we should be clear that everything we are bemoaning here has very secular, social and historical causes. It would be foolish to say that in other places everybody is streaming into church, and that here with a little bit of goodwill and with enough moral appeals it could be exactly the same. I would rather put it the other way around: if in Africa you should ever have the social preconditions for industrialization and the kind of intellectual and scientific way of life that we have, then, to the extent we can measure, more or less the exact same phenomena would show up there as we are now experiencing. That doesn't mean that there wouldn't be notable differences according to the Church's concrete human efforts at the same level and in the same social and historical situation.

Do you think that those bishops are right who, armed with the latest impressions of their travels, put their hopes in the Church of the Third World, when they state that here in Europe the Church is living in a highly secular environment, whereas elsewhere the religious soil reaches down much deeper?

First, to keep your metaphor: if I observe that elsewhere there is deeper soil that permits stronger roots, that doesn't help us very much, because we have to admit we just don't have that soil. Furthermore, Christianity here in Europe shouldn't give up, even when the really clear future of the Church lies in other countries. Something similar occurred in the Middle East which was once the garden spot of Christianity, but where it survives now only with difficulty. Those Christians there would be wrong to give up. As I said: whoever points to the Church in Africa, Latin America, or even Asia, will have to be prepared for the fact that the process of secularization will occur there too at a later time. Even now there certainly must be elite, educated Africans who are already secularized. A forward-looking strategy of the Church would face that fact without delay. The Church can be pleased if a large number of Christians enter it from out-of-the-way areas, but it cannot be any less concerned about how it will reach the secularized, educated groups in Africa.

You'll pardon me if I say that that sounds a lot like Ignatian or Jesuit strategy toward the elite. But if the Church in planning its pastoral stategy is to think and act only about the elite, can it still act only according to a classical European understanding of who make up the elite among the leaders and the educated. Aren't the elite to be found closer to the grass roots, as, for example, in the many small base communities in which the Church today is growing in many different ways?

No doubt we need to be clear that today and tomorrow the people destined to be among the leaders are and will be coming from completely different structures and mentalities than they did in the sixteenth or seventeenth centuries. A Jesuit, to pick up on your remark, must be concerned precisely about those persons who come directly from the base, those representatives and leaders of the base communities or other associations of engaged Christians. But I'm not saying that the Church doesn't have to devote itself to persons who come from among ordinary people, people from the soil, or from the base. I only mean that it ought not forget the others.

For example, I don't know how much longer the Polish intelligentsia will remain Catholic as a large proportion of the whole nation is at the present time. We can't count on the fact that we will have in the foreseeable future a very large number of persons who will be committed, active members of the Church. We will have plenty to do and we will need a lot of optimism and initiative in order to make a large enough proportion of men and women Christian, so that they do not remain simply an unimportant minority in the social order. Therefore it is precisely for that reason that it is essential that the Church cares also for those who belong socially to the leading groups.

You are continually pleading for a Church-wide pastoral strategy that many perceive as constructive. But isn't the situation not only in the Church but also in society altogether too diffuse for such a strategy?
Precisely because the overall situation is vague and diffuse is why we need such a strategy.

Given the differences in the world-Church, is it really possible to have a strategy that focuses in a central way on the overall action of the Church? Shouldn't we start from regional bases, if we don't want to come up against an increased Roman centralism even in pastoral matters?
No, in formulating an overall strategy it must be clearly stated that the traditional Western European or Roman strategy is not everywhere applicable. Regional differences must be seen as obvious.

What would be for you the principal strategic points?
One particularly important point for me concerns my old question whether the Church is well advised to maintain its system of local parishes, or whether it wouldn't be better, granted the problematic character of my metaphor, to create flowering oases even if thereby, from a pastoral and ecclesiological point of view, there would be many areas of desert in between.

Your image is a fascinating one. But isn't it a gamble to concentrate or rely on such oases? In doing so wouldn't you be in the situation of the surrounding deserts abandoning not only what is already dead but also in many cases what is still alive?
The metaphor may be misleading. But it is wiser to use an unavoidably very limited amount of water to produce an oasis somewhere than to sprinkle the limited amount over the whole land.

How do you see this Church strategy in theological or pastoral terms?
I'd formulate it this way. Given the fact that faith is always a faith faced with the challenge of making personal decisions, then the Christian shouldn't find this oasis situation so strange at all. Theologically and historically that means that as long as the Church, by reason of its historical origin, was a small group but one that was destined for the whole world, it could and had

to be relatively dominant in a specific place. But, from the moment the Church became more or less a world-Church, I don't need, by any kind of "heavenly strategy," such compact groups of Christians, who from a social point of view can live their faith without confrontation.

But may I, trusting in the universal salvific will of God, simply abandon what is certainly a sparser remnant but which is still capable of living, as, for example, the Catholic people's Church (Volkskirche)?

No. On the basis of the universal salvific will of God the Church in no way has the right to let people simply fend for themselves and to neglect the possibility of a lively growth of the Church from below. But, given our concrete historical situation, I may not trust that God will make the Church present everywhere, even if there is no longer anywhere an unchallenged Christianity of a regional character.

Did not Vatican II with its more positive hope for salvation occurring beyond the so-called official or ecclesial structures of Christianity play a decisive role here?

I believe that the change in the way of looking at salvation and ecclesiology was particularly clear at Vatican II. From Augustine to about the eighteenth or nineteenth century Christians regarded the whole non-Christian world basically as a *massa damnata* (a mass of people with no salvation in sight). Such was the general attitude, although not exclusively so. Francis Xavier still saw it this way: if I don't save this person from India or Japan, he is lost! Today no missionary goes to Japan with the idea that whomever he doesn't reach is damned. That doesn't mean that I want to play down evangelization or to exempt a mission from the duty of making as many persons as possible explicit Christians. I only mean that I hope with a Christian realism that God also really lives where I myself am not present.

But doesn't it still remain true that the Church would have to withdraw its forces from places where there is still a Christian presence? As far as this new optimism about salvation: Are there not precisely in recent times countermovements that work exactly as oases and understand themselves so, but which presume a Christianity of election and in which the rest of the world, looked at really and biblically, is nothing else but a massa damnata?

I would maintain that we should calmly try to create living, radically cohesive communities that resemble the life of the early Church. And I would hope that from their feeling of being something special there would arise a pronounced sense of mission. The future will show whether we have created truly modern communities inspired by the early Church or simply insular ghettoes that produce a lot of warm nests which don't warm the rest of the world at all. They'd be like thermos bottles that keep warm what is inside but leave anything outside cold.

In my view, behind nearly every such attempt are false premises. The Church must at any rate be open. It may not be made up of people who don't want anything to do with the rest of the world. We need a Church that attracts people because of a truly basic Christian conviction, without the Church becoming clerical in old or new ways.

To return to the first part of my question. Is an overall ecclesial strategy responsible if it concentrates on oases, but neglects traditional Christianity, even if that Christianity is perhaps diffuse or even only Christian by custom or tradition?

You're right when you say that, where there is a traditional and somewhat living Christianity, every effort ought to be made to maintain and continue it into the future. But should, for example, a bishop send a particular priest whom he has at his disposal only once to a remote village parish in the Tyrol that could be cared for very well by a neighboring priest? Or should he educate him to be an alert, modern man, one who is profoundly Christian, and then assign him to a large city? Of course this comparison limps. Still it can indicate that the Church of today really has to have the courage to follow a certain strategy, instead of starting every imaginable approach on all possible fronts, approaches that immediately fail because they were undertaken with limited resources.

The conclusion to be drawn from this is that the only remaining thing for the Church to do is to gather into many disparate ghettoes and to live and rely on providence that somehow a new Christianity will emerge out of this.

They may be disparate but, first of all, they must be true Christian communities. They must live and take shape only from the fundamentals of the Christian gospel. And the more such communities there are, the greater will be the chance for them to approach other neighboring ones, so that after a new start once again they can become a geographical Church. But take only the example of a person from a large city, an ordinary, theologically not very well trained person, somebody, God knows, not particularly religious, but still open to Christianity. At the present time he sees only parishes, but hardly Christian communities. If there were no parish community present, but this lost large-city dweller with his very limited religious potential were to stumble upon such an active group, he would be much better off than if parish X were still officially open with a few elderly ladies attending Mass whom God certainly will save, and with a poor pastor who is stuck and turned off by the bureaucratic running of the Church.

Let's concede that the officially established Church has too one-sidedly stressed the "apparatus" or even the parish system as such. But there is more church life in the existing parish system than you suggest with your example. And just where are these new oases to be developed normally if not in the parishes?

It's obvious that the organized Church has offered historically and still continues to offer anew structures and aids for a vibrant Christianity. I'm the last person who would be so marked by ideologies, so full of illusions and exaggerated enthusiasm, as to assert that the present Church must to a greater or lesser degree be done away with and then new churches and church groups and finally large church systems would again appear. That's not what I mean.

Rather, I'm arguing that the Church should judiciously employ its available but, looked at soberly, very limited potential for religious communities in the right places. That's where the weakness is. Despite numerous investments and incentives from official church quarters hardly anything significant results. I can't peer into the heads and hearts of Roman prelates; I don't know what they are offering as advice to one another behind closed doors. But there must certainly exist something like ecclesial futurology through which various alternatives are discussed.

But just take a look at the new Code of Canon Law. It's simply a revision of the Code of Benedict XV. That was suitable as the canonical book for the Western, West European, Roman Catholic Church. The present world-Church is something other than a West European Church exported to the Third World. The new Code could not have been constructed as it was if it had been conceived with strategic consideration for the future.

While you're on the topic of the Code, I would like to return again to your example of the priest whose bishop should send him to a large city rather than to a village parish. If the bishop sent the priest in question to a large city, the village community would not have to give up on getting a priest. It could perhaps find someone who would be willing by way of exception to take on such a ministry if he were ordained. . . .

To put it concretely: a little while ago a senior bank official came to visit me. He told me he was soon going to retire, that he was in good health and active, and that he would be delighted to become a pastor in a small village somewhere in the mountains. He wouldn't of course attempt later on to become pastor in a large city or even a bishop, or anything like that. But he had the necessary theological formation or he could still manage to acquire it, so as to serve as representative and presider at the eucharistic celebration for this village. Why can't he be ordained? And why shouldn't the pope allow the bishop to ordain this man?

But celibacy is a very strong fixation in the strategic plans of the Church. . . .

It would be a shame if there ever was a Church where heavenly foolishness wouldn't inspire persons to renounce marriage for the sake of Christ. For that reason it is proper to have and want a celibate clergy. Now this, which after all is *a* principle, not *the* principle of the holy Church, has been overextended in an extremely mechanical way. Since there should be a celibate clergy, that doesn't mean the priest in this mountain village sixteen hundred meters high should be celibate. In the Catholic Church nobody requires, just because we have a celibate clergy, that Eastern Catholics may not have married priests.

There is also the possibility of legislating and differentiating different kinds of vocation. An elementary schoolteacher can be happy in her or his vocation even if she or he cannot become a high school teacher. There have been dentists who are not dental surgeons. Even today there are distinctive groups of civil servants with clearly marked differences. What you expect from one you don't automatically expect from another. These kinds of reasonable structures that are in no way hangovers from feudalism could also exist in the clergy.

Your examples presuppose that the Church is lacking less in strategy than in creative, innovative strength. What is the primary reason for that? Is the fault with the institution that is concerned primarily about itself, or with a lack of trust in the future, or with the preferential return to only apparently secure juridical positions, or with an understanding of tradition that does not allow for leaps forward in history?

I think there are a number of such causes at work here. In the last centuries, especially since the Council of Trent, there has doubtlessly been an extraordinary, unprecedented reinforcement of the legal side. The movement to protect against secularism since the Enlightenment has certainly also contributed to that. Also the restoration movements that took place in Europe. The Church has sometimes relied too much on this, and seen itself not as a contributor to the advancement of history but rather as protector of the permanent. To consider the traditional as automatically the valid is all very human. What's new can easily go awry and so innovative experiments have, so to speak, first to prove that they are good.

Hasn't this attitude also been influenced very strongly by theology, especially since after the major breakthroughs before and during Vatican II it has, by and large, restricted itself to church matters?

In regard to theology we must first of all note that there was a movement to get away from that neoscholastic theology favored by the various popes named Pius. Such a thing can't take place every twenty years or so in a clear and spectacular way. This attempt to make a change created the feeling that we had embarked upon a new epoch in theology. This feeling created a certain euphoria among theologians and other persons. But after such break-throughs, just from the nature of things, you get back into the routine and the less spectacular.

I don't mean only that at the present time theology in general has a lower profile, but that it has restricted its efforts too strongly, of course not exclusively, to church related issues.

You could of course say in a maliciously one-sided way that something remarkable happened at Vatican II. The Church wanted to face up to the present social and intellectual situation in a way marked by trust, courage, and much initiative. To achieve that, it naturally reflected on itself, and if I can put it this way, cleaned its own glasses. As long as it was busy with that, it didn't see too well why it was cleaning its glasses, namely, in order to see other things in a clearer, sharper, more colorful way.

Do you mean that these were unavoidable historical and practical effects?

Probably yes, and for that reason the situation will also go away. Even the most conservative theologian thinks and writes nowadays in a different way than, let's say, thirty years ago. Take the latest document of the pope *Salvifici Doloris* (1984). When has there ever been a papal document in two thousand years that even vaguely suggested our Semitic roots? Even for the most conservative representatives of the Church much has changed in mentality and practice. Good people often don't even notice such things, but they produce things as if they were obvious. At the Council, Parente, who later became a cardinal, but at that time was second in command at the Holy Office, insisted without blushing, and in good faith, that the Congregation for the Doctrine of the Faith had never said anything against the corporeal origins of humanity from the animal kingdom. Thereby he was turning history upside down. But such unreflective changes in mentality happen even among conservatives. They talk as though they are doing nothing else but continuing an ancient tradition. The present pope has, for example, spoken about the "Yahwist" (one of the sources of Genesis). If he had said that, let's say, as archbishop of Kracow under Pius X, he would have been removed from office. The history of ideas advances in unreflexive ways.

Mindful of such odd turns of history, one could argue that a decidedly conservative, pastoral pope, who, conscious of the present, could to a certain extent achieve more for the Church by not neglecting the facts than a curial pope who is cautiously turned inward.

In many cases that is quite possible, but I wouldn't count on it.

Father Rahner, you are talking about the pope, but my question about theology is not yet finished. Has theology not restricted itself inasmuch as its "object," God in the totality of the divine life and humanity in all that relates to creaturehood, has not been explored sufficiently or profoundly enough because, to retain your metaphor, it has been cleaning its own ecclesiological glasses?

That is correct. But nowadays it is no longer really possible to think and live from the totality of contemporary thought and knowledge. A prelate in Rome, just as a theologian in Germany, has the right to understand less about many modern things than a scholar or an expert in an appropriate field. Everyone has to live with a piece of knowledge, because one can't integrate everything. Even experts in natural and social disciplines can't pursue learning from the total fund of knowledge in modern times. Consequently, to teach persons to have patience and to develop the ability to ask questions is much more critical than to create a positive synthesis between modern scholarship and theology. The opportunities are enormous. Not only theologians are uncertain, others also feel how little they can say about the totality of their own scientific discipline.

I suppose it is neither possible nor necessary for theology to integrate profane branches of knowledge in a rigorously scientific way. But there is for theology as for the Church a hierarchy of truths. You yourself have given strong warnings to place the question of God at the heart of theology. And for many in a special way your theology is characterized by its existential and theological emphasis on preaching and piety. At present one has the impression that theology is altogether much too busy with Church and social questions, and is leaving its contemporaries alone to deal with the deepest questions about Christianity. . . .

I think that Church and theology should give much more thought and make more effort to bring men and women to realize they can be completely faithful and courageously and unabashedly Christian despite the vast amount of material that has not been synthesized and despite the differences found in present-day consciousness. Modern Christianity can live comfortably with the insight that today a synthesis of humanistic, scientific, and sociological scholarship is impossible. I mean that we must make clearer that Christianity in its true essence, even if it must be realized and objectified in many different ecclesial ways, is not simply one of many rival and partial ways of looking at the world which can no longer be brought into a unity. Rather, Christianity is the acceptance in faith—despite the many aspects of the world that cannot be integrated—of a unity of all reality that comes not from human beings but is grounded in God's self-communication. Faith in God's self-communication precedes all other world views which make one particular aspect of reality into its "god."

Please excuse the simple question, but do theology and Church speak about God too little or not radically enough? And is that perhaps exactly why the Church is experiencing a winter?

I don't have the right to deny a serious and radical Christian position to any actual person, whatever stand or position in the Church he or she assumes, nor do I have the right to suspect him or her. It is something else whether in the actual exercise of theology and Church this radical dimension is made concrete with all its necessary clarity, so that those outside can sit up and take notice. Several times already I've asked why there is no encyclical about God or against atheism. You could say a lot about these topics. One can say to me: "Physician, heal thyself" (Luke 4:23). But if I have done it poorly, others must not also do it poorly. Recently I said clearly that Christianity, with its affirmation of the unknown God, is in fact the most radical form of agnosticism. By comparison, much of what is supposed to be agnosticism is just idle talk, since it doesn't take seriously enough the incomprehensibility of our existence. In this sense one can preach the truth of Christianity much more radically and lively than ordinarily happens. I'm living in a glass house, but where are the bishops who, even as priests, converted a few ordinary persons to Christianity from agnostic relativism? I hope that there are some. Only we can't find many of them.

And once again to return to a previous point. If nobody claims or can seriously claim to have the ideal solution, then the Church needs to have far less anxiety about being overtaken by the profane sciences. From this situation, widely recognized as insecure, the Church could with and through its gospel engage in open dialogue with very many aspects of experience. . . .

To respond concretely and somewhat ironically. There's no need to have proof that somebody's been to confession when you're dealing with somebody who's attending a Catholic university and is studying chemistry or something similar. Wouldn't it be enough if they were persons who manifested a certain openness and sympathy for Christianity as a whole? Who would in fact be more valuable for the Church in the modern world: a gifted professor who unfortunately has been tinged with a deeply skeptical outlook on life and who nonetheless feels at home in Christian circles, or someone who is accepted without hesitation as well disposed to the clergy but in the world itself can scarcely qualify even as a simple popularizer?

But to go beyond your single example, how can the Church not only bear this widely recognized situation but also give shape to it in the light of Christian preaching?

Like a monomaniac, you can never reduce a principle or a rule of life to a single one. I mean that the Church now has more than ever the duty to expose with determination the basic heart of the Christian gospel. And the Church must absolutely protect itself from a watered-down humanism wherever it may appear in any form or other. But theologians (and I'm not saying they have to preach in the lecture hall) must make clear through their lives that they really believe and realize that they are dealing with the improbable and absolute reality of God who is near and who wishes to communicate himself. They must show that for them it is to a certain extent obvious that they pray and that they consider life as meaningful in light of Jesus who was crucified and who rose from the dead. This radical nature of the proper, specific Christian gospel cannot be hidden. If that were sufficiently present in a lively way, then many clerical, bureaucratic, and canonical measures would seem totally superfluous.

To summarize our conversation in a short sentence, if I may, isn't our wintry, crises-filled situation in the Church linked ultimately to our lack of courage to take Christianity completely seriously? And don't precisely the juridical, institutional, church-political side-questions often appear to be the most important, thereby hiding what is the real gospel?

I think so. Because if Christianity really possessed that degree of radical consistency which by nature it demands, then it would be springtime in the Church.

The question is how, with what means can we achieve this necessary intensity about our Christian convictions? An answer to this question is extremely difficult. And so I think it's part too of Christian hope that we don't interpret these wintry times as a prelude to ultimate death. Each one of us should instead see these times as a personal challenge to work so that the inner core of faith becomes alive. Then of course the Church itself will again shine radiantly, and it will again become clear that the Church is intended to be a sacramental sign of the world's salvation.

Translated by Michael A. Fahey, S.J.
University of Saint Michael's College, Toronto

INFORMATION ON THE INTERVIEWS

The number given in the margin corresponds to the interview number as found in the table of contents. The date for the television and radio interviews refers either tó the date of the interview or the first broadcasting date.

1. In *An unsere Freunde: Information der süddeutschen Jesuiten*, Munich, 2/1984, pp. 10–13, 16f.
2. "Gnade als Mitte menschlicher Existenz." Interviewed by *Herder-Korrespondenz* on the occasion of his seventieth birthday, Munich (February 1974). In *Herder-Korrespondenz*, February 1974, pp. 77–92. See also: Karl Rahner, *Herausforderung des Christen* (Freiburg i. Br.: Herder, 1975), pp. 117–53.
3. "Me hubiera gustado haber tenido más amor y valentia" (I would have liked to have had more love and courage), in *Vida Nueva*, nr. 1421 (March 24, 1984), pp. 29f. and 609f.
4. Original production, Innsbruck (May 29, 1982). Also in *Jaarboek 1982* of the "Werkgroep Thomas von Aquino," Utrecht, 1982, pp. 69–94.
5. "Ik bestrijd de verduiveling van de bevrijdingstheologie" (I'll protect myself against the seductions of Liberation Theology), in *de Tijd*, Amsterdam, 5/29 (September 1978), pp. 30–33.
6. "Exorzisten, Psychiater, Theologen" (Exorcists, psychiatrists, theologians), in *Orientierung*, Zurich, 38/17 (September 15, 1974), p. 180. Also see p. 177.
7. Recorded in Munich (September 8, 1976). Previously unpublished.
8. Previously unpublished. Obtained from the Rahner Archives, Innsbruck.
9. Previously unpublished. Obtained from the Rahner Archives, Innsbruck.
10. "Die Friedensbewegung ist eine Hoffnung für viele" (The peace movement is a hope for many), in *Deutsche Volkszeitung*, Innsbruck, 31/2 (January 13, 1983), p. 6.
11. Previously unpublished. Recorded in Innsbruck (May 5, 1983).
12. Women students at the Poor Sisters' Gymnasium am Anger in Munich question Karl Rahner. Part I broadcast on December 8, 1983; Part II, on

December 15, 1983 on SF, SWF, and SR radio stations. Recorded and
edited by Bernd H. Stappert.

13. "Ich habe nie an Gott gezweifelt" (I've Never Had Doubts About God),
    Junge Zeit, Augsburg, 3/1984, pp. 16f. and 33.
14. Original recorded on October 30, 1983. Summary version in *Nachrichten*,
    published by the School Sisters of Notre Dame, St. Pölten (November
    1983), pp. 82–90.
15. On Radio Kossuth, Budapest (December 10, 1983).
16. In *Daily News/Neueste Nachrichten*, Budapest, 18/44 (March 2, 1984), p. 7.
17. Interviewed by Valeria Koch, in *Vigilia*, Budapest, 50/3 (March 1984),
    pp. 255–59.
18. Interviewed by Wenzel Hambuch for the German language program of
    the Hungarian Radio Network, Budapest (March 1, 1984).
19. Previously unpublished. Original recording in November 1983.
20. In *Panorama-Mese*, Milan, 9/1984, pp. 54f.
21. "Le Christianisme, Religion de toutes les Cultures" (Christianity, a re-
    ligion for all cultures), in *La Croix*, Paris (April 13, 1983), p. 9.
22. Original recording on February 3, 1984. Summarized as "Lutheraner auf
    dem Stuhl Petri?" (A Lutheran on the chair of Peter?), in *Deutsches
    Allgemeines Sonntagsblatt*, Hamburg, 37/10 (March 4, 1984), p. 10.
23. "Wir können die Frohbotschaft viel freudiger und mutiger verkünden"
    (We can preach with more life and spirit), in *Rupertusblatt: Kirchenzeitung
    der Erzdiözese Salzburg*, Salzburg, 39/10 (March 4, 1984), pp. 8f.
24. Previously unpublished. Original recording on January 23, 1981.
25. "Wenn nötig, auch kritisch" (If necessary, I can also be critical), in
    Weltbild, Augsburg, 6 (March 16, 1984), pp. 8f.
26. "Otto domande a Karl Rahner" (Eight questions for Karl Rahner), in *Vita
    Trentina*, Trent (May 1, 1983), pp. 1, 12.
27. In *Herder-Korrespondenz*, Freiburg im Breisgau, 38/4, 1984, pp. 165–71.

Index

Abortion, 98
Anonymous Christianity
  on critics of, 181–182
  definition of, 102, 166–168
  and grace, 21
  and missionary activity, 103
  terminology of, 132–133
Anthroegoism, 2
Anthropology, 21, 158
Aquinas, Thomas
  contemporary theologians and, 46
  influence of, 53–57
  on mystery of God, 23
  Rahner as disciple of, 51–53
  Rahner's generation and, 45
  Rahner's theological studies and, 41–44
  Rahner's use of, 47–48
  and theological turn to the world, 50
Arrupe, Pedro, 11, 40, 80
Atheists, 127, 131–132, 135–136. *See also* Marxism
Atomic war. *See* Nuclear war
Atomic Weapons (Cremer and Rahner), 150

Barthel, Manfred, 57
Birth control, 98
Blatty, William Peter, 65–66
Bonaventure, 53
Bühlmann, Walter, 162

Catholic Church. *See* Roman Catholic Church
Celibacy, 196
Charismatic movements, 35
Christianity
  as absolute religion, 159

diaspora of, 177
Marxism and, 128–129, 130–131, 139–140
optimism of, 103, 117, 125
for other cultures, 165–166
and profane branches of knowledge, 198–199
radical, 199
reuniting, 79–80
short credo on, 178–179
structures of, 195.
See also Anonymous Christianity; Christians
Christian living, models of, 121–122
Christians
  communities of, 194
  and flawed Church, 142–143
  learn from non-Christians, 161
  and nuclear weapons, 157–158
  relationship of, to Church, 141–142.
See also Christianity
Christology, 28–29, 50
Churches, as obstacles, 111
Code of Canon Law, 169, 183, 185, 187, 195
Communion, interfaith, 99
Communities, Christian, 194
Confession, sacrament of, 187, 199
Congregation for the Doctrine of the Faith, 101, 154, 197
Conscientious objection, 156
Consensus, theological, 173
Council of Bookkeepers, The (Lorenzer), 173
Cultures, multiplicity of, 165–166

Death, 103–104, 134
Death penalty, 120

203

Translators

(Numbers after the name refer to the number of the interview)

Bernhard A. Asen and Harvey D. Egan, S.J., 2
Robert J. Braunreuther, S.J., 12, 13, 14, 15, 16, 17
Daniel Donovan, Editors' Preface, 9, 10, 11, 18, 19, 20, 21
Michael A. Fahey, S.J., 7, 8, 22, 23, 24, 25, 26, 27
Thomas O'Meara, O.P., 1
Roland J. Teske, S.J., 3, 4, 5, 6